Studies in the History of Medieval Religion

VOLUME VI

William Waynflete

BISHOP AND EDUCATIONALIST

This is the first modern study of William Waynflete, powerful and influential bishop of Winchester from 1447 to 1486. He was one of the great educationalists and patrons of learning of late medieval England, and his career was dominated by his interest in education (which included close involvement with Eton and Magdalen College, Oxford), particularly by his concern with the teaching of grammar. He played a leading role in some of the changes which transformed education in fifteenth century England: the emergence in Oxford and Cambridge of new and larger colleges; the influence of continental humanist ideas which reshaped English thought and learning; the introduction of the teaching of Greek; the composition of new grammars; and the introduction of printing as a means of disseminating the new learning. Coincidentally, his involvement with new foundations led to the construction of several magnificent and often innovative buildings.

This study is a corrective to the view that the medieval church was corrupt and in need of reform; it supports recent research revealing the truth to be more complex, with bishops both politically and pastorally active in varying degrees. Waynflete himself was politically linked to Henry VI and the Lancastrian administration. As this biography records, most of his career was spent in southern England; however, he retained close links with his native county, Lincolnshire, and his extensive commitments there are also fully considered.

VIRGINIA DAVIS is lecturer in history at Queen Mary and Westfield College, University of London.

Studies in the History of Medieval Religion

ISSN 0955–2480

General Editor
Christopher Harper-Bill

William Waynflete

BISHOP AND EDUCATIONALIST

VIRGINIA DAVIS

THE BOYDELL PRESS

First published 1993
The Boydell Press, Woodbridge

ISBN 0 85115 349 6

The Boydell Press is an imprint of Boydell & Brewer Ltd
PO Box 9, Woodbridge, Suffolk IP12 3DF, UK
and of Boydell & Brewer Inc.
PO Box 41026, Rochester, NY 14604, USA

British Library Cataloguing-in-Publication Data
Davis, Virginia
    William Waynflete:Bishop and Educationalist.
    – (Studies in the History of Medieval Religion,
    ISSN 0955–2480;Vol.6)
    I. Title II. Series
    942.04092
    ISBN 0–85115–349–6

Library of Congress Cataloging-in-Publication Data
Davis, Virginia, 1958–
    William Waynflete, bishop and educationalist / Virginia Davis.
        p.   cm. – (Studies in the history of medieval religion ; v. 6)
    Includes bibliographical references and index.
    ISBN 0–85115–349–6 (alk. paper)
    1. Waynflete, William, 1395?–1486. 2. Catholic Church –
England – Winchester Region – Bishops – Biography. 3. Education,
Medieval – England. 4. Winchester Region (England) – Biography.
I. Title. II. Series.
BR754.W3D38   1993
282'.092–dc20
[B]   93–36091

This publication is printed on acid-free paper

Printed in Great Britain by
St Edmundsbury Press Ltd, Bury St Edmunds, Suffolk

Contents

Plates

Plates 4, 5, 6 and 8 are reproduced by permission of RCHME Crown Copyright; Plate 3 by permission of Oxfordshire County Council Leisure and Arts; Plate 1 by permission of the Courtauld Library.

Abbreviations

BIHR	*Bulletin of the Institute of Historical Research*
BRUO/C	A.B. Emden, *Biographical Register of the University of Oxford/ Cambridge to 1500*
BL	British Library
CCR	*Calendar of Close Rolls*
CPR	*Calendar of Patent Rolls*
CPapL	*Calendar of Papal Letters*
Cart St John	*Cartulary of the Hospital of St John the Baptist*
Chandler, *Life*	R. Chandler, *Life of William Waynflete*
ECR	Eton College Records
EHR	*English Historical Review*
HBC	Powicke & Fryde, *Handbook of British Chronology*
HRO	Hampshire Record Office
Hist Mss Com	Historical Manuscripts Commission
JEH	*Journal of Ecclesiastical History*
MC	Magdalen College archives
NMR	National Monuments Record
OHS	Oxford Historical Society
PL	*Paston Letters and Papers of the Fifteenth Century*, ed. N. Davis
PPC	*Proceedings of the Privy Council*
Reg Waynflete	Episcopal register of William Waynflete
RP	*Rotuli Parliamentorum*
TRHS	*Transactions of the Royal Historical Society*
VCH	Victoria County History
WCM	Winchester College Muniments

Place of publication is London unless otherwise stated.

Acknowledgements

This book had its origins in a doctoral thesis at Trinity College Dublin but in the years during which it was being reformulated as a book I have had much further support, encouragement and advice. It was only possible to research and write, first the thesis and then the book with the help of many people and I would like to thank them for their support. Firstly all the staff of the Department of Medieval History in Trinity College Dublin and most especially Professor J.F. Lydon for his consistent encouragement and enthusiasm. The Board of Trinity College awarded me a research grant and I am also grateful for the award of the Luker and Cobbe Bursary which enabled me spend some time at Girton College Cambridge and to Trinity Trust who contributed towards the costs of travel to regional record offices.

I received much help from the staff of numerous libraries and record offices – The British Library, Bodleian Library Oxford, Cambridge University Library, Institute of Historical Research, Public Record Office, Hampshire County Record Office, Lincoln Record Office, Winchester Cathedral Library, Corpus Christi College Cambridge, Magdalen College Oxford, Winchester College and Eton College. Special thanks must go to the staff of Trinity College Dublin Library, to Mrs B. Parry-Jones of Magdalen College archives, and to Patrick Strong, the then archivist at Eton College who was not only exceedingly helpful but who, together with his wife Felicity was most hospitable.

I owe a special debt to Mr John Mills who generously permitted to me to draw heavily on his B.Litt. thesis on the foundation and endowment of Magdalen College for part of chapter 6. I am particularly grateful for comments and advice on early drafts of the book from Dr Gerald Harriss and from Professor Nicholas Orme.

This book would never have been completed without the help and encouragement of many people. I would like to thank all the friends with whom I stayed while travelling around the record offices and libraries of England. In addition to those already mentioned I would like to thank all my medieval colleagues at Queen Mary and Westfield College and also Dr Andrew Ayton; Professor Christopher Brooke; Dr Phil Connolly; Dr Rosemary Hayes; Mr Peter Heath; Dr Phillip Lindley; Professor Joan Greatrex; Professor Roy Haines; Dr Christopher Harper-Bill and Dr Robert Swanson. I owe a special debt to my godparents Hazel and Sandy Saunders. Finally and most especially I must thank my parents – Bill and Marie Davis, my sister Heather and John McLoughlin for their constant help, encouragement and support.

To my parents, Bill and Marie Davis

Introduction

In recent years the image of the fifteenth century episcopate has been changing as individual studies have broken down the impressions of earlier generations who, influenced by reformation polemic, saw the church as in decline or corrupt and in need of reform. This transformation of our view of the episcopate as a group is based on specialised studies of individual bishops which have revealed the diversity of figures who went to make up the episcopal bench. Some, such as George Neville (Exeter 1456–65, York 1465–76) or Robert Stillington (Bath and Wells 1464–99) neglected their dioceses to devote their attention to politics, others like John Carpenter (Worcester 1444–76) concentrated on their pastoral commitments and conscientiously attended to the administration of their dioceses. The variety of men who together constituted the English episcopate can only be established by a combination of prosopographical studies of the episcopate and research into the careers of individual bishops.[1]

One such bishop was William Waynflete, bishop of Winchester 1447–1486. Hitherto he has been seen as rather a shadowy individual, a far less significant figure than either of his two predecessors in the see of Winchester, Cardinal Henry Beaufort and William Wykeham. During his lifetime William Waynflete was involved in a number of important aspects of fifteenth century English life. He was bishop of Winchester, a rich and potentially powerful see, for almost forty years in the later fifteenth century; politically he was linked with Henry VI and the Lancastrian administration in the last years of Henry VI's disastrous first reign; as headmaster of Winchester College, provost of Eton College and founder of Magdalen College Oxford he was closely involved with an educational revolution of the fifteenth century. His patronage of learning attracted the attention of contemporary humanist writers and his extensive investment in architecture resulted among other things, in the construction of a number of magnificent early Renaissance style brick buildings.

Despite the diversity and influence of Waynflete's activities – which make him an attractive figure to study – he has been neglected by recent historians. Three biographies of Waynflete have been written by men who were attached to Magdalen College. The earliest life was that written by John Budden, reader in

---

[1] Prosopographical studies include R.G. Davies, 'The Episcopate', in C.H. Clough, ed., *Profession, Vocation and Culture in Later Medieval England: Essays Dedicated to the Memory of A.R. Myers*, Liverpool 1982; J.T. Rosenthal, 'The Training of an Elite Group: English Bishops in the Fifteenth Century', *Transactions of the American Philosophical Society* ns lx, pt v, 1970; J.T. Rosenthal, 'The Fifteenth Century Episcopate: Careers and Bequests', in D. Baker, ed., *Studies in Church History* x, 1973, 117–28.

philosophy there at the beginning of the seventeenth century.[2] Budden's Latin life was based on a number of primary sources, including documents from the college muniments, but the result is somewhat eulogistic in tone. Budden was at least as concerned to display his own erudition in Latin composition as he was to detail Waynflete's career. The next work concerned with Waynflete, written c.1660, adds little to our historical knowledge of William Waynflete. This is the metrical life of the bishop written by Peter Heylin, a fellow of Magdalen College.[3] Its content was closely based on Budden's *Vita* but it was propagandist and hagiographic in style, being much coloured by Heylin's own political involvements, in particular his support for King Charles I, whom he parallels with Henry VI. It is of negligible historical or literary value as a short extract demonstrates:

> Then Henry was thy murther first made knowen,
> And all deplored thy lamentable state,
> Then Richard was thy tyranny first shown,
> And all abhorred thy most tyrannic state,
> But above all Wainfleet, the heavens did tear,
> With dolororous complaints; he had no mate
> Equal to him in greefe. Thus did he reare
> His plaints on high and with these following cries,
> Did tears extract out of Panicean eyes.

In the late eighteenth century Richard Chandler, D.D., rector of a Hampshire parish and one-time fellow of Magdalen College, wrote another biography of Waynflete.[4] It was solidly founded on detailed research especially amongst letters and charters in the college muniments and in the Winchester diocesan records. Chandler's work has remained the standard biography of Waynflete since it was published posthumously in the early nineteenth century.[5]

William Waynflete was a Lincolnshire man, although his direct residential connection with his native Lincolnshire was broken by the late 1420s. Henceforth he made his career in Southern England but this did not mean that all his links with his native county and particular with the area of his birthplace ceased. His family continued to live there and Waynflete's lasting connection with Lincolnshire can be seen in a number of ways throughout his career; as a

[2] J. Budden, *Gulielmi Patteni, Wintoniensis Ecclesie Presulis Vita Obitusque*, Oxford 1602.
[3] P. Heylin, *Memorial of Bishop Waynflete*, ed. J.R. Bloxam, Caxton Society, 1851. The quotation is taken from stanza 137. The tone of the work evident from the first verse which begins, 'Chant out my muse in thy most pleasing strain, that worthy prelate's fame . . .'.
[4] R. Chandler, *The Life of William Waynflete, Bishop of Winchester*, 1811.
[5] More recent brief biographical entries can be found in the *Dictionary of National Biography* and in A.B. Emden, *A Biographical Register of the University of Oxford to A.D. 1500*, 3 vols (Oxford 1957–9). Recent historians, writing on particular aspects of William Waynflete's activities, have drawn on these entries and additionally on Chandler's *Life* for their information about Waynflete's background and career.

benefactor to the town of Wainfleet and its inhabitants; as executor to Ralph Lord Cromwell, a commitment which involved him closely with Cromwell's foundation, Tattershall college; as co-founder of a chantry in Coningsby[6] and by the promotion of Lincolnshire men within his household circle after he became a bishop.[7] Throughout his adult career, however, William Waynflete's connections with his native Lincolnshire were private rather than public, he did not, for example, serve on royal commissions there. Yet despite the fact that he had few physical links with his birthplace during his lengthy career, it is clear that it remained important to him and that he actively promoted its interests where possible.[8]

William Waynflete's interests in education and in particular his concern with the teaching of grammar derived from his own experience as a teacher, were to dominate his career. His life spanned an important period of change in English educational practices. At the beginning of the century, schooling in England looked backwards to the traditions of previous centuries. Teaching of school-boys was still largely based on adapted versions of works such as Donatus which had been standard texts since the late classical period. The fourteenth century had seen one step forward with the translation of some basic teaching texts into English – John Cornwall's *Speculum Grammaticale* of 1346 was the first work to

---

6 PRO SC/8/251; 'Chantry Certificates Lincolnshire, nos 46, 47', *Lincolnshire Archaeological Society* 1947, 281–2.

7 Three important figures within the bishop's household were Lincolnshire men – William Darset, successively his chaplain, official-principal and chancellor; Simon Aylward, scribe, notary and agent for the bishop in matters connected with Magdalen College; Robert Peverell, notary and official-principal. Both Darset and Aylward had been pupils of Waynflete – Darset at Winchester College and Aylward at Eton – and this personal contact with Waynflete through educational links is likely to have been more important for their promotion than their Lincolnshire connection.

In the political sphere, an emphasis on Lincolnshire men can be seen in the first parliaments where Waynflete had the opportunity of exercising his patronage in the parliamentary boroughs under his control – Hindon and Taunton in Somerset and Downton in Wiltshire. In the parliaments of 1449, three of the men representing these boroughs came, not just from Lincolnshire but from the same coastal area of the county as the bishop himself – John Gibthorpe of Thorpe by Wainfleet, Hugh Witham of Kirton in Holland and Robert Tilney of Boston, J.C. Wedgewood, *History of Parliament 1439–1509*, 2 vols, 1936, *Register*, 109–12, 139, 142; *Biographies*, 61, 373, 856. Tilney continued to represent the borough of Hinton throughout the 1450s but no other Lincolnshire men subsequently represented any of these boroughs for the remaining thirty-five years of his episcopate. It seems that Waynflete who had little previous political experience and thus perhaps knew few suitable representatives had to fall back on men from his native area in these early years. This was not a pattern which was to continue.

8 In March 1457, just six months after Waynflete had become chancellor of England, he promoted a petition from the people of Wainfleet to the king which resulted in the grant of a charter of incorporation and a concomitant grant of freedom from customs and taxes to the town of Wainfleet. 'The Charter of Incorporation of Wainfleet', ed. R.M. Heanley, *Lincolnshire Notes and Queries* ii, 1890, 11–14.

include some explanations in English – but grammar as taught in the schools remained old fashioned.[9]

Contemporary commentators complained of a dire shortage of teachers by the early fifteenth century. This mirrors in some ways, both the general population decline and more particularly the continuing decline in recruitment to the English church.[10] Specific complaints about the shortage of teachers lie behind William Bingham's proposal of 1439 to set up a college in Cambridge which would train grammar teachers. According to Bingham's petition to the king:

> . . . how gretely the Clergie of this youre Reaume, by the which all wysdom, konnyng and gouernaunce standeth in, is like to be empeired and febled, by the defaute and lak of Scholemaistres of Gramer, in so moche that as your seyd poure besecher hath founde now of late ouer the Est partie of the wey ledyng from hampton to Couentre and so forth no ferther north than Rypon, lxx Scoles voide or mo that weren occupied all at ones within l yeres passed, bicause that ther is so grete scarstee of maistres of Gramer, whereof as now ben almost none, nor none mowen be hade in your Uniuersitees ouer those that nedes most ben occupied still there.[11]

Within the universities changes had begun with Bishop William Wykeham's foundation in the 1380s of New College Oxford, later to be linked with his grammar school, Winchester College. Yet the universities were still far from being collegiate institutions; most students were not attached to colleges, many may not even have been attached to the more ephemeral halls. By the end of the fifteenth century considerable changes were beginning to occur. Oxford and Cambridge had more and larger colleges. Continental humanist interests were making an impact on English thought and learning. Greek was beginning to be taught in England. New grammar texts designed to teach schoolboys and young men were being written. The introduction of printing provided an exciting and relatively inexpensive means of disseminating this new learning. In all these developments William Waynflete played a role. By the time of his death he was very much the elder statesman of the educational revolution of the century. Much of his career had been intertwined with educational developments and he deserves recognition as one of the great educationalists and patrons of late medieval England.

---

[9] For a general introduction to the schoolbooks in use in England throughout the middle ages see N. Orme, *English Schools in the Middle Ages*, 1973 and D. Thomson, *A Descriptive Catalogue of Middle English Grammatical Texts*, Oxford 1979.

[10] V. Davis, 'Rivals for Ministry? Ordinations of Secular and Regular Clergy in Southern England, c.1300–1500', in *Ministry: Clerical and Lay*, Studies in Church History xxvi, Oxford 1989, ed. W.J. Sheils and D. Wood, 99–109.

[11] Cambridge, King's College Muniments, quoted in *Educational Charters and Documents 598–1909*, ed. A. Leach, Cambridge 1911, 402–3.

Plate 1 Detail of effigy on Waynflete's tomb, Winchester Cathedral

I

William Waynflete:
Background and Biography

Early Life

Wainfleet, a port near Boston on the coast of Lincolnshire, was the birthplace of William Patten, subsequently William Waynflete bishop of Winchester. He was probably born in the early years of the fifteenth century; a papal dispensation exempting him from the triennial *ad limina* visit to the papal curia in 1470 describes him as 'almost a septuagenarian'.[1]

The history of Waynflete's family is poorly documented and has been further obscured by the work of early modern antiquarians who conflated the Patten family of Waynflete with other, quite separate Patten families, in an attempt to include Waynflete in their descent.[2] He was one of two sons of Richard Patten, also called Barbour. His mother was Margery Brereton, daughter of Sir William Brereton of Cheshire.[3] The Breretons held a Lincolnshire manor at Dalby which lay near Wainfleet[4] which makes the match plausible. Waynflete certainly had connections with the Brereton family in the 1450s and 1470s which suggest that he was related to them.[5] The one attested Brereton relation of William Waynflete was Juliana, his cousin, daughter of his paternal uncle

---

[1] *CPL 1458–71*, 782; this occurs in the context of a petition for a dispensation from the triennial *ad limina* visit to the Curia. Since Waynflete was petitioning on the grounds of his advanced age there was no need for him to understate his age; quite the reverse might in fact be expected. An earlier birth date for William Waynflete would conflict with the known date of his maternal grand-parents marriage, which took place in 1386, BL Harleian MS 2077.

[2] See for example, Lancashire Record Office DD HO 13, an elaborate genealogical roll for Thomas Patten of Bank which erroneously suggests that William Waynflete was brother to Richard Patten of Baselow in Derby; T. Fuller, *The Worthies of England*, 1662, 62; R. Holinshed, *Chronicles*, 1577, ed. Henry Ellis, 6 vols, 1807–8, ii, 627, 'W, eldest brother to John and to Richard that lived and died at Boslo in Derbyshire'.

[3] Budden, *Gulielmi Patteni*, 52; Chandler, *Life* 4.

[4] E. Oldfield, *A Topographical and Historical Account of Wainfleet in the County of Lincoln*, 1829, 311.

[5] MC Deeds Candlesby 19b, 5 April 1451 – Waynflete, his brother John and others were made feoffees to use for Alice Brereton of the manor of Dalby. MC Deeds Candlesby 18, 15 June 1474 – conveyance from William Brereton, knight, to William Waynflete,

Robert. A lost deed cited in Budden's *Life* describes Juliana as '. . . widow of Richard Churchstile deceased . . ., kinswoman and heir of master William de Waynflete, late bishop of Winchester; to wit sole daughter and heir of Robert Patten, brother and heir of Richard Patten, otherwise called Barbour, of Waynflete, father of the bishop.'[6]

There is little evidence for the social status of Richard Patten but he seems to have been of gentry stock. The effigy on his alabaster tomb, once in the parish church of Wainfleet All Saints but moved in the eighteenth century to Magdalen college chapel, shows him dressed in a prosperous manner. He is depicted with his hands clasped in prayer, dressed in a gown with wide puffed sleeves, tied with a decorated belt while on his fingers are two rings. This prosperous-looking attire may, however, owe more to Waynflete's own rise in social status than to the reality of his father's position for although no evidence has survived, it is inconceivable that the bishop was not involved with the construction of his father's tomb.[7]

Waynflete's brother John also entered the church, perhaps in his brother's wake. Certainly his success owed much to William's patronage. Until his brother's promotion to the see of Winchester, John Waynflete appears to have been unbeneficed. His first recorded benefice was the archdeaconry of Surrey to which Waynflete presented him, shortly after becoming bishop. After that, he was regularly promoted to a succession of benefices, reaching the peak of his ecclesiastical career when he became dean of Chichester in 1455.[8] The two brothers are depicted on Richard Patten's tomb, kneeling, one on each side of their father's head. Waynflete is on the right-hand side, distinguishable by his mitre and staff.

From an early date, writers have stated[9] that Waynflete was educated in Winchester at William Wykeham's recently founded Winchester college. Its records of scholars, however, are complete and do not include his name;[10] the

his brother John and Robert Brereton, rector of Brereton parish, Cheshire, of all manors and other lands in Lincolnshire. PRO C1/76/27 [1485–86] – Dame Maud, late wife of William Brereton, brings a case against William Bishop of Winchester, concerning the ownership of the manor of Dalby in Lincolnshire. Alice, William and Robert Brereton may have been Waynflete's cousins.

6 Budden, *Life*, 55. Budden states that the deed was in the Register of Magdalen College. Lancs Record Office DD HO 13 describes it as a lost deed which was in the Remembrancer's Office. Juliana held the manor of Dagenham in Essex.

7 The tomb was originally in the parish church of Wainfleet All Saints but was moved to Magdalen College chapel in the nineteenth century.

8 John Waynflete was presented to the benefice of Wonsyngham [Woldingham?] in the diocese of Winchester on 17 May 1447, by his brother, described as provost of Eton, warden of the temporalities of the diocese of Winchester, Lambeth, Register John Stafford, fo 93v; for John Waynflete's career generally see *BRUO*, 2001; see also W.D. Peckham, 'John Waynflete, Dean of Chichester', *Sussex Notes and Queries* xii, 1949, 7–9.

9 Budden, *Life*; others are listed in Chandler, *Life*, 5.

10 He does not appear under any possible form of his surname – Waynflete, Patten or

Richard Patten,
Bewfino of Lincolnshire,
A.B. Reader of Linco[...]
empowering the authority
of the [...] in the autho[...]
of the Tombing [...]
and [...] in the [...]
D.Part of the [...] Tomb.

Plate 2   Tomb of Waynflete's father in Magdalen College Chapel

names of commoners are not so well recorded but unless he had a local patron, which was not the case, it is unlikely that he attended in this capacity. The source of this tradition can be traced to a misunderstood reference in the theological dictionary of Thomas Chaundler, warden of New College Oxford (d.1490), whose description of one of Henry VI's chaplains William Say as '. . . springing from the root of such a foundation [Winchester college], like a flourishing shoot, by the help and assistance of Thomas Beckington, most beneficent lord, he grew, as it, were into a mighty cedar . . .' has been erroneously taken to refer to William Waynflete.[11] It is far more likely that the future bishop received his early education locally at a school within Lincolnshire.

A similar lack of certainty surrounds William Waynflete's early ecclesiastical career. Wainfleet was a substantial port in the early fifteenth century and a number of men from the town entered the church. This, combined with the fact that John and William were the most popular names for English boys in this period,[12] make it difficult to identify positively references in the Lincoln ordination lists and institutions' registers relating to William Waynflete the future bishop and his brother.

Of the numerous references to men called William Waynflete in the sources, three have been identified with the bishop by various authors. William Waynflete would have been too young to be the man referred to in a papal dispensation of December 1410 which described the recipient as being in his 'eighteenth year'.[13] It has been accepted that he was the man to whom, on 26 September 1416 Philip Repington, bishop of Lincoln, granted a *cum ex eo* licence, enabling him to be absent from the benefice for three years for the purpose of studying at a university.[14] This William Waynflete, is described in the licence as rector of Binbrook. The man who was presented to Binbrook – still only with a first tonsure and not yet ordained to any of the major orders – been presented to Salmonby parish by John Kyghley on 3 January 1416.[15] Three weeks later he had exchanged Salmonby for the parish of Binbrook with a master John Waynflete, not his brother because this man had graduated from Cambridge as a bachelor in Canon Law in 1390 and had held Binbrook since

Barbour. This has been pointed out by Chandler, *Life*, 5 and subsequently by T.F. Kirby, *Annals of Winchester College*, 1892, 198, but the tradition that Waynflete was himself educated at Wykeham's foundation persists in the secondary literature.

[11] Oxford Bodl. MS Lincoln Coll 117; on Chaundler see, *BRUO* 2001.

[12] Over 30% of all entrants to the church recorded in ordination lists in this period were called John, while about 15% were called William, see V. Davis, 'Medieval English clergy database' *History and Computing* ii, 1990, 79–80.

[13] Two dispensations to hold a benefice with cure were issued, one to a John Waynflete and one to a William Waynflete; although it is tempting to identify these with the brothers they would hardly have been old enough and there is no supporting evidence, *CPL* 1405–15, 224.

[14] This identification is provided in Emden, *BRUO*, 2001. Reg Rep fo 154r.

[15] LRO Register xv, [Philip Repington] fo 77v.

1400.[16] Binbrook was still held by a William Waynflete in 1420;[17] by September 1427 it was in the hands of a Thomas Lavenham.[18] While it is not impossible that this may be the future bishop, it is unlikely in view of his age. The man who held Binbrook may more plausibly be identified with the William Waynflete who was a clerk at the Exchequer in the early 1420s and who later became a fellow at King's Hall Cambridge.[19] From a chronological perspective, the most likely of the numerous ordination list references to William Waynflete, to be identified with the future bishop may be those which refer to a man of this name being ordained as an unbeneficed acolyte at Holbeck church in February 1425, as subdeacon with a title from the Lincolnshire priory of Markby in December of the same year and as deacon with the same title in September 1426.[20]

The details of William Waynflete's own university education are similarly obscure. Evidence of Waynflete's Oxford education is provided by the university itself which claimed him as an ex-student in a letter of 1447. Waynflete had recently been promoted to the episcopate and the university authorities requested his help to obtain the benefaction left to them by Humphrey Duke of Gloucester. In their letter to him they describe the university as 'your mother who nourished you in learning'.[21] Beyond this, no collegiate link can be traced. It has usually been accepted that Waynflete was a member of New College Oxford which drew its students from Winchester College but again the collegiate records of scholars are complete and his name does not appear. In his *Description of England*, the sixteenth century chronicler William Harrison stated that Waynflete was a member of Merton College but he is not recorded there either.[22] The fact that his name does not appear in the records of any of the colleges does not mean that he did not go to the University of Oxford. In the early fifteenth century neither Oxford nor Cambridge were essentially collegiate universities. Many students belonged to halls whose ephemeral nature meant that they have left few records; others seem not even to have been attached to halls. Increasingly it is becoming clear that many of the men who were students at Oxford or Cambridge in the fifteenth century are not to be found among the formal records. Before the matriculation statute of 1564/5, it was possible to be a student without leaving any trace in the records; this might occur, for

---

16 Reg Beaufort fo 131; See *BRUC.*

17 LRO Register xv, [Philip Repington] fo 170v.

18 *CPL* 1417–31, 499.

19 This William Waynflete was a BCL, not a BTh, PRO E28/49; E404/37/174; Trinity College Cambridge Library, Account Books of King's Hall, vols vii, viii.

20 LRO Register xvi [Richard Fleming], fos 200v, 203v, 207v.

21 'Credimus enim semper tibi ante occulos esse quanto tenearis amore in matrem, que te spirituali conceptum utere in lucem cognicionis eduxit', *Epistolae academicae Oxon*, ed. H. Anstey, OHS xxxv, 1898, 258.

22 Cited in the *DNB* article on Waynflete; *Merton Muniments*, ed. P.S. Allen and H.W. Garrod, OHS lxxvi, 1928; *The Early Rolls of Merton College*, ed. J.R.L. Highfield, OHS ns xviii, 1963.

example, if a man did not supplicate for a degree or if details of the supplication are missing, or if his hall or college did not keep adequate records or if he was not attached to a hall or college.[23] The term 'chamberdeakin' appears in the fifteenth century to describe a poor clerk at university; it seems likely that this is precisely the category into which an aspirant young scholar like Waynflete fell. Having achieved his arts degree – for which there is no record – Waynflete proceeded to the study of the highest branch of learning, theology. It is not known when he supplicated for the degree; the earliest reference to him as a Bachelor of Theology dates from September 1443, after he had become provost of Eton college.[24]

Clear and unequivocal documentation of William Waynflete's career really only begins his mid-twenties, when in June 1430, he appears as *magister informator* or headmaster at Winchester College.

Winchester College

William Wykeham had founded Winchester College in 1382 as a grammar school. Subsequently he was to link it with his other foundation, New College Oxford and boys from Winchester College proceeded to New College. Some seventy boys were allowed for by the statutes of Winchester College and in addition there were a number of day boys. These students were taught by a grammar master, assisted by an usher. It was not a very senior position. The headmaster was an employee of the college, not a member of the foundation; he was subordinate to the warden of the college but his position was important enough to permit him to dine at high table with the warden and senior fellows.[25]

In September 1429 the College sent one of their fellows to Oxford to seek a master.[26] Waynflete's appointment followed, suggesting that perhaps he had been in Oxford throughout the decade of the 1420s. Oxford was still the great centre for grammar teachers.[27] It is possible that Waynflete had had some teaching experience prior to his appointment as headmaster for Wykeham's statutes had stipulated that the master should be a man *'in gramaticam sufficienter eruditus, habens docendi peritiam, vir bone fame et conversationis.'*[28] However since university learning involved some teaching, that in itself may have been enough and he may not have had any further experience.

Waynflete taught at Winchester College throughout the 1430s. The college

[23] E. Russell, 'The Influx of Commoners into the University of Oxford before 1581: an Optical Illusion?', *EHR* xcii, 1977, 721–45.

[24] ECR 39/30.

[25] Kirby, *Annals of Winchester*, 80.

[26] WCM 22106, bursars' accounts 1429–30.

[27] Br Bonaventure, 'The Teaching of Latin in Later Medieval England', *Mediaeval Studies* xxiii, 1961, 15.

[28] *Annals of Winchester*, 484.

hall books show that he was in residence for the bulk of the time with only two short periods of absence, 18 May – 8 June 1431 and 9 – 16 March 1435.[29] During this time he was assisted by a number of ushers but they rarely stayed for more than a few years and their names have not survived.

Wykeham's statutes were specific about the duties of the master. He was to teach or to supervise the teaching of grammar to the scholars and was also responsible for discipline, for the chastisement of the '*negligentes seu alias delinquentes*'. The scholars themselves ranged in age from eight to eighteen, with Founder's Kin being allowed to remain until the age of twenty-five. Before they were admitted they were supposed to have grasped the rudiments of grammar and plainsong.[30]

Some idea of what Waynflete taught can be derived from a surviving inventory of the college library drawn up by one of the fellows in 1432, not long after Waynflete's appointment as headmaster.[31] This inventory listed the books, their value, the donor where known and the first couple of words of the second folio of each. The list was divided by subject into sections; the final section – *libri grammaticales* – lists nineteen works. Predominant among these were the commonly used texts of Priscian and Peter Helias which formed the basis for the Arts course. Of particular interest are the two works which were described as 'being in the hands of the master of the scholars'.[32] These were *Liber continens librum equivocorum et librum magni doctrinalis* and *Liber continens quandam compilationem de informatione puerorum cum aliis parvis tractatibus*. Neither work survives today in Winchester college library but the *Compilatio de informatione puerorum* to judge from its title was of a type used quite widely by Waynflete's contemporaries.[33] Similar works covered the four principal parts of grammar: etymology, orthography, prosody and syntax. There were almost as many different texts as there were teachers and no one set of texts or glosses was widely used. Prior to the 1480s when the printed works of English grammarians such as John Anwykyll (and later, of John Stanbridge) became available to teachers of Latin in England, masters like Waynflete had to rely either on earlier works produced on the continent which had elaborate glosses adapting them for teaching in England or works like that of the English grammarian John Leland. By the latter half of the fourteenth century the teaching of Latin through English rather than French had become common and it is not therefore surprising to find that this *Compilatio* was in English – the words cited in the catalogue from the beginning of the second folio being 'ablytif case'.

29 WCM 22824–7 Hall Books.

30 Kirby, *Annals of Winchester*, 88.

31 This inventory is printed in 'Catalogue of Books Belonging to the College of St Mary Winchester in the Reign of Henry VI', ed. W.H. Gunner, *Archaeological Journal* xv, 1858, 59–74.

32 *Ibid.*, 74.

33 'The Teaching of Latin in Later Medieval England', 13–18; R.W. Hunt, 'Oxford Grammar Masters of the Later Middle Ages', *Oxford Studies Presented to Daniel Callus*, OHS ns xvi, 1964, 163–93; Orme, *English Schools*, chapter 3.

It must have been while at Winchester that Waynflete was the recipient of a piece of minor patronage from Cardinal Beaufort, Bishop of Winchester. The college lay not far from the episcopal palace of Wolvesey and during this period the Cardinal visited the college on a number of occasions.[34] These visits would have provided an opportunity for Waynflete to come, albeit briefly, to the attention of the cardinal. In the 1430s the Cardinal collated Waynflete to the mastership of the small hospital of Mary Magdalen which was situated just outside the city of Winchester.[35] Such a presentation was not unusual; the first schoolmaster of Winchester College, John Melton, had also held the mastership of Mary Magdalen hospital.[36] Since a substantial part of Beaufort's episcopal register has been lost the precise date of this presentation is not known, but Waynflete was certainly master by 1438, for in that year he was involved in a legal wrangle over its possessions.[37] Waynflete retained this benefice until his elevation to the episcopate; he then resigned it, appointing one of his chaplains in his stead.[38] This early piece of patronage is likely to have been the reason why he subsequently looked to Mary Magdalen as his spiritual patron. She was depicted on his episcopal signet seal, in the *Noli me tangere* scene;[39] he dedicated the college he founded in Oxford to her and the chantry chapel in Winchester Cathedral in which he was to be buried was also dedicated to her.

Waynflete remained headmaster at Winchester for eleven years, a longer period than any of his predecessors. While this lengthy stay may reflect his commitment to the position, it may also have been occasioned by the lack of other opportunities for advancement in this period. Progression within the church without influential patrons was not easy; his brother John Waynflete made equally little career progress at this period, all his prebends and offices were obtained in the wake of his brother's advancement to the episcopate. William Waynflete's subordinate position within the college means that we know little of his activities during this period but clearly he attracted Beaufort's attention, as he was later to attract that of Beaufort's great nephew, Henry VI. It

---

34 *Annals of Winchester*, 176–9.

35 This hospital existed until the late eighteenth century. It consisted of a row of habitations, a chapel and a common hall; it is illustrated in R.M. Clay, *The Medieval Hospitals*, 1909, plate xxi.

36 D. Keene, *Survey of Medieval Winchester*, 2 vols, Oxford 1985, i, 1296. Melton was schoolmaster at Wincester College 1388 to 1394; he seems to have succeeded to the wardenship of the hospital after he ceased to be schoolmaster, rather than holding the two positions concurrently; he was warden from 1394 until his death in 1404, *BRUO* 1257; *CPR* 401–5, 450.

37 [J. Wavell], *The History and Antiquities of Winchester*, 2 vols, Winchester 1773, ii, 177–8. Although the document cited no longer survives, Wavell's information is likely to be accurate for his position as master of the hospital gave him access to its records which no longer survive.

38 Thomas Yon was presented to the mastership on 12 February 1448, Reg Waynflete I fo 3r.

39 W.G. Birch, *Catalogue of Seals in the Department of Manuscripts in the British Museum*, 6 vols, 1887–1900, i, 355.

is possible that Beaufort recommended the young king to consider the *magister informator* of Winchester college when he was planning the foundation of Eton college, although this can be no more than speculation.

In early August 1441, Henry VI visited Winchester College; the college archives record details of the royal visit and the entertainment of the king who attended mass and dined in the College Hall.[40] The following month Waynflete entered the royal service initially in some undefined role connected with the development of Eton College, although subsequently he became provost. Waynflete's move to Eton college was the major step in a progress which was to return him to Winchester; this time as successor to his one-time patron Cardinal Beaufort, a move which would have astounded both men had they had foreknowledge of it in the 1430s. His enormous contribution to the development of the Eton College is discussed in detail below. There can be no doubt that the move to Eton marked a vital turning point in his career; while there he was in regular communication with the king and in contact with other members of the court circle. His success as provost led directly to his promotion to the episcopate, a promotion which arose from Waynflete's success in winning the support and gratitude of Henry VI for his work in developing the King's beloved foundation of Eton College, although it was Waynflete's own abilities and astuteness which turned Henry VI's desire to give him such a reward into a reality. Promotion to the episcopate, and more particularly, promotion to such a rich see as Winchester, gave him the opportunity and equally the resources to indulge his interests in education still further. As bishop of Winchester he exploited his position and the considerable financial resources of his see to become a great founder and educational patron.

Election as Bishop

Waynflete was promoted to the see of Winchester in the spring of 1447, only six years after he had left Winchester college for the royal foundation at Eton. Waynflete's election as bishop took place with remarkable speed. Less than a week elapsed between the death of Cardinal Beaufort and the election of Waynflete as his successor by the chapter of Winchester Cathedral. The letters of provision were dated a month later, 10 May; by the end of July Waynflete had been consecrated bishop of England's richest see. No previous election of a bishop of Winchester had been effected with such haste – a year had elapsed between the death of Edington and the consecration of Wykeham in 1367; six months in 1404 in the case of Beaufort, himself of royal blood and eleven months in that of Peter Courteney, Waynflete's successor.[41] Part of the emphasis on haste came directly from the king: both the chronology of events and the

---

[40] WCM 22992, Liber Albus; WCM 22117, Bursars' accounts 1440–41.
[41] *HBC* 58. There were particular problems in the case of Wykeham, although King Edward III was keen for his elevation, Pope Urban V was reluctant, partly because of

contents of the royal letters to the cathedral chapter show Henry VI to have been enthusiastically encouraging Waynflete's candidature.[42]

The death of Henry Beaufort, Cardinal-priest of St Eusebius and bishop of Winchester since 1404, took place in Wolvesey Palace, his episcopal residence in the city of Winchester, on Tuesday 11 April 1447. Beaufort's death was hardly unexpected; he was an elderly man and had been in decline for some time; a contemporary described him as languishing on the point of death nearly three weeks earlier on 25 March.[43] News of the death of a member of the episcopate would naturally be sent quickly to the king but on this occasion the urgency must have been increased in view of Beaufort's royal blood and his relationship to Henry VI. The King, who was at Windsor Castle when he received the news,[44] responded immediately, dispatching a letter under the signet addressed to the prior and chapter of St Swithun's cathedral licensing them to proceed to the election of a new bishop. It continued,

> . . . And preye you hertily that in alle the haste that ye goodly may, ye wol so do, having by oon assent oure right trusty and welbeloved clerc and concelloure maister William Waynflete Provost of our College Royal of oure lady of Eton at the reverence of us and contemplacion of this oure writing, in your sayd election to be Bisshop of youre sayd chirch before alle other especially recommended, whom as ye knowe wel we have in the most tender favour of oure good grace, wherinne ye shall not oonly provide youre sayd chirch of right a notable clerc and a substantial personne to goddes plesir and to the worship and wele of the same as we truste, but also do unto us right singular plesir and cause us to have bothe you and the sayd chirch in the more special favour of our good grace in tyme to come . . .[45]

Such a recommendation, combined with the veiled threat implied in the promise of special favour can have left no doubt in the minds of the chapter as to the king's desires. Henry VI had moved more precipitately than the chapter itself for its letter, requesting the issue of the *conge d'elire* was not sent until the following day, 12 April.[46] This must have crossed with the king's original letter

Wykeham's reputation as a pluralist, J. Highfield, 'The Promotion of William of Wickham to the See of Winchester,' *JEH* iv, 1953, 37–54.

[42] Details of the election proceedings were recorded in the register of the priory of St Swithun (Winchester Cathedral), *The Register of the Common Seal of the Priory of St Swithun, Winchester*, ed. J. Greatrex, Hampshire Record Series ii, Hampshire County Council 1979, 99–100.

[43] K.B. McFarlane, 'At the Death-Bed of Cardinal Beaufort', in *England in the Fifteenth Century – Collected Essays*, 1981, 115–38, prints two descriptions of Beaufort's death. His own will, with its numerous added codicils, also attests to the long-drawn out nature of his last illness, see G.L. Harriss, *Cardinal Beaufort*, Oxford 1988, 376–9.

[44] Wolffe, *Henry VI*, itinerary 363.

[45] The letter was dated 11 April, the day of Beaufort's death. It is printed in full in Chandler, *Life*, appendix i, 299–300 and calendared in the *Register of the Common Seal*, 99.

[46] *Register of the Common Seal*, 99.

for the arrival of the proctors of the priory with their petition resulted in the issue of a second royal letter. Again the selection of Waynflete was urged and this time it set Saturday 15 April as the date for the election. In addition Henry's letter stated that the election was to proceed without waiting for, 'eny lettres under oure grete seel for we have in such wise ordeined that ye shal not nede theym at that tyme but have theym in goodly haast after bering date before . . .'[47] The chancellor, archbishop Stafford, was in his cathedral city at that time and the election would have had to be delayed if the chapter had waited for formal authorization under the great seal. When issued later, the letters were backdated as promised to 15 April, despite the fact that a recent statute had forbidden this practice.[48]

The chapter met as suggested on Saturday 15 April, having formally agreed at a meeting on the Friday that the following day would be suitable. After a Mass sung at the High Altar in Winchester Cathedral, the bells were rung and the community assembled in the chapter house. In addition to the prior William Aulton and thirty-six monks, the archdeacon of Winchester, a representative of John de la Bere who was archdeacon of Surrey and Richard Petworth, a notary public, were present. The archdeacon of Winchester, Stephen Wilton had also received a letter from the king requesting that he assist the monks in the election.[49] Presumably the king wished Wilton to be particularly careful to ensure the canonical legality of the election in order to reduce the possibility that it might be subsequently challenged. After Wilton had read the general constitution, '. . . all felt themselves to be immediately inspired by the Holy Spirit to cast their votes for M. William Waynflete . . .'. The *Te Deum* was sung and finally, to conclude the proceedings, the chapter processed to the high altar where the archdeacon announced their choice in English to the waiting people. Proctors were then sent to Eton College where provost Waynflete, apparently after an initial show of reluctance, gave his formal acceptance.[50]

On Monday 17 April, less than a week after Beaufort's death, the chapter of St Swithun's priory addressed a letter to the king, rounding off their part in the proceedings by petitioning for royal assent to their choice.[51] Prior Aulton wrote to Pope Nicholas V informing him of Beaufort's death and the subsequent election.[52] On 10 May, letters of provision were issued to Waynflete, the pope

---

[47] *Register of the Common Seal*, 100.

[48] *CPR 1446–52*, 44.

[49] This letter is no longer extant but is mentioned in Henry's second letter to the chapter; presumably the king wished Wilton to be particularly careful to ensure the canonical legality of the election to reduce the possibility that it might be subsequently challenged.

[50] *Register of the Common Seal*, 101.

[51] *Ibid.*, 100–1.

[52] *Ibid.*, 101–2.

thus maintaining his prerogative with regard to his nomination of members of the English episcopate.[53]

The final stage in the transformation of William Waynflete from schoolmaster and provost of Eton College to bishop of Winchester took place in Eton College chapel where, on 30 July, his consecration was held.[54] The temporalities had been restored to him on 4 June, which may have been the date on which the king had received the news of papal approval of the new bishop[55] although in reality Waynflete had had jurisdiction of the temporalities of his future see since Beaufort's death, for Henry VI appointed him custodian of them on 11 April.[56] Once Waynflete's position as bishop was assured, the need for haste had passed and there seems to have been a lull in the proceedings. His installation in Winchester cathedral did not take place until January 1449, eighteen months later.[57] His episcopal register begins recording his activities from the end of October 1447, by which time he was resident in the episcopal palace in Southwark.[58]

It is clear that William Waynflete's election as bishop was not merely efficiently conducted, it was rushed. The proceedings surrounding the requests for congé d'elire and royal assent to the choice of the chapter were usually conducted in a slower and more cumbersome manner. Why on this occasion was the king so emphatic about the need for speed?

A formal reason is given by the king in his second letter to the monks of St Swithun's where he indicates his reluctance to allow the cathedral church of Winchester should to be vacant for any length of time and encourages the monks to 'proceed to election in all goodly haste . . .'[59] Such consideration was rarely to be found in royal dealings with these matters and, although Henry VI has a reputation for piety, his anxiety for the good ordering of the church can hardly have been the sole cause of the haste shown in pressing the election of his provost of Eton College as bishop of Winchester. The real reason must lie in Henry VI's previous conspicuous lack of success in promoting his candidates to the episcopal bench. Although in 1437 the young king had announced his

53 *CPL 1447–55*, 298; the letters of provision state that the see had been reserved to the pope during Beaufort's lifetime.
54 *Registrum Sacrum Anglicanum*, 90.
55 *CPR 1446–52*, 55.
56 *Ibid.*, 53. Waynflete was active as custodian of the temporalities, presenting to benefices in the gift of the bishop as can be seen from *sede vacante* Winchester entries in the archiepiscopal register of John Stafford, Lambeth, Register Stafford 1443–1452.
57 The *Liber Albus* of Winchester College (WCM 22992) records the visit of Henry VI to the college on the occasion of Waynflete's installation; the bursars' accounts for 1448–9 (WCM 22123) itemise the college's expenditure on celebrations. Among the guests were the provosts of Eton and King's colleges and the bishop of Bath and Wells, Thomas Beckington, an ex-pupil of the college and a man closely associated with Waynflete in the foundation of Eton.
58 Reg Waynflete, i, fo 1r, 28 October 1447.
59 Calendared in *Register of the Common Seal*, 100, and printed in apppendix iii, Chandler, *Life*.

intention of exercising his prerogative especially in matters relating to the dispensing of patronage,[60] in reality he had often failed to realise this desire. He had been particularly unsuccessful in the important area of the episcopate. In 1445, two years before Waynflete's election, Henry had been out-manoeuvred by his council when he failed to secure the much less important bishopric of Norwich for his confessor John Stanbury. Instead Norwich went to Walter Lyhert, the chaplain of the Duke of Suffolk.[61] Stanbury had to wait until 1448 for episcopal promotion; it was not until then that he became bishop of Bangor. 'It is clear that the king's prerogative in making ecclesiastical appointments was subject to Suffolk's approval' was the conclusion of one study of the appointment of bishops under Lancastrian rule.[62] The speed with which the king acted in the case of Winchester must have been designed to present his advisers with a fait accompli: a completed and canonical election which would be difficult to challenge and overturn.

Waynflete had been in close contact with Suffolk in matters relating to the foundation of Eton College[63] but he was not amongst that powerful figure's proteges. Waynflete, as a schoolmaster with no experience either of diocesan or royal administration, must have been viewed by his contemporaries as an unexpected and perhaps even unsuitable choice. Even if Suffolk approved of Waynflete personally there is likely to have been doubt, in view of this lack of experience, of his ability to fill what was the richest and one of the most influential sees of England. Unfortunately there is no evidence as to Suffolk's whereabouts during this week in April and it is impossible to know whether he was aware of Henry VI's speedy reaction to the news of Beaufort's death before the election of Waynflete by the cathedral chapter took place.

In these circumstances, an apparently apocryphal story told by Waynflete's first biographer about his election has a ring of truth. According to this anecdote, the king came to Waynflete at Eton College and asked him whether he thought that he could manage to retain a benefice if he were to be given one. Waynflete apparently replied that he could certainly do his best whereupon Henry VI informed him that he was making him bishop of Winchester.[64] Such an incident might well have taken place prior to the death of Beaufort for the evidence shows Waynflete well prepared to 'do his best' to retain the benefice, demonstrating at this early stage in his career the shrewd and efficient business behaviour which can be seen later in his lifetime.[65] On this occasion he left little

60 Wolffe, *Henry VI*, 91–92.

61 *HBC*, 243.

62 L. Betcherman, 'The Making of Bishops in the Lancastrian Period', *Speculum* xli, 1966, 416.

63 Suffolk had been one of the chief advisors to the king about the fabric of Eton College, see Lyte, *Eton College*, 11.

64 Budden, *Gulielmi Patteni*, 34; although Budden cites this story he does not appear to believe it.

65 See for example his astute behaviour while executor of the will of Sir John Fastolf which resulted in Fastolf's inheritance going to Magdalen College Oxford, below, pp. 131–38.

to chance. While the letter from the cathedral chapter to Pope Nicholas V records his initial reluctance to accept the bishopric[66] – the expected and customary response to such an offer – evidence from the Vatican archives shows him to have been ready and indeed waiting to accept such a position.

On 15 May 1447 William Radclyff B.C.L.[67] and Antonious de Caxa, a Florentine merchant, proctors on behalf of Waynflete paid 12,000 florins in services to the Apostolic Camera.[68] This was in response to the issue of the letters of provision which made Waynflete bishop elect of Winchester. There was nothing unusual in his choice of these men as proctors; both had acted at the Roman Curia on behalf of other Englishmen.[69] However, proxy instruments which gave them authority to act on Waynflete's behalf had been drawn up on 9 March,[70] a month before Beaufort's death and the ensuing vacancy in the see of Winchester. Clearly Waynflete had his proctors waiting at the curia, ready to act on his behalf as soon as news of Beaufort's death reached Rome.

Waynflete can hardly have been the expected successor to Cardinal Beaufort. Although it may have been felt that his services to the king as provost of Eton College deserved some reward, the see of Winchester was a most singular prize. At most he might have expected to have been rewarded like John Langton who was elevated to the bishopric of St David's in May 1447, or Stanbury, the king's confessor, who got Bangor in 1448. Some of the men already holding sees could have expected translation to Winchester. One such was Marmaduke Lumley, the bishop of Carlisle who was treasurer and who had been bishop of Carlisle for seventeen years. Lumley had owed his original promotion to the patronage of Beaufort. Other possible candidates were Robert Neville, bishop of Durham and another Beaufort protege; William Alnwick, bishop of Lincoln since 1437; the king's confessor and Suffolk's close associate William Ayscough, bishop of Salisbury since 1438 or even Adam Moleyns, recently promoted bishop of Chichester. Bishop Bourgchier of Ely and and Bishop Lacy of Exeter were also experienced members of the episcopate, although Lacy was perhaps too old; the former in particular clearly had the potential to rise since in 1454 he was to become Archbishop of Canterbury. Waynflete, however competent he may have been in his position as provost of Eton College would seem to have had little chance of competing successfully with these men for the bishopric of Winchester. The fact that he succeeded Beaufort with apparent ease should lead us to view his prowess as a skilled political manoeuvrer with considerable respect.

While the elevation to such a position could not have been achieved single-

[66] *Register of the Common Seal*, 101.

[67] *BRUC*, 469.

[68] H. Hoberg, *Taxae pro Communibus Servitiis 1295–1455*, Rome 1938, 133; W.M. Brady, *The Episcopal Succession in England, Scotland and Wales*, 3 vols, Rome 1876–7, i, 11.

[69] William Booth, bishop of Coventry and Lichfield also used Radclyff as a proctor in 1447.

[70] Brady, *Episcopal Succession* i, 11.

handedly, even with the rather broken reed of royal support,[71] the main credit must remain with Waynflete himself whose rapidity of action and political acumen succeeded against the odds. His distribution of ecclesiastical patronage in the year after his promotion does not suggest that he had debts to pay to supporters. The first collation recorded in his episcopal register was to one of the most important benefices in his gift – the archdeaconry of Surrey.[72] To this he presented his own brother, John Waynflete, a definite assertion of his own independence from patrons.

Waynflete's successful election as bishop of Winchester in 1447 was not therefore a casual appointment but the result of careful efforts on the part of both Waynflete and the king. In view of Henry VI's previous failures in this sphere, it is clear that much of the credit for his succession this occasion must be attributed to Waynflete's own efforts.

> A man whose discretion, knowledge and blameless way of life are to be commended; he is in priest's orders and meets the requirements with regard to his legitimate birth, age and free status. In addition his prudence, both in spiritual and secular affairs and his remarkable virtues and abilities will enable him to defend the rights of their church.[73]

This laudatory statement of Waynflete's virtues is to be found in the letter of the prior of St Swithun to Pope Nicholas V, advancing the reasons for their choice of prelate. While the factual essentials can be taken as true, the fact that the priory were seeking approval of their election may have coloured their description of Waynflete. How did he compare with other fifteenth century prelates and what was the contemporary opinion of his elevation?

This latter question cannot be satisfactorily answered for what contemporary comments exist largely postdate his election, being written after he had proved himself a conscientious member of the episcopate. Chronicles refer to the death of Beaufort but little is said of the choice of Waynflete or his performance as bishop until his own obit comes to be written. The chronicle of John Benet is typical, merely mentioning that the cardinal of Winchester was succeeded by master William Waynflete, provost of Eton college.[74]

In 1447 William Waynflete was a man in early midde-age, a theologian by training, a schoolmaster by vocation. He was in priest's orders but had little experience of pastoral work. For the previous six years he had served Henry VI as provost of Eton College and during that time he had become a trusted royal

---

71 Thomas Gascoigne in *Loci e Libro Veritatum* implies that Henry VI was not even aware of how a man could become a bishop when he recounts the story of his own meeting with the king at Windsor Castle. Henry VI apparently asked Gascoigne on this occasion why he was not yet a bishop!, *Loci e Libro Veritatum*, ed. J.T. Rogers, 1881, xlv.

72 Reg Waynflete, i fo 1v.

73 *Register of the Common Seal*, 101.

74 'John Benet's Chronicle for the Years 1400–1462', ed. G.L. & M.A. Harriss, *Camden Miscellany* xxiv, Camden Society 1972, 193.

councillor. Prior to 1441 he had been schoolmaster in Winchester college. All in all the impression is that he was competent and acceptable to the king but there is nothing to suggest that he was the ideal choice for the next bishop of Winchester, to replace a man who was not only of royal blood but an assured international figure. How does Waynflete fit into the pattern of episcopal promotion under the Lancastrians?

His social origins present no problem; they can be roughly summed up as middle class gentry, not aristocratic but not unduly humble. Although some members of the episcopal bench were of aristocratic blood, others such as John Carpenter were of obscurer parentage. Carpenter, bishop of Worcester 1444–76 was the son of a tenant on the estates of the bishopric of Worcester.[75] Neither did his theological training make Waynflete an unusual choice for the episcopate. The last decades of Lancastrian rule were a favourable period for the elevation of theologians; of the twenty five bishops created between 1443–61 sixteen were theologians. Prior to 1443 the theologians, many of whom were members of the regular clergy, were presented to the less well-endowed sees; after that date they had a virtual monopoly over the lesser and middling sees. Winchester, however, was a see of prime importance and Waynflete was the first graduate in theology to be appointed to it.[76]

While Waynflete was a bachelor of theology, most of the men with theological degrees promoted between 1385–1461 were doctors of theology.[77] That Waynflete was not, reflects the fact that although his higher degree was in theology it would be misleading to describe him as a theologian. Vocationally he was a schoolmaster. A recent study of schoolmasters in the later middle ages pointed out that '. . . hardly anyone who had been a schoolmaster reached a high position between 1307–1509, either in church or state . . . teaching evidently did little to forward their ambitions and may even have done them harm.'[78] Two other teachers reached the forefront of public life under Henry VI – John Chedworth, bishop of Lincoln 1452–71 and John Somerset, Chancellor of the Exchequer. Neither, however, had been a schoolmaster. Chedworth had been tutor to Robert, Lord Hungerford and Somerset had been master of Bury St Edmunds and tutor to the king. Waynflete was the only episcopal figure in this period known to have taught in a public school. He was the sole exception to the rule that teachers 'were overlooked, forgotten and unnoticed.'[79]

Waynflete was also unusual in his to his lack of previous church preferments; royal and governmental servants who were rewarded with a bishopric as the climax of their careers had usually held a number of lesser church preferments at the earlier stages of their careers. One group of bishops in the fifteenth

[75] C. Dyer, *Lords and Peasants in a Changing Society*, Cambridge 1980, 154.
[76] Davies, 'The Episcopate' in *Profession, Vocation and Culture in the Fifteenth Century*, 59.
[77] *Ibid.*, 56.
[78] N. Orme, 'Schoolmasters 1307–1509', in Clough, ed. *Profession, Vocation and Culture in the Fifteenth Century*, 226.
[79] *Ibid.*, 227.

century who had averaged twenty-two years in the church prior to their promotion to the episcopate, averaged five rectories and four prebends each.[80] By comparison Waynflete had only held one hospital mastership. As a schoolmaster and a secular clerk without other church or governmental connections if not as a theologian, Waynflete was an unusual choice for the important see of Winchester. His elevation must be attributed entirely to his fortune in attracting Henry VI's attention, initially during the first royal visit to Winchester College and subsequently as provost of Eton college. It would have been difficult to predict in 1447 what sort of bishop he would prove to be.

Episcopate, 1447–1486

Any attempt made to view a late medieval bishop in the role of spiritual leader within his diocese is fraught with difficulties created by a lack of evidence. Except in rare cases where sermons or other spiritual writings have survived, our picture of late medieval bishops in their dioceses is drawn essentially from administrative documents and thus the episcopate is presented primarily in an administrative role. This does not pose as great a problem of balance as might be supposed, for most bishops' administrative activities, both inside their dioceses and in the central government clearly filled their lives, not as a rule leaving great lacuna which might or might not be filled with spiritual thoughts. The aim of this section is not to study the diocese of Winchester during Waynflete's episcopate but rather to provide a brief overall assessment of Waynflete's attitude toward his pastoral role as bishop and his performance as bishop.

In Winchester, as elsewhere, within the diocese there existed a comprehensive administrative structure which could operate, if required, with minimal involvement by the bishop. The presence of a conscientious bishop however added to its efficiency. In Winchester during William Waynflete's episcopate the direction of affairs came clearly from the top; the bishop had a circle of administrators but policies and actions were the result of his personal initiative.

The major body of clergy under the bishop's jurisdiction were the men who served, or who were supposed to serve, the cure of souls – the rectors, vicars and chaplains attached to the parishes in the diocese. They comprised a large body of men, there were over three hundred and sixty parishes in the diocese and it was important for Waynflete to be able to exercise proper control and authority

---

[80] J.T. Rosenthal, 'The Fifteenth Century Episcopate: Careers and Bequests', in D. Baker, ed. *Studies in Church History* x, 1973, 124. Waynflete was included in the group of bishops mentioned; if he were to be excluded the average would be even higher. George Neville, just prior to his promotion to the see of Exeter in 1455, held five canonries, four prebends, one rectory, two archdeaconries and was chancellor of Oxford, G. Keir, 'The Ecclesiastical Career of George Neville', Oxford B.Litt. thesis 1973, unpublished, 85.

over these men for the spiritual welfare of the laity lay in their hands. If they were permitted to neglect the divine office and the cure of souls, the spiritual welfare of the diocese would suffer.

Over one thousand presentations are recorded in Waynflete's register but in only three is particular mention made of examination. Relatively little is known of the procedure for assessing the suitability of candidates for presentations; episcopal registers rarely refer to an examination process. For presentees to fulfill canonical requirements they had to be at least twenty-four years old and known for the quality of their learning and the commendable nature of their lives, very undefined criteria.[81] It is likely that presentees were examined as a matter of course but that the registrar only noted this exercise when some particular problem arose of which a record was required. Three out of a thousand, however, suggests either very high standards among the clergy or, more probably, low standards of achievement required. In August 1448 the presentee to Shirfield parish, Richard Glover, was described as being deficient in his knowledge of grammar and he was ordered to study for a period before being examined again by the bishop or his deputy.[82] No further references occur to this problem until July 1471 when the vicar of Walton-on-Thames was commissioned to examine John Flete who had been promoted to Little Bookham.[83] In September 1478 a presentee of Westminster Abbey to the Surrey parish of Wandsworth, John Jordan, was ordered to appear before either the bishop or his chancellor to undergo examination of his knowledge. He was ordered to spend some time studying before he appeared.[84]

Within the diocese of Winchester, the most important single figure in the distribution of ecclesiastical patronage was the bishop. William Waynflete is recorded as presenting to over sixty benefices, about one-fifth of the total number of benefices in the diocese. In addition he held the advowsons of a number of benefices scattered throughout other dioceses, primarily in neighbouring Salisbury but also in the dioceses of Bath and Wells, Norwich, and Lincoln. As ordinary he also possessed the right of collation when the usual patron was absent or negligent. A consideration of the group of one hundred and seventy-six men recorded as being presented by Waynflete provides a general idea of the type of men he favoured.[85] Almost two-thirds of them were graduates, mostly of Oxford or Cambridge; only a handful of continental graduates are mentioned. Waynflete's own training was as a theologian and men with a theological training had a slight preponderance over legists while those described simply as magister accounted for over one third of all graduates.

[81] Lyndwood's Provinciale, ed. J.V. Bullard and H.C. Bell 1929, 7–10.
[82] Reg Waynflete, i, fo 7r.
[83] Reg Waynflete, ii, fo 6r.
[84] Ibid., fo 63v.
[85] This section is based on a detailed study of the presentations recorded in Waynflete's episcopal register; fuller details are to be found in V. Davis, 'The Life and Career of William Waynflete', unpublished Ph.D. thesis Dublin 1985, chapter 8.

While at first sight the ratio of graduate to non-graduate seems not to give graduates a huge advantage, of those collated to more than one benefice by Waynflete the great majority were graduates. Forty men held more than one of the bishop's benefices and thirty-two of these were graduates. Additionally, as might be expected, the more valuable benefices tended to go to the better qualified men. Meonstoke and Droxford valued at fifty marks and sixty marks per annum respectively were held solely by graduates in this period while Highclere, valued at only twelve marks, had no graduate incumbents. The benefice lists viewed as a whole show clearly a predominance of graduates holding the more valuable livings.

That Waynflete relied heavily on personal knowledge and on recommendations from connections for the benefices in his gift seems clear. A quarter of the graduates he presented had attended Wykeham's dual foundation, first Winchester College and then New College Oxford. Half of the old Wykehamists Waynflete presented had been at the College during Waynflete's period as headmaster there. The same pattern of promotion of boys that he had taught can be seen to an even greater extent in the case of Eton college. Over half of the Etonians he presented had been at the college during the relatively short period during which Waynflete had been provost there. This is all the more surprising because these were the earliest years of the college; it began initially with small numbers of pupils, not attaining its full complement of seventy boys until 1447.

Bishop William Waynflete spread his patronage across a variety of men in accordance with the diversity of the parishes in his gift. His preference, which can be seen in the careers of men whom he favoured most highly, was for men whose background was quite similar to his own. Of undistinguished birth, neither noble nor particularly humble, his proteges were highly educated, a number with theological training; men who were primarily administrators in either the diocesan or educational sphere.

Both when conducting ordinations[86] and when seeking candidates to present to the benefices in his gift Waynflete could hardly have failed to be conscious of the problems caused by low recruitment levels to the clergy, although since inadequate clerical recruitment had been a chronic problem since the last decades of the previous century[87] it was perhaps a state of affairs which would

---

[86] Waynflete carried out the first ordination ceremony after he had become bishop, in Eton College chapel in December 1447 by special licence of the bishop of Lincoln in whose diocese the college was situated. During the first decade of his episcopate, except in 1452 Waynflete presided personally over ordinations which took place wherever he happened to be in residence when one of the *quatour tempora* fell. His practice altered with the appointment of William Westcarre as his suffragan bishop late in 1457. Since he was chancellor at this period the handing over of the regular and quite possibly tedious duties of ordination is understandable but in fact he never returned to carrying out ordinations himself on a regular basis, even after his chancellorship had ceased. Throughout the remainder of his lengthy episcopate he presided at only two ordination ceremonies.

not have seemed to Waynflete particularly unusual or striking. The 1440s and 1450s were the period when Winchester, like dioceses elsewhere in England reached their nadir with regard to attracting recruits. Only a handful of men were being ordained as priests at the quarterly ordination ceremonies. A combination of low recruitment levels and the extension of non-parochial means for clergy to earn their living – serving chantries or acting as clerks in noble or gentry households for example – could mean that it was difficult to find men, especially to fill the poorer parochial livings. In this context, pluralism may have been less of an abuse than might initially appear, if the alternative was benefices left vacant for lack of priests. There is no evidence that Waynflete conducted any sort of recruitment campaign within his diocese but his reluctance to issue *cum ex eo* licences, allowing men to leave their benefices for the purposes of study, may reflect his concern – seen also in his attack on absenteeism – that men holding benefices should reside and carry out their parochial duties. If suitable deputies were difficult to obtain, this is all the more understandable. Against this background of continuing decline of recruits for the church, Waynflete's statement in his 1448 foundation charter for Magdalen Hall that one of his intentions was to encourage a 'fitting increase of clergy'[88] rings true as an authentic desire: and should not be summarily dismissed as a conventional formula taken thoughtlessly from the statutes of other similar foundations.

The selection of and vetting of men inducted into parochial benefices for canonical, educational and moral suitability was one side of controlling the clerical population; the necessary corollary, ensuring that they diligently fulfilled their duties, was more difficult. General visitations gave a bishop the opportunity to see for himself the state of his diocese. Few fifteenth century bishops adhered strictly to the requirement that such visitations should be held triennially and Waynflete was no exception.[89] The only general visitation recorded in Waynflete's episcopal register is that of 1451 which was carried out by his official-principal Richard Manning.[90] However, he was in residence in the diocese for most of his episcopate and fairly itinerant, particularly in the eastern half (Surrey and East Hampshire) and his journeys between manors enabled him to observe the diocese on a casual basis. Although no other visitations are referred to as such, Waynflete's itinerary shows that on occasion he deviated from his normal routes between manors to visit the more out-of-the-way parts

---

[87] J.H. Moran, 'Clerical Recruitment in the Diocese of York, 1340–1530', *JEH* xxxiv, 1983, 19–54; R.L. Storey, 'Recruitment of English Clergy in the Period of the Conciliar Movement', *Annuarium Historiae Conciliorum* vii, 1975, 290–313; V. Davis, 'Rivals for Ministry? Ordinations of Secular and Regular Clergy in Southern England, c.1300–1500', *Ministry, Clerical and Lay*, ed. D. Wood, Studies in Church History xxvi, Oxford 1989, 99–109.

[88] *Cart St John*, 425.

[89] Thomas Langley, bishop of Durham 1406–37, only carried out one general visitation of his diocese during his episcopate although he paid less formal visits on other occasions, R.L. Storey, *Thomas Langley and the Bishopric of Durham*, 1961, 183.

[90] Reg Waynflete i, fo 14*v.

of his diocese.[91] In the summer of 1464 he visited Cheriton, East Meon, Chertsey and Highclere. Highclere lay in the north-western area of the diocese in which he was otherwise rarely seen. Before Christmas of 1468 he visited Ropley (in the extreme south-west) and Alresford. Clearly he did make an effort to visit areas of the diocese which he did not pass through on a regular basis.[92] His mere presence within the diocese would help to keep the clergy on their toes. Such itinerations were regarded as important by late medieval writers; in the late fourteenth century Langland had written, 'Every bishop who carries a crosier is thereby bound to travel through his diocese and show himself to his people.'[93] In the early years of the sixteenth century, Bishop Smith of Lincoln was concerned about the welfare of his diocese because he was being called from it too frequently to fulfil his responsibilities on the Welsh Marches.[94] While deputies had the authority to act for the bishop, their work – no matter how dutiful – would not have had the same weight as personal action by the bishop himself.

Non-residence by clergy was a perennial problem in the English church but it was no less serious for that. Thomas Gascoigne, a severe mid-fifteenth century critic of the church hierarchy, pointed out that a parish needed a good rector just as much as a sinking ship required a good sailor.[95] From the point of view of Waynflete and fellow members of the episcopate, non-residence presented a two-fold problem. Firstly it meant the neglect of the spiritual needs of the people for whom the bishop was ultimately responsible and secondly, since there existed a licensing system, to overlook unlicensed absence by parish clergy was to undermine his own authority. Waynflete himself set a good example by his regular residence in the diocese. In sees where the bishop was rarely present it must have been difficult for his administrators to emphasise the dangers of non-residence to the lesser clergy.

A commission from bishop Waynflete to the archdeacon of Surrey on 9 April 1453 launched an attack on both non-residence and the holding of incompatible benefices which was a concomitant abuse. The archdeacon was sent a list of rectors and vicars who were absent from their benefices without permission and was ordered to cite them to appear before the bishop himself in his chapel at Southwark manor on 11 May. In this commission Waynflete warned that a parish with an absent vicar is left open to the ravages of wolves.[96] Fifteen men were listed. The success of this attack on the abuse is unclear but at least one of the men cited on this occasion, Thomas Copte, rector of Streatham, proved

---

91 Appendix 2, Waynflete's itinerary.
92 His episcopal register does not indicate any great increase in judicial activity as a result of these travels but since many of the matters arising would have been dealt with in the consistory court rather than in the audience court, the lack of surviving records for the former means that it is difficult to be sure of the direct effects of his peregrinations.
93 *Langland, Piers the Ploughman*, ed. J.F. Goodridge, 1959, 195, Passus xv, ll. 561–2.
94 M.Bowker, *The Secular Clergy in the Diocese of Lincoln 1495–1520*, Cambridge 1968, 4.
95 *Loci e Libro Veritatum*, 139.
96 Reg Waynflete i, fo 25*v.

obdurate and had to be cited to appear again before the bishop later the same year. Another, master John Concham, was subsequently refused a licence to be absent.[97] This mass attack on the abuse is unique but throughout his episcopate action was regularly taken on Waynflete's orders against individual examples of non-residence and in obstinate cases sequestration was initiated.[98] Waynflete clearly attempted to ensure that the parishes in his diocese were adequately served.

While non-residence was frowned upon, the existence of a licensing system meant that it was seen as acceptable under certain circumstances. In 1453 Waynflete's attack had been on those absent without reasonable cause. The most common reasonable causes were the service of a bishop or king or for the purposes of study. *Cum ex eo* licences, introduced by Pope Boniface VIII to enable clerks to use their benefices as a source of support while at university, were declining in number in the fifteenth century.[99] In view of his own promotion of education it is surprising to find that Waynflete granted very few such licences. Only nine were issued during his forty year episcopate and these were all for short periods, one, two or three years, not for the maximum of seven years. In the early years of his episcopate Waynflete apparently pursued a policy of encouraging study by the issue of such licences – seven of the nine licences were issued prior to 1455.[100] The decline in the number of licences issued after 1455 may have been a result of the bishop's experience of parochial problems which could arise from non residence. There is, of course, a problem of how far he turned a blind eye to absences but he certainly did not exercise a 'rubber-stamp' approach to petitioners for licences. Master John Southell, one of the rectors cited for absence in 1453, was refused a *cum ex eo* licence in 1454.[101]

Much of the problem of non-residence was closely tied to the holding of multiple benefices, although the vicarage system and the existence of benefices not involving cure of souls which could help to support students and administrators, mitigated some of the evils which could arise from a single cleric simultaneously amassing a number of benefices. Although the poor value of many rural parishes has been adduced as a justification for this practice, it was more often the case that it was the valuable benefices which were held together. The other justification, that the collection of benefices was necessary to support adequately men performing valuable services within the church and central

97 *Ibid.*, fos 28*r–v; 30*r.
98 *Ibid.* In December 1464 the goods of Rotherhithe were seized because the rector was absent fos 84*r; in 1468 the absence of the vicar of Morden resulted in the same action, fo 95*v.
99 R.M. Haines, 'The Education of the English Clergy in the Later Middle Ages', *Canadian Journal of History* iv, 1969, 1–22; L.E. Boyle, 'The Constitution *Cum ex eo* of Boniface VIII', *Mediaeval Studies* xxiv, 1962, 263–302.
100 Reg Waynflete i, fos 2*r, 9*v, 16*r, 19*r, 26*r, 30*v, 32*r. It has been suggested that more licences may have been issued than were recorded but the Winchester episcopal registrar appears to have been conscientious in recording such matters.
101 *Ibid.*, fo 30*r.

government, should not be dismissed so summarily since it was widely accepted at the time.

Waynflete in this, as in the case of non-residence, set a good example to his clergy; upon taking office as bishop he resigned the single mastership which was all that he held. His major officials had dispensations allowing them to hold two or three incompatible benefices but they were not serious abusers of the system.[102] There is no evidence that Waynflete attacked such pluralists or excluded them from the benefices he collated to; to feel that he should have done so would be to expect him to undermine the accepted church structure. It was, however, clearly a problem in which he was interested because among the few books we know he possessed was a copy of Richard Rotherham's *De pluralitate beneficiorum*, a series of lectures specifically concerned with pluralism and its problems.[103]

It is clear from a study of the episcopal registers of Winchester for this period that Waynflete as bishop of Winchester was conscious of the problems which could arise within the parochial system and he attempted to hold them in check. Action against abuses was taken by his deputies but it was initiated by personal episcopal mandates and numerous commissaries were authorised to act on his behalf. Incumbents of parishes were frequently instituted in his presence. Similarly Waynflete's personal interest was demonstrated when he himself witnessed such actions as the signing of compositions between religious houses and appropriated parishes. Yet there is no evidence that Waynflete made any particular efforts to improve the standards of education in his diocese, no suggestion that he was particularly rigorous in his examination of the parochial clergy prior to their institutions to parishes. He did appoint graduates extensively to the more valuable parishes in his gift but these were often people from within his household circle or those of whom he had particular knowledge and in particular, people he had known while at Eton college. Men who had obtained degrees while at Magdalen College were slow to appear among his presentees. He was reluctant to issue *cum ex eo* licences to benefice holders to enable them to pursue their studies. It seems in fact that Waynflete's interests in education were divorced from his diocesan cares, they represented two sides of his interests and rarely met.

Unlike Bishop Beaufort, whose extensive political and diplomatic activities meant that frequently his attention was directed to non-diocesan matters, Waynflete, despite his educational interests and occasional political involvements, was consistently concerned with fulfilling his episcopal duties and personally directing the administration of his diocese. The long record of his episcopal register demonstrates this beyond doubt – his almost uninterrupted

[102] An exception was Vincent Clement, the papal choice as archdeacon of Surrey 1459–75, whose absences and pluralism were notorious – he attracted the disapprobation of Gascoigne – but his appointment had been out of Waynflete's control.
[103] BL Egerton MS 2892; see below chapter 5.

residence within the boundaries of his see; the lack of any vicar-general[104] throughout the forty years of his episcopate; the regularity with which his register records his personal involvement in the most routine of matters such as the granting of probate and receiving of resignations of rectors. While many of his contemporaries were careerists for whom a bishopric was a reward offered for political services and a means of support for a man involved in politics, Waynflete proved himself a conscientious diocesan figure. In neither parochial affairs nor those of religious houses was he an innovator or reformer but he upheld the status quo to the best of his ability, issuing mandates to his administrators and intervening personally where necessary. In general he made his presence felt within the diocese of Winchester and his vigilance was rewarded in that few major or widespread problems arose during his episcopate. Within his diocese Waynflete's priorities would seem to have been administrative ones and under his strict eye the diocese was effectively administered with particular concern being paid to the cure of souls in parishes. His register provides details of a well-ordered diocese with occasional less turgid flashes, as for example, in the description of the procession and processes surrounding the translation of the relics of St Swithun in the summer of 1476.[105]

There is no evidence that Waynflete was a particularly devout figure; he was not, for example, known as a great preacher and no spiritual writings or sermons written by him have survived. He was, however, loyally committed to his diocese and his cathedral. An attack, legal and physical, made on him by his tenants on East Meon manor in 1461 arose out of the efficiency of the temporal administration of the diocese of Winchester under his supervision.[106] It is an incident which reinforces an impression of Waynflete as an efficient administrator

[104] Although in many English dioceses the vicar-general was the cornerstone of diocesan administration, – deputising for the bishop, often himself taking action rather than merely carrying out direct orders from the bishop – Waynflete only once appointed a vicar-general. He was rarely out of his diocese for any length of time and he never left England, an action which would have made the appointment of a vicar-general essential. John Hermondswerth abbot of Chertsey Abbey was vicar-general in the spring of 1450 and he is the only vicar-general of whom there is any record, Reg Waynflete i, fo 20v. Hermondswerth had acted in the same capacity for Cardinal Beaufort.

[105] Reg Waynflete ii, fo 173. An account of the same event is also recorded in *The Register of John Morton, Archbishop of Canterbury 1486–1500*, ed. C. Harper-Bill, Canterbury & York Society lxxv, 1987, no. 284.

[106] The tenants of East Meon had been a source of trouble to Waynflete from the very beginning of his episcopate. In 1448, within a year of his becoming bishop, they withdrew the services due to him from their holdings. Subsequently Waynflete held a lengthy inquisition at Winchester which ascertained in minute detail all the services due to him. He may have gained the upper hand in 1448 for the tenants were quiescent during the 1450s but in the late summer of 1461 the East Meon tenants made a complaint to the king which was adjudged serious enough to be referred to the judgement of parliament. Although the Lords upheld Waynflete's case, the matter was followed up by the tenants who made a second complaint the following year, see Davis, 'The Life and Career of William Waynflete', 222–6. Waynflete was also in dispute with his tenants on the manor of Alverstoke in Hampshire in 1462, *CCR 1461–68*, 230–34.

but it also suggests that he could be harsh and over-zealous as steward of God's temporal lands. The chapter of St Swithun's cathedral would seem to have been correct when in 1447 they assured the pope that Waynflete's 'prudence in both spiritual and secular affairs and his remarkable virtues and abilities will enable him to defend the rights of their church'. The diocese of Winchester during his episcopate saw no great flowering of religious devotion but was efficiently and quite effectively administered.

Political Activities[107]

William Waynflete was essentially a public rather than a political figure, a man with considerable personal loyalty to the person of Henry VI but whose ties with the political interests within the court circle were loose. Critics of Henry VI's court and councils did not see the bishop of Winchester as being unduly influential or at least his influence does not appear to have provoked popular resentment. He was not listed among those whom the parliament of 1450–51 desired to be removed from the king's presence[108] and neither did he suffer from attacks such as those which caused the deaths of bishops Ayscough and Moleyns in 1450 in an extreme expression of popular disapproval of their role in government and their responsibility for England's reversal of fortune in French affairs. A bishop in the fifteenth century could not, however, divorce himself from public affairs; his role as a spiritual lord carried with it obligations as part of the 'body politic'.[109] As bishop of Winchester from 1447 to 1486 William Waynflete held an important see throughout a period of considerable political strife, from the reign of Henry VI to that of Henry VII. In such circumstances, therefore, Waynflete could hardly avoid being caught up in politics on occasion. He applied himself conscientiously to the public and political duties expected of him but at the same time it is clear that political activities were not his driving interest. His primary interests lay elsewhere, outside the political sphere. He himself admitted this in 1454 in his response to a request to serve on the Duke of York's protectorate council. He proposed a rota of councillors stating that, while he was prepared to serve for a period, 'his consyence [concerning his involvements elsewhere] wold not suffer hym contynualy to serve'.[110] While this reply may have been an excuse to escape an irksome political burden, seen in the light of his extensive educational concerns and of his active participation in

---

107 Waynflete's political career is discussed in detail in V. Davis, 'William Waynflete and the Wars of the Roses', *Southern History* xi, 1990, 1–22.

108 *RP* v, 216–17.

109 The role of other members of the episcopate during this period is described in R.J. Knecht, 'The Episcopate and the Wars of the Roses', *University of Birmingham Historical Journal* vi, 1957–8, 108–31. See also J.A.F. Thompson, 'Bishop Lionel Woodville and Richard III', *BIHR* lix, 1986, 130–35.

110 R. Griffiths, 'The King's Council and the First Protectorate of the Duke of York', *EHR* lxxxxix, 1984, 80.

diocesan affairs, it rings true. Despite this, it is impossible to look at his activities as an educationalist and patron without taking into consideration the contemporary political scene. Being in or out of favour with the establishment could play an important role in determining the fate of foundations and educational projects. In the 1450s, when Waynflete had close ties with the court, it was easier for him to smooth the path of obtaining writs and licences to amortise land, than was the case in the early Yorkist period.

There is no doubt that Waynflete was closely identified with the Lancastrian monarchy through his personal relationship with Henry VI which had arisen from Waynflete's connections with the embryonic foundation of Eton college. However their relationship existed primarily on a personal basis for much of Henry VI's reign. Only in the early 1450s did he begin to play a role in royal government.[111]

Throughout the 1450s, even after his appointment as chancellor in the autumn of 1456, William Waynflete played an important if low key role as a mediator in a period dominated by increasing political polarisation. During Cade's revolt in 1450 he was one of the emissaries sent to persuade the rebels to seek pardons and later negotiated with them in St Margaret's church in Southwark, within the bounds of his own diocese.[112] Again at Dartford in March 1452, in an atmosphere of growing political tension, Waynflete was dispatched together with Lord Sourton and Henry Bourgchier to attempt to dissuade the Duke of York from hasty action.[113] At the end of the decade, in 1459, his sermon, preached at the opening of the Coventry Parliament on the text, 'Let peace and unity be given unto you'; reflects what he saw as the aim of his endeavours whether as bishop or chancellor.[114]

Waynflete's period of real, active political power was during the period 1456–60. The reshuffle of Henry VI's advisers which took place at the Coventry council of September/October 1456 brought the bishop to the forefront of the royal administration. Waynflete was appointed chancellor[115] and thereby became the king's foremost adviser, head of the Privy Council and potentially a man of great political influence. This power could be and was used to further

---

[111] In 1454–5 he was present at forty-four meetings of the council out of a total of sixty-four; this was in contrast to the period 22 March 1450 to 19 August 1453 when he attended only eighteen of fifty sessions of the council, R. Virgoe, 'The Composition of the King's Council 1437–61', *BIHR* xliii, 1970, 157–60. His attendance can be traced in the *Proceedings of the Privy Council* vi and by his signature on warrants issued by the council, PRO C81/1546 and PRO E 28.

[112] 'Wilhelmi Wyrcester Annales Rerum Anglicarum', in *Letters and Papers Illustrative of the Wars of the English in France During the Reign of Henry VI*, ed. J. Stevenson, 2 vols, Rolls Series 1861–4, ii, 768.

[113] 'John Benet's Chronicle for the Years 1400–1462', ed. G.L. and M.A. Harriss, *Camden Miscellany* xxiv, Camden Society iv series, ix, 1972, 206. His mission met with no success. Subsequently Waynflete was one of the arbitrators in the recognisance between Somerset and York on 13 March 1452, *CCR 1447–54*, 327.

[114] *RP* v, 345; 'Gratia vobis et pax multiplicetur', 1 Peter, 2.

[115] *CCR 1454–61*, 211.

his educational interests. In September 1456, just before Waynflete became chancellor and thus a period when he was very much in favour, Magdalen Hall was granted a mortmain licence allowing it to acquire lands worth up to £100 per annum.[116] Shortly after his appointment, on 27 October 1456 he was granted the patronage and advowson of the Hospital of St John the Baptist in Oxford and along with this grant of patronage was a licence to enable him to re-grant his newly-acquired rights over the hospital to Magdalen Hall.[117] The formal grant of the hospital to Magdalen Hall was made on 5 July 1457.[118] All this facilitated his plans to refound the hall in a more substantial form as a college. Mortmain licences were not easily come by, as the extensive efforts of Sir John Fastolf to obtain one for his projected foundation at Caister Castle demonstrated, despite the fact that Fastolf had, as he himself pleaded, 'long seruice contynued and doon vnto the Kyng and to his noble fader'.[119] Others of Waynflete's interests benefitted during his period of chancellor; in November 1457 a grant of money from customs collected in the ports of London and Boston was made to Waynflete in repayment of a loan of £220 he had made to the king.[120] Repayment must have been welcome as the expenses of collegiate foundation began to be felt. Together with Ralph Legh, a member of his household, he obtained a licence to found a chantry in the church of Lambeth St Mary.[121] Most of the letters patent issued concerning matters of especial interest to Waynflete in this period[122] were authorised by the signet, that is, the order for the issue of the appropriate letters patent came directly from the king, bypassing the office of privy seal and going directly to the chancery.

This period of ease of access to royal power was not to last. Waynflete resigned the chancellorship on the eve of the battle of Northampton in June 1460.[123] Henry VI was in the custody of the Yorkist earls after the battle; this Yorkist supremacy and the subsequent deposition of Henry VI in 1461 dramatically undermined Waynflete's position. Instead of being intimately connected with the king he was now outside the favoured circle, regarded with some suspicion by the Yorkists and he had to work to win favour, to gain 'insurance' through a judicious choice of friends and careful use of the patronage at his disposal in order to safeguard his position as bishop of Winchester and by extension, to safeguard his educational interests. Between 1460 and 1467 his educational projects were in a sort of limbo. Between 1459 and 1468 Waynflete appears to have ceased to collect land for the endowment of his college;[124] the

---

116 *CPR 1452–61*, 324.
117 *Ibid.*, 343.
118 *Cart St John* i, 263–6.
119 *PL* no. 570.
120 *CPR 1452–61*, 420.
121 *Ibid.*, 343.
122 Davis, 'The Life and Career of William Waynflete', 251–6.
123 *CCR 1454–61*, 459.
124 See chapter 6.

development of the college itself made little progress and Waynflete seems also to have detached himself from the interests of Eton college.[125]

In the period after his accession to the throne, Edward IV was wooing the support of the episcopate and was reluctant to alienate it unessarily. There is little evidence to suggest that Waynflete was made to suffer by Edward IV for his earlier support of the Lancastrian cause. However Waynflete's connections with the court and royal government were slight and his political influence decreased accordingly. Clearly he felt himself vulnerable. His itinerary shows him spending an ever-increasing amount of time within his diocese. This withdrawal from Yorkist politics must have come from the bishop himself rather than occurring as a result of deliberate exclusion of ex-Lancastrians by Edward IV. Apart from regular attendance at parliament, as befitted his position as a senior member of the episcopate, Waynflete remained uninvolved in political life.[126]

During this period Waynflete made judicious use of the patronage at his disposal to gain allies in the political sphere.[127] In the 1470s, when once again his educational interests were proceeding apace, he appears to have been doing likewise in order to gain valuable allies for his educational interests. On the death of his own brother John Waynflete, in 1479, the bishop appointed the King's brother-in-law, Lionel Woodville, to be archdeacon of Surrey.[128] Lionel Woodville was already a well-beneficed figure and a man to whom Waynflete had in April of the same year given the Oxfordshire benefice of Witney which was in his gift.[129] The grant by Waynflete of the archdeaconry of Surrey to such a notorious pluralist and a man with close royal connections suggests a greater regard for the advantages to be gleaned from the royal connection than concern for the ecclesiastical duties to be carried out. In making this choice Waynflete must have been influenced by the fact that earlier that year Woodville had been elected chancellor of the University of Oxford. In this position he would be a powerful friend for Waynflete's foundation of Magdalen College, the welfare of which dominated Waynflete's actions in the last decade of his life.

By the time of Edward IV's untimely death in 1483, Bishop Waynflete was the longest survivor on the episcopal bench. He played no part in the political events of Richard's reign or in his overthrow. By now he was over eighty and increasingly sedentary. His non-involvement in politics perhaps ensured that he was on good terms with Richard III and he entertained the king at Magdalen

---

[125] See below pp. 50–3.

[126] He seems to have attended conscientiously and acted when required as one of the triers of English petitions; *RP* v, 461, 1461–2; 496 1463–5; 571 1467–8; *RP* vi, 3 1472–3; 167, 1477; 237 1485, for references to Waynflete as a trier of petitions. Unfortunately records recording the membership of Edward IV's Privy Council are few in number but Waynflete's name does not occur as a member of the council prior to 1473, *CCR 1468–77*, 319–20.

[127] See Davis, 'William Waynflete and the Wars of the Roses', 11–16.

[128] Reg Waynflete ii, fo 88r; for Woodville's career see *BRUO* 1320–1.

[129] LRO Register xxi (Rotherham) fos 84r, 88v.

College in 1483 when the king was making a major royal progress around England in pursuit of support. Two years previously Edward IV had been entertained in the college.[130] Such actions were an active attempt to attract royal favour for the college.

As incumbent of the see of Winchester. William Waynflete was potentially an important force in English political life. That for more than half of his episcopate – from 1460, he played little part in politics reflects his personal preference. Other Lancastrian sympathizers had had active political careers under Edward IV and his earlier loyalties would have been of little disadvantage had Waynflete wished to follow suit. Instead he largely withdrew from politics although he did attend parliament and fulfill public duties as a commissioner of the peace. He had, he considered, more important things to do than to become embroiled in political affairs after 1460. His sporadic attempts to win friends within government circles position reflect not so much his personal need for survival but also his concern for the success and continuance of his foundations. When Waynflete was out of favour, he was unable to do anything to ease the plight of Eton college, threatened by Edward IV with merger with St George's chapel; Waynflete's Oxford foundations, lacking both statutes and endowments until the 1480s would not have lasted long without the support of their founder. The vulnerability of such foundations in a time of political crises was aptly summed up by John Gygour, Master of Tattershall college, when he wrote to Waynflete in April 1483, emphasising the uncertain position of Tattershall College now that the king was dead and his successor unknown. Gygour advised Waynflete in these circumstances to

> . . . spede your maters and utterli to conclude them that concern your worschipful college of Oxenford as wel as of Eton and pore Tateshale . . .[131]

---

130 Richard III's visit is discussed in more detail in chapter 3.
131 MC MS 367, no. 4, printed in C. Richmond, 'A letter of 19 April 1483 from John Gigur to William Wainfleet', *Historical Research* 65, 1992, 112–16. I am grateful to Dr Richmond for sending me a pre-publication copy of this article.

II

Eton College

Waynflete at Eton College, 1441–1447

The later development of Eton College, its links with Winchester College and the presence of Wykehamists such as Thomas Beckington and Henry Chichele among Henry VI's circle of advisers have all over-shadowed the fact that the king's original scheme for Eton College did not suggest that it was to duplicate Wykeham's foundation. Having acquired the advowson of the parochial church of Eton in September 1440[1] Henry VI issued a foundation charter on 11 October of the same year. This charter emphasised the king's desire to demonstrate his devotion to the church by copying the pious works of his ancestors and shows that he saw his collegiate foundation as a symbol of his having grasped the full reins of power, which he had done in November 1437:

> Wherefore it is that we, who, by the will of the same king of kings by whom all kings reign, have just taken into our hands the governance of both our kingdoms, have from the very beginning of our riper age turned over in earnest thought in our mind how and in what manner and by what royal gift suitable to the measure of our devotion, and following the fashion of our elders, we could do fitting honour to our lady and most holy mother, to the pleasure of her great spouse; and at length, while thinking such things in inmost thought, it became settled in our heart, that we would found a college in the honour and for the support of our great and most holy mother in the parish church of Eton by Windsor, which is not far removed from the place of our birth.[2]

The nature of Henry's foundation as religious college, almshouse and charity school is outlined in the charter; it was to consist of a provost, ten priests, four clerks, six choristers, twenty-five poor scholars and the same number of bedesmen. In addition a master was to be appointed to teach grammar to all who wished to attend the school, freely and without exactions.[3] Although people to fill the positions of provost, priests and choristers were named in the foundation

---

[1] Lyte, *Eton College*, 4.
[2] *Educational Charters and Documents*, 404.
[3] Lyte, *Eton College*, 6.

charter and several boys were designated scholars, the reference to the master comes almost as an afterthought and no-one was nominated to take the position. A royal chapel school and the Cambridge college of King's Hall already provided schooling for court proteges and future servants of the crown;[4] there was no actual need for the king to establish a school. Neither in 1440 was any reference made to a second university foundation to complement the school as would have been expected if Henry's foundation had been designed to rival that of Wykeham. Six months later, in February 1441, Henry VI did establish a Cambridge college, consisting of a rector and twelve scholars.[5] This may indicate a growing interest in the idea of a dual foundation but such a link can only be seen with hindsight; no reference was made to any connection between Eton College and the Cambridge college dedicated to St Nicholas. The school element of Eton College was secondary;[6] the whole tone of the foundation charter clearly demonstrates that the king's intention in the autumn of 1440 was to found an ecclesiastical college, imitating the foundations of his ancestors. Henry VI did not set out to emulate Wykeham's dual educational establishment, despite the fact that within five years of 1440 they were closely linked in fact and in form. This development was primarily orchestrated by William Waynflete.

Just under a year after he issued his foundation charter, in early August 1441, Henry VI visited Winchester College. This visit resulted in his employment of William Waynflete, then headmaster of Winchester College, initially in some undefined role connected with the development of Eton College. Details of the royal visit and the entertainment of the king on this occasion appear in the White Book of Winchester College and the account rolls but they shed no light on the king's motives, merely recording that he attended mass and dined in the College Hall.[7] Henry may have gone to Winchester for the express purpose of visiting the College as has been suggested,[8] but it must not be assumed that because the visit resulted in the employment of William Waynflete, its purpose was to seek a master for Eton. The following month Waynflete entered the royal service. This was evidently at short notice for Winchester College, deprived of its headmaster by the king, had hastily to send a messenger to Thomas Alewyn, Waynflete's predecessor, requesting his return. Waynflete's stipend was paid until Michaelmas 1441 and Alewyn was paid thereafter.[9]

His single visit to Winchester was Henry VI's only documented connection

4   A. Cobban, *The King's Hall Within the University of Cambridge in the Later Middle Ages*, Cambridge 1969, 1.
5   *VCH Cambridge*, iii, 376–7.
6   Cf. R. Griffiths, *The Reign of Henry VI*, 1981, 244 where he states that the prime purpose of Eton College was educational; B. Wolffe, *Henry VI*, 1981, 137 emphasises that Henry did not envisage Eton's developement principally as an educational institution.
7   WCM 22992, Liber Albus; WCM 22117, Bursars' accounts 1440–41.
8   *Annals of Winchester*, 192.
9   WCM 22117.

with Waynflete prior to his appointment but that his decision had been taken impetuously seems unlikely. As far as Eton College was concerned, the king was consistently meticulous in the details of his arrangements. The king's secretary, Thomas Beckington, an old Wykehamist, may have known Waynflete and recommended him to the king. In addition Waynflete had previously been the recipient of a minor piece of patronage from Cardinal Beaufort who had appointed him to the mastership of the Hospital of Mary Magdalen in Winchester.[10]

No evidence supports the later tradition that Waynflete was accompanied by five fellows and thirty-five scholars of Winchester College when he moved to the new royal foundation.[11] In fact only six scholars moved to Eton with their headmaster.[12] Neither is there evidence to support the description of Waynflete as first headmaster of Eton.[13] He may have done a little teaching for two scholars were named in the foundation charter but it is unlikely that much formal teaching was required until the school started to expand. When this happened the following spring, William Westbury, a fellow of New College Oxford, resigned his fellowship and came to Eton as the first headmaster; he was an ex-pupil of Waynflete's having been at Winchester College in the first years of Waynflete's headmastership.[14]

Waynflete was not been brought to Eton to act as schoolmaster. When he set his new foundation in motion Henry VI was not yet twenty years of age. In Waynflete he found what he needed, a mature man with appropriate experience, able to carry out the royal desires and to supervise the future development of the college. Henry Sever, named as provost in the foundation charter seems to have made little impact on the new foundation and may have proved unsatisfactory in the role as provost. Certainly that is the implication of a letter written by some members of the university of Oxford to the papal curia in 1443, requesting that the pope use his influence with the king in Sever's favour.[15] This was a surprising request in view of the fact that not only had Sever served the king at Eton but also as his confessor in the 1430s; had he won royal favour in these activities such a letter would hardly have been necessary. No formal record of Waynflete's appointment as his successor has survived but it took place in early March 1442. Sever is last referred to as provost in a deed of 5 March 1442[16] while a manor court roll for the Oxfordshire manor of Cottisford dated 13 March 1442, describes the court as being the first one held under

10 Wavell, *History and Antiquities of Winchester*, ii, 177.
11 Kirby, *Annals of Winchester*, 199 pointed out that this was not the case but the tradition, supporting the idea that Henry was consciously following Wykeham's example, continues to be repeated in the secondary literature, as in J. Simon, *Education and Society in Tudor England*, 13.
12 *Annals of Winchester*, 199.
13 *Ibid.*, 198.
14 *BRUO*, 2020–1.
15 *Epistolae Academicae Oxon.* i, 223–5.
16 *CPR 1441–6*, 50.

Waynflete's provostship.[17] Between these two dates Henry VI was in residence at Sheen,[18] a day's ride from Eton and the appointment may have been ordered from there. The formal swearing in of Waynflete as provost did not take place until after a code of statutes for the college had been drawn up; on 23 December 1443 Waynflete and the other members of the foundation at a ceremony held in the partially built chapel of the college, swore to observe the statutes.[19]

William Waynflete's provostship was a time of great change for the royal college of Eton. Conceived under the king's original plan as a fairly modest establishment, during Waynflete's provostship it developed into a much more grandiose body upon which much royal time, energy and revenue were expended. Two men in particular were in a position to influence the direction of Eton's development, Thomas Beckington and William Waynflete. Beckington, the king's secretary,[20] was a Wykehamist and although he had no later experience of the college after he had ceased to be a schoolboy there, he could have encouraged the king to look at Wykeham's foundations as a model. He himself was primarily involved with the diplomatic negotiations with the papacy necessary to obtain the extensive indulgence privileges which Henry wanted for his college.[21] The emphasis on indulgences shows how highly the king regarded the religious and pious side of his foundation.

Waynflete, by virtue both of his experience at Winchester College and his appointment at Eton was in a strong position to influence Henry's plans. The trust which Henry came to place in Waynflete's judgement, zeal and abilities is clearly demonstrated in the 'King's Will'.[22] Since Waynflete's experience hitherto had been solely at Winchester College, it was not surprising that he directed the king along similar lines. His own continuing approval of the idea of linking a university college with a grammar school can be seen from the form of his own later foundation at Oxford which was supplied by two schools.[23]

The great year of change for Eton College was 1443; this was the year when statutes were drawn up and in which Eton was modelled closely on Wykeham's model and linked with a much altered King's College Cambridge. A link

17 ECR 26/120.
18 Wolffe, *Henry VI*, itinerary, 363.
19 ECR 54/10. The original of the statutes sworn to on this occasion have not survived, but a copy exists in ECR MS 300. This manuscript is incomplete and highly interlined and corrected. I am grateful to Patrick Strong, retired archivist, Eton College for this information.
20 *BRUO*, 157–8.
21 Beckington's letters relating to the diplomatic negotiations with the papacy can be found in *Official Correspondence of Thomas Beckington*, ed. G. Williams, 2 vols, Rolls Series 1872.
22 The King's Will stated Henry VI's intentions concerning the development of his two foundations; it is discussed in more detail below, pp. 47–49.
23 Magdalen College School was situated in Oxford as an integral part of Magdalen College; a second foundation was established along similar lines in Waynflete's Lincolnshire birthplace, Wainfleet. Both of these foundations will be discussed in more detail later.

between the English kings and Cambridge dated back to the fourteenth century when Edward II founded King's Hall but despite the existence of this college in addition to Henry VI's new foundation, there was no intention at first that the early scholars of Eton College should automatically proceed to Cambridge. That their options remained open can be seen from a grant made in February 1442 by John Carpenter, master of the Hospital of St Anthony in London, to sustain five boys studying the arts in Oxford at the rate of 10d per week, 'provided that they have been instructed in the rudiments of the arts faculty at Eton College'.[24]

On 10 July 1443 William Millington, rector of the College of St Nicholas in Cambridge, was appointed provost of a reconstituted body, the royal college of St Mary and St Nicholas at Cambridge.[25] On the same day the original commissioners appointed by the king to draw up its statutes were released from their obligations.[26] A public instrument made in the chapel in Eton on 13 September 1443 shows links between the two royal foundations being forged for the first time, three years after their initial establishment:

> The venerable Master William Waynflete . . . provost, sitting, reciting and declaring the intention, mandate and will of the king . . . that the poor and indigent scholars of the said Royal College of the Blessed Mary of Eton, after they have firstly been sufficiently imbued in the rudiments of grammar, are to proceed to the said Royal College of the Blessed Mary and St Nicholas in Cambridge, in the diocese of Ely, there to be imbued in liberal studies, other sciences and profitable subjects according to the ordinance and statute of the most serene prince and lord . . . in this part declared.[27]

The statutes which were being drawn up at this time were instituted three months later in December 1443. The earliest statutes no longer exist; those now extant and printed as *Ancient Fifteenth Century Laws . . . for the public school of Eton College* date from the period c.1447–55. These later statutes, as far as can be seen from the later copies, were extremely closely modelled on those of Winchester College; some small changes were made, for example to cover the bedesmen who were unique to Eton College or to delete Wykeham's references to founder's kin – inappropriate at Eton – but in effect such alterations were minor.[28]

The position of provost of Eton College was very different to that of *magister*

---

[24] *VCH Buckinghamshire* ii, 153.

[25] *Syllabus of Rymer's Foedera*, ed. T.D. Hardy, 3 vols, 1869–85, ii, 672.

[26] *CPR 1441–6*, 97.

[27] ECR 39/30.

[28] The notarial instrument of 21 December 1443 – ECR 54/10 – which records this ceremony refers to still earlier statutes. The original of these has not survived but an incomplete copy, highly corrected and interlined survives in ECR MS 300. The Eton statutes are not quite as Leach described them in *VCH Buckinghamshire* ii, 157, '. . . a mere transcript of those of Winchester'; a careful comparison reveals some changes but these are primarily of phrasing, to fit the royal status of the founder.

informator at Winchester College. At Winchester Waynflete's duties had been those of teaching and disciplining the scholars and his status within the college was that of a paid subordinate, not a member of the governing body. At Eton, Waynflete was in control of the day-to-day management of the college; he was in regular communication with the young king and with leading royal advisers, in particular the powerful Duke of Suffolk, himself a founder of a school at Ewelme. Although Eton College was still a fledgling foundation, the constant personal interest shown by the king in its development made the provost an important figure.

The sources for the provost's duties in these early years are fragmentary. The earliest surviving audit roll is that of 1445–6; the next is from 1446–7 while the first Lease Book which also records early college *acta* begins in 1445. The College register does not begin until 1457.[29] Some light is also shed on these early years by official government records such as the patent and close rolls. Initially the college was small in size but it quickly began to grow. The first election of scholars, held in 1444, resulted in the election of 25 boys. By 1447 when Waynflete left Eton the full complement of seventy scholars and sixteen choristers had been attained although the almshouse element remained small, there being only six bedesmen at that time.[30] The provost was responsible for all aspects of collegiate internal affairs although many external matters, especially negotiations with the papal curia for grants of indulgences, were managed by the king and his secretary.

The oath sworn by William Waynflete as provost on 23 December 1443 before the king's commissioners gives some idea of his obligations.[31] The duties, with some slight changes, resembled those of the warden of Winchester College. He had precedence over all the fellows and full authority over the whole college although (as was the case in Winchester also), the fellows had to be consulted in important matters. He appointed internal college officers – bursars' officials and other servants of the college. Every second year at least he had to visit all the college estates. In the religious sphere the provost was responsible for the cure of souls, not only of members of the college but also of all the parishioners of the parish of Eton. Periods of absence totalling more than sixty days a year were not permitted unless required by urgent college business. In this matter the Eton statutes contain an additional clause not found in those of Wykeham which reflects the emphasis on religious observance and piety in the royal foundation – the provost was required to be in the college on the occasions of the major

[29] ECR/61/AR/1, audit roll 1444–5; ECR/61/AR/2, audit roll 1446–7. The extensive building accounts for this period are described in D. Knoop and G.P. Jones, 'The Building of Eton College 1442–60', *Transactions Quatuor Cornati Lodge* xlvi, 1933, 3–43; H. Colvin, *The History of the King's Works*, 2 vols, 1963, i, 280, n. 3 refers to the earliest surviving account not seen by Knoop and Jones.

[30] Lyte, *Eton College*, 20.

[31] ECR 54/10.

religious festivals of the year, Christmas, Easter, Pentecost and the Assumption of the Virgin being particularly specified.[32]

The daily activities of the provost connected with the running of the college were wide-ranging and manifold. Matters as diverse as the purchase of cloth for liveries, the provision of books for scholars and fellows and the organisation of temporary and permanent buildings all fell within the range of his responsibilities. As a matter of course there were daily services to be attended. The duties of other members had to be supervised. It was the duty of the bursars to purchase cloth for gowns but the ultimate responsibility was Waynflete's; the choice of a Winchester clothier for supplies of cloth suggests the provost's involvement in this matter.[33] In the early years before the buildings had been completed, arrangements had to be made for the scholars to be boarded out locally[34] – another responsibility for the provost.

During the 1440s the site of the college was overrun by a large number of workmen, about sixty on average at any one time under the supervision of a clerk of works. The first clerk of works was William Lynde but several men filled the position in succession during Waynflete's years at Eton.[35] While the daily business of building and the employment and payment of masons and labourers was the clerk's responsibility, the provost was involved in directing the course of building and in matters such as the employment of leading craftsmen. On 30 November 1443 Waynflete and Lynde contracted with a carpenter, Robert Wheatley, for the carpentry work in ten chambers, a hall and several towers and turrets. The original contract has disappeared and is known only because it is referred to in the accounts for 1445–6 when the final payment to Wheatley was made.[36] Waynflete must have been involved in numerous such contracts relating to building works. Such experience was to stand him in good stead later in his own career. It would be he as provost who would act as a liaison figure between the king and royal advisers and the clerk of the works and the masons. The 'King's Will' drawn up in February 1448 shows that Henry VI had very definite ideas about the physical form his buildings should take.[37] The need for the king to produce such a document in 1448, the year after Waynflete left Eton, may have been made more urgent because the king did not have the same personal relationship with the new provost that he had established with Waynflete in whom he placed great trust.

As well as dealing with the affairs of internal college administration and building, the provost had to oversee the administration of the estates and manors which made up part of the endowment in order to safeguard and

---

32 *Ancient Laws*, 507.
33 ECR/61/A/1, m4; 61/AR/A/2, m3; 61/AR/A/3, m7.
34 Lyte, *Eton College*, 32.
35 'The Building of Eton College', 4, 6–7; the clerks of this period were John Vady, John Medehill, Richard Burton and William Lynde.
36 Willis and Clark, *Architectural History* i, 389.
37 Willis and Clark described the king's building plans in detail in *Architectural History*, i, 313–27.

maintain income from them. The accounts record personal visits by the provost and some of the fellows to outlying estates, as in November 1445 when expenses were paid to the provost, eight fellows and their servants who visited Stokensay, Leighton Buzzard and other manors to inspect them. In July of the same year the provost had been to the manor of Tooting Bec while in January 1447 he went to Beckford and Deerhurst manors.[38] The holding of manorial courts had to be organised and bailiffs appointed.[39] Landholding brought with it numerous responsibilities which devolved to the provost. The Lease Book of the college shows him making indentures on behalf of the college.[40] He also received grants for the college; in December 1444 Waynflete was named, along with the Earl of Suffolk and John Hampton, as recipient of the custody of the lands of John Speke which were in the King's hands by reason of Speke's death.[41]

Eton College also held a number of advowsons which had previously belonged to the alien priories with which Henry VI had endowed his foundation.[42] Clerks had to be found to be presented to these benefices.[43] Another responsibility towards the church was the provost's holding of archidiaconal jurisdiction over the parish of Eton which arose from the exemption of the parish and college from the jurisdiction of the Archdeacon of Buckingham in exchange for an annual payment of £1 2s 11d.[44]

William Waynflete was also involved in obtaining writs and confirmations of

[38] ECR 61/AR/A/1, m5; ECR/61/AR/A/2, m6.

[39] ECR/VR/A/1 – this is a valor of estates but it includes a memorandum of the appointment of a bailiff of the liberties of Eton College estates in Northamptonshire, 29 April 1443.

[40] In 1446, for example, indentures were made between provost Waynflete and Edward and Eleanor Hulle and between Waynflete and William Marshall concerning Leominster Priory, ECR/60/LB/1, fos 6r, 7r.

[41] *CPR 1441–6*, 314, 316.

[42] Over a hundred alien cells and priories which had not taken out charters of denization were seized by Act of Parliament in 1414; their revenues were mostly given to new religious and educational establishments. Both Eton College and King's College benefited from this redistribution. The main properties which went to Eton were Grovebury, Bedfordshire which belonged to the Order of Fontevrault; St Helen's, Isle of Wight one of the few Cluniac houses which had not taken out a charter of denization; the Benedictine alien cells of Stogursey in Somerset; Sporle in Norfolk; Ogbourne St George in Wiltshire; Modbury in Devon; Minster Lovell and Cogges in Oxfordshire; Brimpsfield in Gloucestershire; the Benedictine houses of Cowick in Devon; Deerhurst in Gloucestershire and Goldcliff in Monmouthshire. Decayed or allegedly decayed religous houses were a fruitful source of property which had the advantage of already having been amortised, throughout the fifteenth century. Bishop Waynflete acquired the property of a number of religous houses for Magdalen College and other founders did likewise. Cardinal Wolsey in 1518 and 1524–5 suppressed a number of priories whose revenues were then devoted primarily to his educational projects.

[43] From 1447 details of presentations to advowsons are recorded in the lease book but they do not start until after Waynflete had ceased to be provost.

[44] ECR 39/21; *CPR 1441–6*, 205.

privileges from the chancery.[45] He attended parliament as the representative of the college.[46] He had regular communication with the king about the affairs of Eton. When the king was at Windsor Castle, as was often the case, this presented no problem but at other times the provost had to ride in search of him. The accounts record such journeys, both to the king and to the chancery and exchequer in London.[47] When in London Waynflete had to stay in a house rented from Chertsey Abbey for it was not until 1449 that Henry VI gave the college the Hospital of St James in the Fields at Westminster which could act as a London residence.[48]

Some of these visits were for purposes of public relations rather than business. In April 1445 Waynflete attended the king's wedding to Margaret of Anjou at Titchfield Abbey in Hampshire and subsequently the queen's coronation in Westminster Abbey.[49] The involvement of the provost of Eton in these ceremonies was due to the high regard in which the king held his foundation and its provost. Such occasions were to Waynflete's advantage also, for they brought him into contact with the leading figures of the land.[50]

The educational side of Eton College was just one aspect of the provost's responsibilities, although Waynflete's special interest as an ex-schoolmaster may have meant that he concerned himself more with the educational aspects of the foundation than would otherwise have been the case. Thus although no longer involved in the teaching of the scholars he was still closely involved with educational affairs. William Westbury, headmaster from 1443, had been a pupil of Waynflete's at Winchester, and as such he must have been familiar with the sort of curriculum which had been taught there.[51] There were particular problems associated with the fact that Eton was such a recent foundation; one must have been the temporary schoolroom, another the shortage of books – a contrast with the well-stocked library at Winchester College. A library building had been completed at Eton in 1445 but in 1447 the provost had to complain to the king of an acute shortage of books.[52]

Each year in July the provost of King's College Cambridge rode to Eton

[45] PRO SC/8/44/12 – a letter from Waynflete to the chancellor requesting the issue of writs for Eton and King's colleges, August 1445.

[46] ECR 61/AR/A/2/, m6, account of Waynflete's expenses while attending parliament at Bury St Edmunds in 1447.

[47] ECR 61/AR/A/2, m5 records a lengthy period spent by Waynflete in London, 5 November – 10 December 1446. On this occasion his expenses totalled £7 12s 8d. Normally his visits were of shorter duration, a week or ten days.

[48] Lyte, *Eton College*, 51–2; although Waynflete never stayed in St James' Hospital while provost, he spent much of the winter of 1451–2 there, after he had become bishop of Winchester.

[49] ECR 61/AR/A/1, m5.

[50] He was also present at the consecration of the cemetery of King's College Cambridge in 1447, see Harriss, *Cardinal Beaufort*, 359, n. 30.

[51] *BRUO*, 2020–1.

[52] R. Birley, 'The History of Eton College Library', *The Library* v s, xi, 1956, 232–4; an inventory of 1465 shows that the library possessed forty-two books by that date. G.

College for the annual election of Eton scholars to fill vacancies in its Cambridge counterpart. At the same time new scholars were elected to Eton. Procedures for both elections were laid down in the statutes.[53] This visit was one of the high points of the year, requiring extensive preparations by the provost to receive the visitors. The following month came the feast of the Assumption of the Virgin Mary (15 August), one of the most important days in the Eton calendar, for the college was dedicated to the Virgin. Further visitors could be expected on this occasion: Henry VI later insisted that fellows of the college who had been raised to the episcopate should return to Eton for this feast day.[54]

In his final year as provost Waynflete acquired an additional educational responsibility when the king granted to the provosts of Eton and King's colleges the right to nominate to vacancies in the older Cambridge royal college, King's Hall. The provosts were to exercise their rights alternately when vacancies arose. Nine months later Henry VI extended this subordination of the old college to the new by granting the patronage of the wardenship of King's Hall to Eton and King's Colleges.[55]

By selecting Waynflete as his future provost from Winchester College in 1441, Henry VI linked the two collegiate bodies, initially so different in form, through the person of Waynflete. This personal link continued above and beyond the formal connections which was subsequently to develop but at the same time it was reinforced by the king's periodic visits to the older foundation and the reconstruction of Eton along Wykehamist lines. The single most important link, the person who contributed most to the bond, remained Waynflete.

The ex-headmaster did not lose touch with Winchester College after his departure from it. He, his brother John Waynflete and members of his household are recorded occasionally dining at the older foundation.[56] Part of the strength of the connection must be attributed to the warden and fellows of Winchester College. Their headmaster had risen from a relatively humble teaching post to a position where he was close to the king and where he was able to be useful to them. Evidence of their use of Waynflete in this manner can be seen in the bursars' accounts of Winchester College. These show that Waynflete was approached for advice and on occasion feted or given presents. In 1442–3, after the receipt of royal licence permitting the amortising of land to the value of £100 a year, the accounts record a payment of 11s 4d for a breakfast given to Waynflete, master William Say and others for their help in obtaining the licence.[57] In February 1444 a barrel of wine was given to Waynflete. Late in

Williams, 'Ecclesiastical Vestments, Books and Furniture in the Collegiate Church of King's College Cambridge in the Fifteenth Century', *The Ecclesiologist* xx, 1859, 305–6.

[53] *Ancient Laws*, 481–8.

[54] *Ibid.*, 619.

[55] ECR 39/51.

[56] WCM 22828–30.

[57] The accounts for this year also record a visit by fellows of Winchester to Eton to discuss

1444 the same accounts refer to expenses being paid to members of Winchester College who went to consult John Somerset and William Waynflete about obtaining a writ from the king.[58] Evidently there was enthusiasm to retain the goodwill of a man so close to the king and doubtless if Waynflete sought advice from Winchester College in his turn, it would have been readily given.

It is against this background that the *Amicabilis Corcordia* of 1444 must be considered. Most discussions of this document, which bound together Eton, King's, Winchester and New Colleges for their mutual defence, imply that it marks yet another step in Henry VI's modelling of Eton College on Wykehamist lines.[59] The initiative is more likely to have come from the Wykeham's foundations for the pragmatic reason that it had the most to gain. It is clear that the compact, being made for mutual support, would have benefited Winchester and New College far more than the new foundations which were already being nurtured by the king. It would enable Winchester to retain its position with access to the king which they had already achieved through the person of Waynflete.

The *Amicabilis Corcordia* formalised relations between the four bodies. Its preamble described the colleges as having much in common:

> . . . that each and every of the aforesaid colleges, though situated in diverse places, nonetheless bear almost one and the same name in their titles, nor do they seem to disagree or differ in the intentions of their founders or the fruits of their work. . . .[60]

The agreement allowed for mutual defence in law before any judges, secular or ecclesiastical and for mutual assistance where necessary against outsiders. Dated 1 July 1444 it was signed by the heads of all four colleges but the details of where it was drawn up and signed are not given. Possibly it was discussed in March of the same year when the warden of Winchester College rode to Eton for discussion.[61] On 1 July 1444 the vice-provost of Eton was dining at Winchester College; his visit on this occasion must have been connected with the agreement and he may have brought a copy of the concordat to them.[62]

While the agreement was being drawn up the advantages to be gleaned from it must have seemed to lie on the side of Winchester College and New College. In the long term it was Eton which was to come under attack after the deposition of Henry VI while Wykeham's foundations remained unscathed. In

---

other problems with Waynflete; later the same year they made Waynflete a present of six yards of 'revsey' cloth, WCM 22118, *Custus necessariorum forensicorum*.

58 WCM 22119, *Custus liberacionum defensionis*.

59 Lyte, *Eton College*, 20 describes the concordat as resulting from the friendship existing between the colleges.

60 M. Walcott, *William of Wykeham and his Colleges*, 1854, 141–3 prints the Latin text of the concordat.

61 WCM 22119, *Custus necessariorum forensicorum*.

62 WCM 22830, hall book for 1444.

the 1460s the *Amicabilis Corcordia* proved to be of little practical aid to Eton and King's colleges.[63]

The provostship of Eton College into which Henry VI thrust William Waynflete in the spring of 1442 was a challenging position. The responsibilities it carried were both numerous and onerous, being not only administrative but also diplomatic and social, requiring an ability to work successfully with a variety of people – papal envoys, magnates, bishops, bailiffs, carpenters and small boys. For Waynflete the problems were increased by the newly-founded status of the college; it would have been considerably easier to administer a well-established collegiate body which had already developed traditions and routines than it was to establish such traditions. In addition during this period the college was changing, both in size and in the conception of its nature, from an essentially religious foundation to one where education was of prime importance. Waynflete presided over and influenced this transformation. His experience at Winchester College enabled him to guide the development of Eton along similar lines. It was a difficult and challenging task – the problems of which can only have been added to by the personality of the young king. That William Waynflete was successful in rising to the challenge is witness to his wide-ranging abilities. Had he not satisfied Henry VI's exacting requirements it is likely that Waynflete, like Sever, would have faded into relative obscurity. Instead, in April 1447, he was promoted by the king to the see of Winchester – a reward for his achievement in developing Eton within six years into a collegiate body along the same lines as the older Winchester College.

Waynflete and Eton 1447–1461

The ties between William Waynflete and Eton College remained close in the immediate aftermath of his elevation to the see of Winchester. In the presence of the king on 30 July 1447 Waynflete was consecrated bishop in the half-built chapel of the college. The chapel, despite its newness, had already seen the consecration of two men – Thomas Beckington as bishop of Bath and Wells in 1443 and John Carpenter as bishop of Worcester in 1444.[64] In December of the same year bishop Waynflete held his first ordination ceremony in Eton chapel, by special permission of the ordinary, the bishop of Lincoln.[65] In the following years many of Waynflete's visits to the college took place on formal occasions, for celebrations of feast days, in particular for the feast of the Assumption of the Virgin Mary on 15 August, an important day in the Eton calendar.[66] On a

---

[63] For a discussion of the problems faced by Eton in the early 1460s see Lyte, *Eton College*, 62.

[64] ECR 60/LB/1, fo 2r; W. Stubbs, *Registrum Sacrum Anglicanum*, 2nd edn, Oxford 1897, 89.

[65] Reg Waynflete, i fo Ar, 23 December 1447.

[66] 1448, 1450, 1451, see itinerary; this was before the 1453 addition made to the statutes

number of occasions Waynflete seems also to have visited Eton College in April when, in his ex-officio role as prelate to the Order of the Garter, he was at nearby Windsor for the St George's day ceremonies.[67] These visits to the college occurred more frequently in the first four years of his episcopate than thereafter. However, Waynflete's dealings with the college in these years were not confined to formal and ceremonial appearances. He remained involved in the more practical and administrative aspects of the college's affairs.

A visit by Waynflete to Eton in early January 1448[68] was possibly the occasion for the discussion of documents which were to outline the royal plans for the future development of the foundation. Documents dated at Eton on 7 February 1448 foreshadowed the issuing of the 'King's Will' by Henry VI the following month. These first documents, endorsed, 'For the edification of the Quere of the Kinges colege of oure lady . . .'[69] were witnessed by Waynflete, the Duke of Suffolk (who as chief adviser to the young king had been involved with both Eton and King's Colleges since their inception) and others who were not named. They seem to have been a draft for the more detailed 'King's Will' which followed, although the specifications for the architectural plans which they contained were to be altered in some respects.[70]

The 'King's Will' itself was a detailed and specific document.[71] It consisted of a preamble describing the motives for the foundation; details of the arrangements which had been made to finance the building works; a careful description of the architectural schemes for both colleges; the legal provisions concerning the number of feoffees. It concluded with a section which entrusted the overall supervision of the scheme to William Waynflete.

After the preamble the 'King's Will' begins by reciting the names of men already enfeoffed on behalf of both colleges with land from the Duchy of Lancaster. These men were to ensure an annual payment of £1000 from these lands to each college for a twenty year period or longer if necessary. The total issue of castles, manors and other properties was described as being worth £3395 11s 7d annually.[72] The feoffees who included both archbishops and nine

of the college by Henry VI which made it mandatory for fellows who had been raised to the episcopate to return to Eton on that day, *Ancient Laws*, 619–20.

67 1450, 1451, see itinerary.

68 Reg Waynflete, i fo 1*r.

69 ECR 39/4. 39/75. 39/87; ECR 39/75 consists of three texts bound together and endorsed as quoted above. It is dated 7 February, the only named witnesses are Waynflete and Suffolk, m5. EC39/74 is undated but from this period and deals with 'The appointment towching the demensions of the housing of his colege Roial of oure lady of Eton . . .'. ECR 39/87 also deals with the dimensions of the buildings. The plans are discussed in Willis and Clark, *Architectural History* i, 350–68.

70 The main differences between the drafts and the 'Will' are in the dimensions ascribed to the different buildings, Willis and Clark, *Architectural History* i, 352.

71 ECR 39/78, printed in full in *A Collection of the Wills of the Kings and Queens of England*, ed. J. Nichols, 1780, 291–313 but his text was derived from an inaccurate transcript, BL Harl MS 7032.

72 ECR 39/78, m1.

other prelates had been enfeoffed by a number of letters patent, beginning 29 November 1444. These royal grants had been reiterated in a consolidation charter confirmed by parliament at Westminster on 5 March 1446.[73] The major part of the 'King's Will' was taken up by the detailed plans for building works in both colleges which Henry VI desired, '. . . to be doon and performed by my same feoffees . . .'. Until these buildings had been completed, whether achieved during the king's lifetime or not until after his death, the lands were to remain in the feoffees' hands; subsequently they were to revert to the Crown. Another section was concerned with legal safeguards; Henry VI was concerned to ensure that the body of feoffees would not be wiped out by death and he provided that if their number fell to three or less new men were to be appointed. He listed the men he wished to be included among the new feofees. The list was headed by William Waynflete as bishop of Winchester and included Reginald Pecock, bishop of St Asaph, William Westbury who was provost of Eton College and John Chedworth, subsequently bishop of Lincoln (1452–71) but at that time provost of King's College Cambridge.[74] The inclusion of Waynflete in this list is not particularly significant since the existing feoffees included the holders of all the most important English and Welsh sees. It was in the final section of the 'King's Will' that the king expressed his great regard for Waynflete and his belief in the abilities of the new bishop.

> Furthermore, for the final perfourmyng of my seid wil to be put effectuelly in execution, I, consideryng the greate discrecion of the seide worshepful fader in God, William nowe bisshop of Wynchestre, his high trougth and fervent zele whiche at all tymes he hath hadde and hath unto my weel and whiche I have founde and proved in hym and for the grete and hool confidence whiche I have unto hym for thoo causes, wol that he, not oonly as Surveour but also as executor and director of my seid wil, be privee into alle and every execucion of the perfourmyng of my same wil and his consente in any wide be had therto . . . I yeue and graunt unto the seid bisshop of Wynchestre by thes presents, plain power and auctorite . . .[75]

Waynflete was given the supreme executive power; his was to be the deciding voice in any dispute; if required he could select new feoffees. He was directed to choose before his own death, if he outlived the king, a successor whose qualifications were to be that he was '. . . best and most godly disposed and most fervent in zeal to the performing of my seid wil . . .'[76] Faithful adherence to the king's wishes was the crucial factor and that must have been the criterion applied by Henry VI to Waynflete himself.

William Waynflete's departure from the provostship of Eton College may have made the production of a document such as the 'King's Will' a matter of

73 *RP* V, 70–3.
74 ECR 39/78 m1.
75 ECR 39/78, m2.
76 *Ibid.*

urgency and importance. He had worked closely with the king and had been party to Henry VI's plans and ideas which he could be trusted to fulfill. William Westbury, his successor, although a successful and dedicated provost,[77] had not the same intimate links with the king. King's College Cambridge had also lost its original head during 1447 when William Millington resigned rather than accept the statutes provided in that year.[78] Having thus lost both of these well-established and trusted provosts it is likely that Henry VI felt the need to express, in detailed written form, his desires and arrangements for the development of both colleges.

The 'King's Will' is not the sole evidence for Waynflete's active connection with and participation in matters relating to Eton College after his elevation to the episcopate. This remained considerable in the late 1440s, despite the demands laid upon him by his new diocesan and political commitments. In June 1448 Waynflete, together with provost Westbury, the Duke of Suffolk, Richard Andrew and William Tresham, was chosen to act as an arbitrator in a dispute which had arisen between college tenants in the Gloucester village of Aston and other inhabitants of the same town.[79] Nothing is known of the outcome of this case but it indicates Waynflete's continuing involvement with, and importance in college affairs.

This involvement was reinforced by commitments which Waynflete had shouldered while still provost and which could not be easily shaken off. In association with the Duke of Suffolk he was involved in a long-running controversy with the abbey of St Albans over some jewels which Humphrey, Duke of Gloucester had arranged to purchase but which Henry VI determined to acquire for Eton's treasury after the death of the Duke. Henry was slow to pay over the required £600 to the abbey and the matter dragged on until 1457 when it was agreed that the abbey should receive the money owed out of tenths granted by the clergy.[80]

Waynflete's continuing involvement with Eton was not restricted to formal arbitration procedures. He appears to have remained involved with more intimate daily college affairs. In 1449 £75 15s was paid to the college by Waynflete, the estimated cost of the wages of twenty men working on the chancel of the new church.[81] He visited the college in both April and June of that year,[82] while on 30 May at Westminster he witnessed the confirmation of various grants previously made to the college.[83]

There was a marked decline in Waynflete's links with Eton College as the

---

[77] *BRUO*, 2020; Westbury's dedication to Eton College was displayed in the efforts he made during the early 1460s to preserve the college, Lyte, *Eton College*, 63–4.

[78] J. Saltmarsh, 'The Founder's Statutes of King's College Cambridge', *Studies Presented to Sir Hilary Jenkinson*, ed. J. Conway Davies.

[79] *CCR 1446–52*, 66.

[80] *CPR 1452–61*, 395.

[81] Willis and Clark, *Architectural History* i, 401.

[82] See itinerary.

[83] *CPR 1446–52*, 471.

1450s progressed. In 1450 he visited the college in April and August,[84] the latter on the occasion of the feast of the Assumption. In 1451 there was a similar pattern; visits were made while at Windsor to attend the meeting of the Order of the Garter in April and again in August.[85] The bursars' accounts record that a large fish was given to the bishop as a present, probably during the summer.[86] In 1453 his only apparent connection was the witnessing of grant of a weekly fair to the college, made at Westminster on 20 June.[87] The visit of 1451 were the last regular recorded visits to the college by Waynflete although brief and casual visits cannot be entirely ruled out. References to Eton College only occur in the Winchester episcopal register because of episcopal acta made there. Thus it is possible and likely that Waynflete may have paid visits to the college which have gone unrecorded.

His involvement with Eton College revived briefly in 1455 when Henry VI appointed him (together with the ex-provost of King's, John Chedworth, now bishop of Lincoln), to reform the statutes of both royal colleges. The royal letters patent concerning the reform of the statutes state that practical usage of the existing statutes had shown up some defects which needed to be removed and that since the king was not able to devote himself to the matter with complete attention he had chosen Waynflete and Chedworth to act in his stead.[88] Provost Westbury visited Waynflete at Esher manor in 1455[89] perhaps to discuss the matter, for the reforms were supposed to be carried out in consultation with the provosts of both foundations. Waynflete's visit to the college in May of the same year[90] preceded the grant of authority to reform but may well have been connected with it.

Waynflete's appointment as chancellor of England following the reshuffle of royal ministers in September-October 1456[91] made him an even more useful potential patron to the College. In this guise they sought his patronage on several occasions; two visits to the chancellor in 1458 and one in 1459 were recorded in the bursars' accounts.[92] These visits culminated with confirmation of royal grants to the college made on 20 November 1459.[93]

By this time Waynflete no longer had the intimate connection with the college which could be seen ten years earlier just after his promotion to the episcopate. This decline is understandable. Henry VI's period of mental instability in 1453-4 must have helped to break the link. Other personal ties

[84] See itinerary.
[85] *Ibid.*
[86] ECR 61/AR/A/5, m8.
[87] ECR 39/103.
[88] *CPR 1452-61*, 241; the letter patent is printed in full in *Ancient Laws* 624-5 where however it is wrongly ascribed to 1445.
[89] ECR 61/BD/A/2, m13.
[90] See itinerary, appendix 2.
[91] *CCR 1454-61*, 211.
[92] ECR 61/AR/B/1, m5.
[93] ECR 39/122.

between the bishop and the college weakened as new pupils and fellows came to the college. His foundation of Magdalen Hall in Oxford in 1448 and subsequently of Magdalen College in 1458 provided a new channel for Waynflete's educational interests, a channel which moreover, together with his episcopal responsibilities as visitor of New College Oxford, directed his attention away from Eton and Cambridge towards Oxford.

Benefactor, 1461–1486

It would be reasonable therefore to expect that Waynflete's attention and his financial resources would continue to be directed away from Eton College to these other heavy commitments. The reality – Waynflete's response to the poor state in which Eton College found itself by the late 1460s – suggests that a considerable loyalty remained to Henry VI's favoured foundation, the college which had provided the opportunity for the advancement of Waynflete's own career.

The deposition of Henry VI in 1461 was the beginning of a period of great difficulty for his two royal foundations. The promise of protection made by the future Edward IV on 27 February 1461 that, '. . . We have by thees our lettres taken and receyved the Provoste and felaship of the Collage of Eyton into oure defense and saveguard . . .'[94] was to prove of little comfort in the long term. The problems Eton faced in the next half decade when its annual revenues fell from approximately £1,500 to £370 and when a union with the royal chapel of St George at nearby Windsor was mooted, have been described elsewhere,[95] although the almost complete absence of collegiate records during this period leaves the course of the crisis obscure.

Traditionally Edward IV's hostility towards Eton College has been widely accepted; 'As time went on Edward's jealously of Henry VI increased and he resolved to discredit everything that could rebound to the fame of his rival'.[96] In fact there is little evidence to show that Edward acted in this fashion. His promise of 1461 suggests initial good intentions, further evidence of which was displayed by his action in re-granting some estates to the college after the sweeping resumptions of 1462.[97] Eton College had been Henry VI's particular project and he had showered possessions and endowments upon it; Edward IV on the other hand treated the college much less lavishly, dramatically reducing the scale of royal support. Thus while Edward IV should not be portrayed as attacking Eton College because it was the foundation of his predecessor, neither did he show it the munificence displayed by Henry VI.

In this context the proposal that Eton be united with the collegiate church of

[94] Cited in Lyte, *Eton College*, 62.
[95] *Ibid.*, 62–7; *VCH Buckinghamshire* ii, 167–8.
[96] Lyte, *Eton College*, 62.
[97] *CPR 1461–7*, 73.

St George at Windsor should be taken at its face value. In 1463 Edward IV petitioned Pope Pius II for permission to suppress the college and to transfer its endowments to St George's chapel. This petition pointed out that the college was not likely to fulfil the aims of its founder in view of the incomplete state of the buildings and its lack of revenue.[98] Without the generosity of Henry VI and with the endowment reduced to a more usual level this claim was quite true. Although the chivalric values behind the Order of the Garter were closer to Edward IV's own tastes than the pious and educational aspirations attached to Eton and King's Colleges, it must not be assumed that Edward IV actively sought to crush Eton. Edward IV's patronage of St George's chapel was independent of his attitude to Eton College – in 1473 when Eton was no longer under threat of suppression, the king began to rebuild St George's chapel and he continued to favour the college there while remaining on friendly terms with Eton College.[99]

The severe dilapidation of the revenues of Eton College did for a period make the prospect of union with St George's chapel dangerously likely. A Bull of Union was issued by the pope on 13 November 1463[100] and although there is little evidence that any practical attempts were made to enforce it, it was not withdrawn until late in 1470.[101] The survival of the college during this period has been attributed to various causes; one colourful legend assigns the credit to pleading on behalf of the college by Jane Shore, mistress to Edward IV.[102] It seems in fact that what saved Eton was primarily the determination of the provost William Westbury and a small group of fellows to fight the proposed union.[103] Their efforts showed that the college was viable (albeit on a smaller scale than hitherto) and thus gave the lie to the suggestion that it could not survive with reduced resources.

Although William Waynflete was to be of great assistance to Eton College from c.1467 onwards there is no evidence for Lyte's assertion that, '. . . we may probably ascribe the eventual preservation of Eton to his unceasing exertions . . .'[104] As has been seen, by the late 1450s the connections between Waynflete and Eton College were weakening. After the deposition of Henry VI, Waynflete as a known Lancastrian partisan no longer held a position of influence in the court circle. He was hardly in a position to aid Eton College. His episcopal register for this period suggests that in the early years of the Yorkist regime Waynflete spent much of his time quietly in his diocese, avoiding political entanglements and other sensitive issues. Provost Westbury seems to have made an attempt to enlist Waynflete's aid in 1464 for in May and June of that year he

98   *CPL 1455–64*, 655–7.
99   M. Bond, 'Chapter Adminstration and Archives at Windsor', *JEH* viii, 1957, 173.
100 *CPL 1455–64*, 655–7.
101 *CPL 1458–71*, 342–4.
102 N. Baker and R. Birley, 'The Story of Jane Shore', *Etoniana*, 1972, 342–4.
103 Lyte, *Eton College*, 63–5.
104 *Ibid.*, 64.

visited the bishop but his appeal had no visible result. In June of the same year, Westbury visited the bishop of Lincoln, presumably also seeking support from that quarter.[105] It was not until 1467 when initial memories of the early years of the decade were beginning to fade and when Eton's position was already beginning to improve, that Waynflete again became closely involved with the welfare of the college.

Waynflete's documented connection with Eton College resumed with the visit he paid to the college in February 1467.[106] No supporting evidence is available from the bursars' accounts which are missing for this period,[107] but his visit may have been exploratory, to discover the needs of the college. It has been suggested that Waynflete's political position improved in 1467 due to the decline in influence of the powerful Neville family; George Neville, archbishop of York was dismissed from the chancellorship on 8 June 1467.[108] Certainly Waynflete had more friendly connections with the Woodvilles whose influence increased as that of the Nevilles declined. However, while these political developments may have eased the bishop's position, they hardly affected his involvement with Eton for this initial resumption of contact took place before the Nevilles' decline.

From 1467 Waynflete acted as a generous patron and benefactor to Eton College. He concentrated his resources on the building and decorating of the chapel which had been the project closest to the heart to Henry VI. Essentially the relationship was a financial one; Waynflete paid for the building materials and the labour, a benefcation which allowed him largely to 'call the tune' with regard to the form the building should take. Henry VI's ambitious schemes had envisaged the finished chapel at Eton College as rivalling many English cathedrals in size and magnificence but while the chapel was not constructed on the scale envisaged by its founder, considerable care was taken by Waynflete in its design and decoration.

The audit rolls of Eton College from early 1468 onwards record frequent journeys being made by the Provost or fellows of the college to the bishop of Winchester. The purpose of these visits is usually given as '. . . pro operibus ecclesie inchoandi . . .' or '. . . pro pecuniis adquirendi pro operibus ecclesie . . .'[109] To take two years as examples – in 1472 Provost Westbury rode to London in March to see Waynflete and later in the summer went to Farnham, the bishop's manor in Surrey, for a similar purpose. This second visit, for which expenses totalled 6s 2d, was described as lasting three days and three nights.[110] Seven visits of this kind were made in 1479–80 – in November, December,

[105] ECR 61/BD/C/1, fo 7.
[106] See itinerary.
[107] They do not resume again until January 1468.
[108] Mills, 'Foundation, Endowment and Early Administration', 18; HBC, 85.
[109] Willis and Clarke print extracts from the college audit rolls detailing these visits to bishop Waynflete; both of these phrases occur regularly, Architectural History i, 406–11.
[110] ECR 61/BD/C/8, m6.

February, April, June, August and on one unspecified occasion – and the expense of two presents given to the bishop in this year was also recorded.[111] The audit rolls are not complete for this period but the extant rolls from 1468 until Waynflete's death in 1486 record such visits taking place each year.

The frequency of these visits suggests that Waynflete retained tight control over the progress of building, paying out money in small amounts at any one time. The amounts paid by Waynflete to the college for building purposes cannot be estimated for the audit rolls do not record the amounts given to the college. On occasion, particular contracts refer to specific sums; 100 marks was paid over a two year period for the construction of the rood loft. This was in addition to the cost of materials and provision of accommodation for the labourers.[112] Clearly he did not hand over a substantial sum of money to the college to be used for building works at the provost's discretion. Had there been a cash flow problem preventing Waynflete giving large sums of money to the college at one time, it is likely that an arrangement could have been made to pay over regular installments which would not have necessitated these 'begging trips' to the bishop by the provost. It is likely that these arose from a reluctance to relinquish control over the works rather than from a shortage of money. Waynflete can be seen behaving in a similar manner with regard to Magdalen College Oxford which did not gain full control over the endowment amassed for it by the bishop until after Waynflete's death.[113]

This desire to direct affairs at Eton personally can also be seen in the fact that the bishop was party to contracts made with the building workers. In August 1475 he made a contract with Walter Nicholl of Southwark for the erection of a roodloft in the chapel which was to extend the whole breadth of the choir.[114] Under this contract Waynflete retained full responsibility for the cost of supplying materials, paying the labourers, providing their accommodation and a workshop and paying Nicholl.

Waynflete was no newcomer to the details of architectural projects. While provost of Eton he had been involved with the construction of the earliest buildings on the site; as bishop of Winchester, with considerable resources at his disposal, he proved a lavish patron of building, involved with major projects at his manors of Esher and Farnham, at Magdalen College Oxford and at Wainfleet and Tattershall in Lincolnshire.[115] On occasion he employed the same men to work on different projects and it is likely that William Orchard, master of the works at Magdalen College from 1468, was in charge of the works at Eton as

---

111 ECR 61/AR/C/6, m8, 9.
112 Between 1468–86 the audit rolls are missing for the years 1472–3; 1473–4; 1476–7; 1477–8; 1478–9.
113 ECR 38/309.
114 ECR 38/309, printed in full in Willis and Clark, *Architectural History* i, 596–8.
115 See below chapter 5.

well. In 1479 Orchard undertook to supply Eton College as well as Magdalen with stone from the quarry he leased from the king at Headington.[116]

In addition to retaining financial control over the building works at Eton, Waynflete concerned himself with the actual design and decoration of the building. The resulting chapel was smaller than the one envisaged by Henry VI but that does not mean that its decoration was neglected or that it was built without forethought, on an ad hoc basis. Pevsener says of the building that it, 'achieves greatness by means of an uncompromising consistency'.[117] Waynflete evidently attempted to maintain a similar style to that planned by Henry VI – the general similarity between Eton Chapel and that of King's College Cambridge suggests this, although neither was completed according to Henry VI's plans.[118] It is clear that Waynflete was responsible for the major cost of the paintings in the chapel which were carried out between 1477–88; not until after his death in 1486 did the full cost of those still to be completed fall upon the college.[119]

William Waynflete's links with Eton College did not finally cease until his death in 1486. The impact of his death can be seen in the account rolls of the college as it was forced to assume responsibility for projects previously financed by the bishop. The audit roll for 1486–7, the year after Waynflete's death, lists pigments for the completion of the wall paintings in the chapel being paid for by the college for the first time. Eton was left nothing in Waynflete's will; all his benefactions to the college were made during his lifetime, at a period when money was urgently required to restore its viability as a college.

Waynflete was cautious in his attitude towards the college in the early years of Edward IV's reign. He did not leap up in its defence at a time when his own influence was slight and the college seemed unlikely to survive at all. He waited until the future of the college seemed secure and a good investment before he became involved with it again. When he did so his money went primarily towards the construction and decoration of the church; the project to which Henry VI had been particularly attached.

Why did William Waynflete expend so much money and energy on behalf of Eton College? The answer must lie in a combination of two things – the moral obligation to fulfil the trust laid upon him by Henry VI and the debt which he felt personally towards the college which had been the means of his own advancement. Waynflete's adoption of the lilies of Eton College as part of his

[116] '. . . And also unto the werke he hathe at Etone . . .' Willis and Clark, *Architectural History* i, 410; for Orchard's career see J. Harvey and A. Oswald, *English Medieval Architects: a Biographical Dictionary down to 1550*, 2nd edn, Gloucester 1984, 220–3; MC CP/2/67 (2) includes among the Magdalen College building accounts some references to the works of Eton.

[117] N. Pevsner, *Buckinghamshire*, 1960, 123.

[118] F. Woodman, *The Architectural History of King's College Cambridge*, 1986.

[119] ECR 61/AR/F/2 m2.

episcopal arms symbolised his regard and his appreciation of the part the college had played in his promotion to the episcopate.[120] His years there brought him royal favour; he repaid this by helping to fill the financial void created by Henry VI's deposition.

[120] W.K.R. Bedford, *The Blazon of Episcopacy*, 2nd edn, Oxford 1897, plate lx.

III

Oxford Foundations, 1448–1486

Magdalen Hall

Waynflete set in motion the foundation of Magdalen Hall in Oxford very shortly after having been promoted to the bishopric of Winchester. His consecration as bishop took place in July 1447, by the following June at the latest the first steps had been taken to acquire the land and site necessary as a prerequisite to the foundation. On 20 August 1448 a foundation charter was issued which established a hall for a president and fifty graduate scholars.[1] From the first therefore Waynflete envisaged his foundation on a substantial scale. The motives of many medieval founders are difficult to establish. Founders of chantries had a more clearly avowed (and perhaps more selfish) motive than can be seen in the case of founders of secular colleges. While the preamble to foundation charters usually contains some indication of the reasons in the founder's mind, such reasons are often obscured by the limitations of the legal form in which they are couched.[2]

William Waynflete's avowed intentions were clear enough – he gave as his reasons for establishing Magdalen Hall the dual and not uncommon motives of wishing to stamp out heresy and to provide well-educated and suitable clergy to serve in parishes.[3] Were these his only reasons? The speed at which he moved provides a clue to his further intentions. It was more common for episcopal founders to wait until they were well established in their dioceses and were fully conversant with the extent of their resources before they embarked on the long and complex business of founding a college. Richard Fleming, bishop of Lincoln from 1420, acted quickly by episcopal standards in founding Lincoln College in 1427.[4] Henry Chichele became archbishop of Canterbury in 1414, but All Souls College Oxford was not founded until 1437.[5] In 1487 Richard Fox was made bishop of Exeter but he waited until he had been translated several times and finally had been bishop of Winchester for fourteen years

[1] MC Deeds, Chartae Regiae 50, printed in Chandler, *Life*, appendix ix, 323–30.
[2] E.F. Jacob, 'Founders and Foundations in the Middle Ages', in *Essays in the Later Middle Ages*, Manchester 1968, 154–74.
[3] Chandler, *Life*, appendix ix, 323.
[4] V.H. Green, *The Commonwealth of Lincoln College 1427–1977*, Oxford 1979, 1–20.
[5] E.J. Jacob, *Archbishop Henry Chichele*, 1967, 377–8.

motion the foundation of Corpus Christi College in Oxford.[6] Waynflete's predecessor William Wykeham had been bishop since 1367 but waited until 1379 before establishing New College Oxford.[7] Thus William Waynflete was most unusual in taking such precipitate action to found Magdalen Hall. The most likely explanation is that, like his patron Henry VI who founded a royal college at Eton partly as a demonstration of his having assumed the reins of power,[8] Waynflete founded his Oxford hall quickly to demonstrate in a most concrete form that he had been elevated to the see of Winchester (a see with strong educational ties with Oxford) and was now able to promote his own educational projects.

Any episcopal founder whose interests would be spread over a wide range of activities and whose other duties would prevent him from devoting himself whole-time to his foundation, required reliable agents to act for him in the slow process of gathering together endowments to support the fellows and the community and in finding a suitable site for the institution. William Waynflete relied on the Godmanston family, John and Simon, father and son, to act for him in this way. There are no clues to indicate how Waynflete initially came in contact with this family of minor Essex gentry but the connection may have been made through the Duke of Buckingham, for Godmanston was one of the stewards of the central circuit for the Duke.[9] The Godmanstons continued to serve the bishop well. Simon Godmanston who was named among the graduate scholars in the foundation charter of Magdalen Hall was later appointed chaplain to Waynflete and remained in the bishop's service for the rest of his life.[10]

The first indication that the new bishop of Winchester might be considering a foundation in Oxford occurred in the summer of 1448. On 19 June John Godmanston was granted twelve properties by the hospital of St John the Baptist,[11] an Augustinian foundation situated just outside the east gate of Oxford. This grant was confirmed by the king in letters patent dated 25 July 1448 and these letters refer to the proposed foundation of a hall by Waynflete.[12] The hospital of St John the Baptist was to become very important in the later history of Magdalen Hall and from the first it provided the nucleus of Magdalen's property. In addition to these twelve sites, on 1 August John

6 *BRUO*, 3716–17.
7 From 1369 however, Wykeham was collecting properties which were to form part of the site of his future college; at the same time he was housing in Oxford at his own expense, a community of scholars, R.L. Storey, 'The Foundation of the Medieval College', in J. Buxton and P. Williams, *New College Oxford 1379–1979*, Oxford 1979, 6.
8 *Educational Charters and Documents*, 405.
9 C. Rawcliffe, *The Staffords, Earls of Stafford and Dukes and Buckingham*, Cambridge 1978, 203.
10 *BRUO*, 779.
11 *Cart St John* i, 248.
12 *Ibid.*, 3.254–7; MC Deeds, Misc. 372.

Godmanston granted two halls, Bostar Hall and Hare Hall to Waynflete.[13] Such halls were a common feature of both Oxford and Cambridge; they provided accommodation and perhaps a little teaching for the bulk of the undergraduate students.[14] They were usually ephemeral and short-lived, springing up under an individual who was licensed by the university authorities and they kept few records.[15]

On 20 August 1448 Waynflete issued the foundation charter for Magdalen Hall.[16] In it he named as president John Hornley,[17] and a number of graduate scholars. On 8 September Godmanston conveyed the properties which he had obtained from the hospital of St John the Baptist.[18] These, together with the two aforementioned halls were to comprise the major part of the property of Magdalen Hall. No administrative or financial records have survived relating to this foundation and neither are there any extant statutes. It is unlikely that there ever were any formal statutes prior to those issued by Waynflete much later in the 1480s. Knowledge of the composition and activities of the community of Magdalen Hall depends on evidence from its foundation charter and from what is known of the careers of the early members of the hall. In his foundation charter Waynflete described the community as a perpetual hall founded for the increase of knowledge; the emphasis was away from legal studies, philosophy and theology were the subjects to be followed,[19] reflecting the bishop's own training as a theologian. The community was to consist of a president and fifty scholars, making it a substantial body although not as large as Wykeham's New College which provided for seventy scholars. Initially Magdalen Hall was smaller than the charter provided for, only twenty men were named as scholars in the charter.[20] Of these men thirteen were already masters of arts.

No mention was made in the charter of any preference as to the geographical origins of the students; the only stipulation was that they were to be graduates. It is difficult to establish any connection between the bishop and most of the men named in the foundation charter as scholars.[21] With the exception of Simon Godmanston whose inclusion may well have been in gratitude for his

13 *Cart St John* i, 257.
14 See A.B. Emden, *A Medieval Oxford Hall*, Oxford 1927; T. Aston, 'Oxford's Medieval Alumni', *Past & Present* lxxiv, 1977, 36–40; A mid-fifteenth-century list of Oxford halls compiled by the antiquarian John Rous is printed as part of appendix F in *Survey of the Antiquities of the City of Oxford Composed in 1661–6 by Anthony Wood*, ed. A. Clark, OHS 1889, 638–41.
15 Licenses to keep halls were granted annually and were recorded in the register kept by the chancellor of the University, see for example, *Registrum Cancellarii Oxon.* ed. H.E. Salter, 2 vols, OHS 1930–31, i, 50.
16 MC Deeds, Chartae Regiae 50; printed in Chandler, *Life*, appendix ix, 323–30.
17 *BRUO*, 966.
18 *Cart St John* i, 258–9.
19 Chandler, *Life*, appendix ix, 324.
20 Chandler, *Life*, appendix ix, 327.
21 Biographical details of the early scholars are given in Macray, *Register of Magdalen* I and *BRUO* None of these men had previous connections with Waynflete; they had not been

and his father's efforts on the bishop's behalf, the remainder had no previous connection with Waynflete. Some, it can be conjectured may have come from the residential halls it absorbed. This was certainly true for William Elys who came from Hare Hall; Thomas Chapelyn who came from Brasenose; John Forman who came from St Thomas Hall and William Heward who was from Nun Hall.[22] Of the others nothing is known. In so far as their academic progress can be traced, three of the bachelors of arts had become masters of arts by 1449 while the fourth had followed suit by 1452.[23] As a corporation licensed by the king the community could hold land and it had its own seal. The limited evidence which exists relating to its activities in the years after 1448 show Magdalen Hall to be functioning as a corporate, land-holding body, collecting rents and receiving property.[24]

From Hall to College: The Hospital of St John the Baptist

Although the proceedings relating to the amalgamation of Magdalen Hall and the Augustinian hospital of St John the Baptist were not finally concluded until 1458 Waynflete may have envisaged close connections between the two bodies at a much earlier stage. The properties rented from the hospital were the nucleus of the Hall's premises from 1448. Waynflete, after his years at Eton College was familiar with Henry VI's practice of suppressing run-down hospitals and other religious foundations and transferring their endowments to other uses. Such suppressed houses, in particular alien priories, had been widely utilised by the king to endow both Eton and Kings Colleges.[25] The hospital of St John the Baptist had been endowed by Henry III in 1234 on a site outside the east gate of Oxford.[26] It was still of royal patronage in the mid fifteenth century but by that time, like many other such houses, the size of the community was much reduced, consisting only of a master and four canons instead of the original fifteen men.[27] It was not a poor community by any standards, possessing extensive properties which made it potentially a rich prize. By the mid fifteenth century it was worth approximately £75 per annum. In 1451 Henry VI granted the advowson of Horsepath (just outside the city) to the

at either Eton or Wichester colleges and were not holders of benefices in the diocese of Winchester.
22 Their involvement had been in these other halls during the early 1440s, see *BRUO*.
23 William Delyn, William Heward and John Forman (later a substantial benefactor to the college) had become M.A.s by 1449. Philip Rugge had followed suit by 1452, see *BRUO*.
24 Draft deeds and receipts for rent are recorded in *Cart St John* I, 260–65; II, 247–8; MC Deeds Candlesby 29a is a bequest from Thomas Ingyll, 5 August 1450.
25 Lyte, *Eton College*, 17–19.
26 *Cart St John* iii, preface, p. vi.
27 *Ibid.*, xvi–xvii

community,[28] a rare gesture on his part towards a house to which he had hitherto paid little attention. This may have been the first move towards unification of the hospital and Magdalen Hall – subsequently the master of the hospital Richard Vise rented the rectory of Horsepath from Magdalen College[29] and it is possible that this was part of an agreement made earlier, with Waynflete persuading the king to release the advowson of Horsepath to the hospital, perhaps as an encouragement to Vise to look favourably on the idea of amalgamation.

The first steps towards the unification of hospital and hall were taken in the spring of 1456, before Waynflete became chancellor although at a time when his political influence was strong. On 5 May 1456 Henry VI issued a commission appointing several influential men in the university of Oxford to inquire into the state of the house. The commissioners were Luke Laycock, D.Cn.L; John Boteller, D.Cn&C.L.; John Moreton, D.Cn&C.L.; William Godeyere, B.Cn&C.L. and John Wynterburn, B.C.L. These were men with strong Oxford connections; they had all acted on occasion as commissaries for the university chancellor. They were also men likely to be on the spot in Oxford and therefore able to carry out the investigation personally. The wording of the commission painted a sorry picture, stating that the house was dilapidated, its property was being dissipated and that the chalices and precious ornaments belonging to the house had been sold.[30]

No reports of this commission of inquiry have survived but since the dilapidation of the hospital was one of the reasons given to justify the amalgamation this visitation presumably confirmed the reports which had prompted the issuing of the commission. At the same time four lawyers were, on behalf of Waynflete, looking into the feasibility of suppressing the hospital. These lawyers were Hugh Sugar (vicar-general of Bath and Wells), John Holland who was attached to Waynflete's household, William Say and John Druel.[31] Their report concluded that the suppression would be able to take place provided that, (i) the consent of the patron was obtained; (ii) papal authorisation was forthcoming; (iii) its worship and hospitality were not diminished and (iv) the remaining members of the community were adequately provided for.[32] Unfortunately this legal opinion cannot be precisely dated but it seems likely that it

---

[28] MC Deeds, Horsepath 13.

[29] MC Deeds, Horsepath 1, 17; the lease was originally made on 27 July for two years and was renewed in November 1458 after the establishment of Magdalen College, for the term of Vise's life for a nominal annual rent of one red rose.

[30] CPR 1452–61, 303.

[31] Cart St John ii, 448–9.

[32] On 20 August 1457, President Hornley and the scholars of Magdalen Hall granted annual pensions of £10 each to the three remaining chaplains of the hospital Cart St John ii, 449; this grant was sealed with the hospital seal, suggesting that the Hall did not as yet have a formal seal of its own. On 20 July 1457 Waynflete collated the master Richard Vise, to the Hampshire rectory of Falley which Vise was to hold until his death in 1483, Reg Waynflete i, fo 88r.

post-dated the grant of the patronage and advowson of the hospital to Waynflete made in October 1456. Waynflete had become chancellor in early October
1456 and thus was in a position to facilitate the amalgamation proceedings. He
lost little time in so doing. On 27 October 1456 he was granted by the king,
the patronage and advowson of the hospital of St John the Baptist. Along with
this grant of patronage was a licence to enable him to re-grant his newly-
acquired rights over the hospital to Magdalen Hall. The final clause of this grant
shows Waynflete wielding his power as chancellor for it stated that if the letters
are mislaid the chancellor shall issue new ones without charge.[33]

The major problem facing potential founders in late medieval England was
the obtaining of mortmain licenses to amortise large amounts of land. It was Sir
John Fastolf's failure to obtain such a licence, despite repeated efforts, that
prevented him establishing Caister College during his lifetime.[34] In September
1456 presumably through Waynflete's influence, Magdalen Hall obtained a
licence enabling it to acquire lands worth £100 annually.[35] Since the potential
annual income of the hospital was £75, this covered its acquisition comfortably.
The requisite licenses having been obtained, the formal grant of the hospital to
Magdalen Hall was made on 5 July 1457.[36] The Hall now held the patronage of
the hospital but as yet the latter could not be suppressed. The opinion of the
lawyers mentioned above may date from this period. The next stage was to
petition the pope for authorisation to proceed with the suppression. This
Waynflete did in the late autumn of 1457 and a papal commission was issued
on 14 March 1458 which directed a number of English bishops to inquire into
the proposed suppression and to authorise it if all was in order.[37] This papal
commission is the first intimation that Waynflete's intention was to found a
new college. It seems possible that in order to justify the suppression of St John's
Hospital, he had to present the suppression as essential to the establishment of
an institution which was in fact already in existence.[38]

From Hall to College: the Refoundation

A comparison of the foundation charter of Magdalen College issued in 1458
with that of Magdalen Hall issued by Waynflete ten years earlier provides
further clues to the advantages he saw in re-founding his Oxford community.
Such a re-foundation was not actually necessary for Magdalen Hall did not lack

33 CPR 1452–61, 343.
34 See below pp. 131–2.
35 CPR 1452–61, 324.
36 Cart St John i, 263–6.
37 CPL 1455–64, 369–70; the authorisation of the foundation of Magdalen College by
the papal delegate John, Bishop of Hereford is printed in Cart St John ii, 424.
38 MC Chartae Regiae 50.5; 81. The 1448 charter is printed in Chandler, Life, appendix ix,
323–30, that for 1458 in Cart St John ii, 425–9.

any essential 'collegiate' ingredient; it could and did function adequately. Thus Waynflete must have had his own reasons for wishing to begin again from the beginning. The wording of the two charters is very similar but the few changes which were made help to elucidate the bishop's motives.

Two major changes appear in the charter of 1458. The first was the reference to the college having a papal licence. This was the licence to suppress the hospital and annex it to the newly-founded college which the bishops delegated by the pope to investigate the matter had granted.[39] This having been carried out, the foundation charter of Magdalen College was able to refer to '. . . the authority and licence of the Apostolic See granted to us in this business.'[40] No papal sanction had been included in the original foundation charter. This sanction of 1458 however referred only to the amalgamation of the hospital and the college and did not give the foundation of 1458 any special privilege. The most important papal grant, that of exemption from the authority of the bishop of Lincoln in whose diocese Magdalen College lay and the transference of it to the jurisdiction of the bishop of Winchester, did not occur until more than twenty years later, in 1481.[41]

From the viewpoint of Waynflete's control over the college during his own lifetime the college charter of 1458 had considerable advantages over that of the hall. The latter had made no mention of what authority the bishop as founder could exercise over his foundation. That of 1458 on the other hand specifically reserved to Waynflete complete authority,

> . . . reserving to ourselves for the duration of our own life, the full power of removing the president in this way and our scholars in the said college who have been appointed by us or who may be appointed in the future, as well as the full power of altering, adding, correcting and reducing as often and whenever it seems to us to be beneficial, all and any of the statutes and ordinances decreed or to be decreed by us.[42]

It might be expected that the members of the foundation would show due respect to the ideas and preferences of the founder, but under the original charter Waynflete would have been powerless if opposition to his ideas had arisen from members of the community between 1448–58. He must have welcomed the greatly increased endowment provided by the acquisition of the hospital as an opportunity to compile a more watertight foundation charter.

---

[39] *CPL 1455–64*, 369–70.
[40] *Cart St John* ii, 427.
[41] 13 February 1481, *CPL 1471–84*, 97.
[42] '. . . reservata tamen nobis durante vita nostra plenaria potestate presidentem huius-modi et alios scolares in collegium predictum per nos assumptos seu imposterum assumendos mouendi necnon omnia et singula statuta et ordinactiones per nos edita et edensa quociens et quando opus nobis visum fuerit mutandi, addendi, corrigendi et diminuendi.' *Cart St John* ii, 429.

The haste with which Magdalen Hall had been founded may have led him to omit such a provision in the earlier charter.

The foundation established by the 1458 charter was more flexible in terms of size than was the case with the earlier one. While Magdalen Hall had been described as consisting of a president and fifty graduate scholars, the community established in 1458 was described as consisting of a president and graduate scholars, a statement which allowed the exact number of members to be determined at a later stage.[43] A number of other slight changes appear in the charter of 1458 which although of minor importance in themselves are interesting, showing a shift in some of the bishop's attitudes since the first charter ten years previously. The use of the word *illuminatio* in place of the more pedestrian *instructio*[44] when referring to the educational purpose of the college implies an increased enthusiasm towards the idea of the education provided by the college.

The 1458 charter also demonstrates how, after ten years as bishop of Winchester, Waynflete had come to identify more closely with his diocese. Although his personal patron saint Mary Magdalen continued to be foremost in the dedication and provided the popular name for the college, the later charter entrusted the college to the favour not only of St John the Baptist but also the apostles Peter and Paul and all the patrons of Winchester cathedral.[45] When in the 1470s an archway was constructed at the entrance to the college chapel the statutes placed in niches above the door included one of St Swithun. By 1458 therefore Waynflete was identifying himself with his diocese and the patron saints of his cathedral church to an extent not seen ten years earlier. While there was nothing to prevent the hall functioning as a legal corporation, under the charter of 1448,[46] the charter issued by bishop Waynflete for his new foundation in 1458 was improved and revised in a number of ways. The most important was the reservation to the bishop of power over the administration and form of the college. This additional reservation paragraph could have been in itself enough to justify the re-foundation of the hall of 1448 as the college of 1458.

Waynflete and Magdalen College, 1458–c.1477

Waynflete's refounded community of 1458 was initially a small body of men. In addition to the president William Tibard only six men were named foundation fellows; all but one of these (Robert Rous) had been fellows of Magdalen Hall.[47] Simon Godmanston was also one of the bishop's chaplains while Henry Fisher

43 *Ibid.*, 426; Chandler, *Life*, appendix ix, 326.
44 Chandler, *Life*, appendix ix, 323; *Cart St John* ii, 425.
45 *Cart St John* ii, 427.
46 Cf. J. Mills, 'But Magdalen Hall was clearly a temporary arrangement, the first step on a larger plan . . .', 'The Foundation, Endowment and Early Administration of Magdalen College Oxford', Oxford B.Litt. thesis, 1973, 8.
47 *BRUO*, 1874–5. The six were Robert Calthorpe, William Laughtone, Henry Fisshere, Simon Godmanston, Richard Bernys and Robert Rous, *Cart St John* ii, 429.

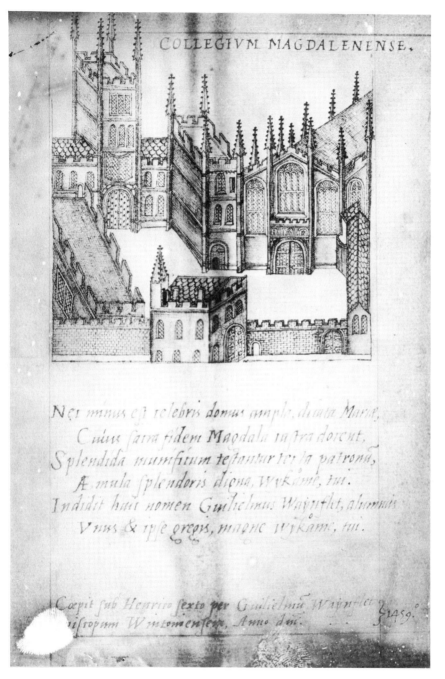

COLLEGIVM MAGDALENENSE.

Nec minus est celebris domus ampli, dicata Mariae,
Cuius fama fidem Magdala nostra docent,
Splendida munificum testantur tecta patronā,
Aemula splendoris digna, Wykame, tui.
Indidit haic nomen Guilielmus Waynflet, alumnus
Vnus & ipse gregis, magne Wykame, tui.

Coepit sub Henrico sexto per Guilielmū Waynflet
Episcopum Wintoniensem, Anno dni. . . . . 1459.

Plate 3 View of Magdalen College in 1459

was also involved in the bishop's household.[48] A third man, Richard Bernys, retained close connections with Waynflete acting as a co-feoffee with him on a number of occasions.[49] Between 1458 and 1480 (when administrative records began formally to be kept) the absence of evidence makes it difficult not only to chart the growth and development of the college but also to see how closely Waynflete as founder involved himself in internal collegiate affairs. It is not known what role he played in the choice of graduate scholars, direction of college affairs, or the ordering of the educational aspects of the college. There is some post-1480 evidence which shows him directing the fellows to elect certain men as members of the college[50] and his influence in this sphere as in others would have been stronger prior to the promulgation of statutes in the early 1480s. To judge from his heavy financial involvement which is well documented, his other involvement is likely to have been extensive.

From 1458 until his death one of bishop Waynflete's major preoccupations was the collections of lands and advowsons to ensure a lavish endowment worth over £675 a year for his foundation.[51] There were three major periods of acquisition; 1455–59 when 30% of the total endowment was amassed; 1469–70 when 25% of the total was amassed and 1479–86 when 40% of the total was amassed. In between these main periods Waynflete was on occasion involved with negotiations which led eventually to the acquisition of lands, as during the 1460s when the problems surrounding Sir John Fastolf's inheritance was one of his major concerns. Waynflete was constantly concerned with seizing opportunities to gather together endowments. Although Waynflete was collecting these properties for the college from the 1450s onwards, he was slow to hand them over to the foundation, an action which would have made the community financially independent.[52] Throughout this period and indeed until 1481 (later if building costs are included), Waynflete retained control of the purse strings. Instead the college was funded directly from his temporal estates, particularly from four manors in Oxfordshire and Berkshire – Adderbury, Brightwell, Harwell and Witney – which between them contributed an average of £123 annually to the college.[53] Money was also paid directly to the college

---

48 *Ibid.*, 687.
49 Richard Bernys was a stalwart of the colleges administration; he was on the foundation of Magdalen Hall and although he never took a further degree he was vice-president from 1458 until his death in 1499, *BRUO*, 179–80.
50 MC MS 367.
51 Details of his acquisitions, the sources of the property and the bishop's main agents in these transactions are traced in Mills, 'The Foundation, Endowment and Early Administration of Magdalen College Oxford'; the percentages are taken from this thesis, 34.
52 20% of the total amount of property amassed by Waynflete had been conveyed to the college by 1480, 60% had been conveyed by 1483 and 83% had been conveyed by the time of the founder's death in 1486, Mills, 'The Foundation, Endowment and Early Administration of Magdalen College', 34.

from the central episcopal treasury at Wolvesey.[54] These payments to the college from either source were only made on receipt of the bishop's personal warrant. The transactions appear irregularly in the ministers' accounts for the bishop's temporal estates.[55]

His policy of tight control over the release of money to Tibard and the fellows of Magdalen College gave Waynflete the opportunity to exercise authority over the development of his college. He would have to be consulted before the college could enter into any arrangement involving major expenditure. This kept him in touch with, and in a position able to direct affairs in Oxford. Waynflete's enthusiasm for the development of Magdalen College is reflected in the fact that his denial of financial independence to it did not stifle the foundation; he kept himself aware of its needs. However it may initially have slowed its growth; only twenty-eight fellows were in residence in 1477 compared to substanitally larger numbers in 1481 when funds were beginning to be released to the college.[56] The college made little apparent impact within the university prior to the 1470s. The earliest that a fellow of Magdalen College is found as a university proctor is 1471 when Nicholas Good was chosen.[57] Henceforth Magdalen fellows appear regularly in lists of university officers.

The bishop also concerned himself with the details and progress of the collegiate buildings which from c.1467 were being constructed on the site of the hospital of St John the Baptist.[58] Richard Bernys, the vice-president, was in charge of the buildings on the spot but again the directive force came from Waynflete. Bernys, whose accounts have survived for the earliest period of building, 1467–74, accounted directly to Waynflete.[59] Waynflete used as architect William Orchard, a mason who served him elsewhere. Surviving contracts for building works at Magdalen College were made between Waynflete and the architect, not as might have been expected between the college authorities and the architect.[60] That Orchard was the choice of Waynflete, not the college is suggested by the fact that although Orchard remained active as a mason in Oxford after Waynflete's death in 1486 he was no longer employed by the college after that date. Between 1486 and 1504 when Orchard died, the president's lodgings and a house for use by the song school were built under the

---

[53] *Ibid.*, 21.

[54] *Ibid.*, 22–4.

[55] HRO EC/2/155834–42; e.g. EC/2/155834, fo 65r records payment of £10 to Tibard and Bernys on receipt of the warrant of Waynflete.

[56] MC C8/49 – accounts of those present for commons, draft *libri computi* and memoranda 1477–86.

[57] *Historical Register of the University of Oxford to 1900*, Oxford 1900, 30; John Ekys, referred to as a proctor and member of Magdalen in 1452 was in fact principal of Glasen Hall in that year, not yet a member of Magdalen, *Registrum Cancellarii Oxoniensis 1434–69*, ed. H.E. Salter, OHS xciv, 1932, 248.

[58] See below chapter 5 for details of the building works.

[59] MC CP/2/67, 1, 2.

[60] J. Harvey and A. Oswald, *English Medieval Architects*, 199–200.

direction of a chief mason named William Reynold, a competent but lesser figure than Orchard.[61]

Waynflete used his influence with the king to the benefit of Magdalen College. When Edward IV, preoccupied with his own building projects at Windsor during the late 1470s, commandeered all skilled stonemasons thus depriving Oxford of their services, he granted permission to Waynflete to employ some of the men to enable the building works at Magdalen College to continue.[62] Without such favour the college would have been left, as the university authorities were, in the awkward position of hunting around for competent masons to complete the half-finished divinity schools.[63] The university authorities also recognised that Waynflete was the crucial power within Magdalen College when in 1478 they addressed a petition to him requesting the loan of cranes being used in the construction of his 'most beautiful college'; explaining that they could not afford to acquire their own building machines of this sort.[64]

Much of the work relating to the business affairs of Magdalen College, especially in the gathering of endowments, was carried out by members of the bishop's personal household. In this way too he was able to control strictly the college's financial position and its freedom to act independently. His main agent from the 1450s was Thomas Danvers,[65] treasurer of Wolvesey c.1478–86, but other household figures, Stephen Tyler,[66] the episcopal supervisor, the chancellor David Husband,[67] his chaplains and various notaries occur regularly, acting as co-feoffees or attorneys in these matters.[68] Of the fellows of Magdalen College only the president William Tibard and the vice-president Richard Bernys were involved in this process of endowment gathering – they occur occasionally receiving land on behalf of the college. Otherwise such matters were beyond the control of the fellows of the community.

While the bishop drew heavily on the revenues of Winchester episcopal manors to cover running and capital building costs of Magdalen College there was little contact between the diocese and the college. Magdalen College fellows (unlike those of New College which also had Winchester connections) are rarely found being ordained within the diocese.[69] Neither are Magdalen fellows

61 *VCH Oxon*, iii, 204.
62 *Epistolae Academicae Oxon*, ii, 446.
63 *VCH Oxon* iii, 344–5.
64 *Epistolae Academicae Oxon*, ii, 443.
65 Mills, 'The Foundation, Endowment and Early Administration of Magdalen College', 26–7; for Danvers, see F.N. MacNamara, *Memorials of the Danvers Family*, 1895.
66 *BRUO*, 1992.
67 *Ibid.*, 989.
68 This statement is based on my study of the witness lists of the charters relating to Waynflete's acquisition of lands and their conveyance to Magdalen College. The deeds were calendared in 49 typescript volumes by William Macray at the end of the nineteenth century and their calendars are available in the college archives.
69 Reg Waynflete ii, fo 197v. This supports the idea that there were not close ties between Magdalen College and the diocese of Winchester.

collated to benefices within the diocese. Although one of the avowed aims of the college was the provision of suitable men to act as parish clergy, Waynflete did not innundate his diocese with men educated in his college. The diocesan-collegiate link was almost entirely financial and restricted to the person of Waynflete and his immediate household.

The Last Phase, 1477–1486

About 1477 Magdalen College appears to have been gaining strength. While this may partly be due to the fact that this is the first year for which a bursary book survives, other external evidence reinforces this impression. University records begin to mention graduates of Magdalen in greatly increased numbers from this period. At the same time a few Magdalen graduates begin to be recorded being ordained within the diocese of Winchester. This was the beginning of a period of rapid expansion. Thirty fellows including the president were in residence in 1477 while by 1482 the community consisted of eighty-seven members and this was the first year in which the college had some financial independence.[70] The presence of lecturers in theology and philosophy in 1477[71] implies that Waynflete's college had begun to approximate to its final form which was enshrined in the statutes promulgated in the early 1480s.[72] Physically building works were proceeding apace during these years under the supervision of Bernys and the expertise of Orchard.

It is difficult to compare fairly Waynflete's involvement with his college in the pre and post 1480 period since records are so much more plentiful for the last six years of the bishop's life. For example, there are for this period descriptions of two visits he paid to Oxford; his itinerary drawn from his episcopal register shows he visited Oxford in 1476 and 1479 as well but these visits are not recorded in surviving college records. The appointment of Richard Mayew to replace William Tibard as president in 1480 marked the beginning of a new phase in the history of the college. Tibard was an elderly man; he died in November 1480 less than three months after having relinquished his duties.[73] Mayew on the other hand was a young man and extremely competent as his effective quashing of initial opposition to his arrival in the college demonstrated. He was Waynflete's choice as a suitable figure to rule the college after his own death.

The process of preparing Magdalen College to cope after the death of its founder dominated this last phase of Waynflete's relations with his college. Although Waynflete was physically active until early 1486, from the beginning

---

[70] Mills, 'The Foundation, Endowment and Early Administration of Magdalen College', 29.
[71] MC Ms CP/8/49, fo 5r.
[72] See below pp. 79–85.
[73] *BRUO*, 1874.

of that decade he was slowly making preparations for the future. Two major moves in particular can be seen: the formulation of statutes to govern the college and the transference to the college of endowments collected over the previous quarter century. Together these developments prepared the college for financial and administrative autonomy. The actual transfer of property was not completed during Waynflete's lifetime; at his death some twenty per cent remained in his possession to be conveyed to the college by his executors. It was fortunate for the future of his foundation that Waynflete lived so long. Had he died in the late sixties or even in the late seventies, the college would have been left in an under-endowed and confused state with only verbal directions left by the founder to guide its administration. It was fortunate also that Waynflete began in good time before his death to make preparations for the future of the college.[74]

Two successful attempts were made by Waynflete in the early 1480s to bring Magdalen College to the attention of the reigning sovereign and thus to ensure for it some royal benevolence. Both Edward IV and Richard III visited the college in the company of the bishop and were lavishly entertained. While these visits were successful as far as they went, the unexpected deaths of both kings shortly afterwards prevented the college from reaping any material gain from its newly-made connection.

Edward IV's visit to Magdalen College in 1481 came as the culmination of a formal visit paid by bishop Waynflete to his college during which decisive steps towards giving the college its independence were taken. An account of the visit was recorded in the college register.[75] This states that Waynflete arrived in Oxford on 20 September 1481 in order to inspect the state of the college and the new buildings. He had sent before him a number of cartloads of books, eight hundred books in all, destined for the new library. Clearly he remembered his days as provost of Eton when the college was forced to complain to the king that it could not function properly due to a shortage of books. Waynflete also brought with him a number of deeds, conveyances and other documents concerning the transference of properties to the college. Waynflete was greeted by the president and fellows not only as founder and patron but also as ordinary of the college by virtue of the recent grant of Pope Sixtus IV which exempted the college from the jurisdiction of the bishop of Lincoln in whose diocese Oxford University lay and placed it under the bishop of Winchester.[76] This was Waynflete's first visit in this new role.

Two days later Edward IV arrived with his entourage to pay the college its first royal visit:

---

[74] On the problems created by the premature death of founders, see V. Davis, 'The Making of Collegiate Statutes in Later Medieval England', *History of Universities* xiii, 1993, forthcoming.

[75] MC Register A, fo 8r.

[76] *CPL 1455–64*, 97; MC Register A, fo 6r.

On 22 day of this month, the lord founder went to [the royal manor at] Wodestock to the most illustrious lord, the lord king, Edward IV, and the lord king spontaneously by his special favour promised to the lord founder that he would inspect the college founded anew at Oxford and there to stay overnight, which things pleased the lord founder exceedingly.

That night, after sunset the most illustrious lord king with a multitude of lights was firstly honorably received outside the university by the lord chancellor of the university and by the regents and non-regents; then he was received honorably and brought in procession to the college of the Blessed Mary Magdalen by the said Lord founder and by the president and scholars and there he stayed overnight and on the morrow, which was a Sunday remained, with many lords spiritual and temporal and other nobles as was fitting, until after lunch and after midday.[77]

Edward's interests were different to those of Henry VI and did not lie primarily in educational foundations. His visit to Magdalen College must have been made out of respect for the elderly bishop; the account in the college register emphasises that it was a considerable achievement on Waynflete's part that he agreed to come. Edward had already demonstrated his goodwill towards the college through Waynflete when he granted to him the right to use masons for the building works in progress there, at a time when his own building projects at Windsor were monopolising their services. Waynflete honoured Edward IV by including him amongst the statues which were placed in niches above the grand archway leading into the college chapel.[78]

The second royal visit, that of King Richard III, took place two years later. Richard's coronation on 6 July 1483 was followed by a major royal progress.[79] By 24 July he had reached Oxford where Waynflete entertained him at Magdalen College. Richard had a genuine interest in the patronage of learning[80] which explains why his entertainment took a different and more learned form from that provided for his predecessor. Like Edward IV, on his arrival in Oxford he was greeted by representatives of the university before he proceeded to Magdalen College. He spent two nights there (24, 25 July) and on the second evening was entertained by a disputation in which three Magdalen men, Thomas Kerver, William Groceyn and John Taylor all took part.

> . . . by the order and wish of the lord king two solemn disputations were held in the great hall of the college; firstly in moral philosophy between Master Thomas Kerver and a certain bachelor of the same college; secondly, still in the presence of the king, a disputation in theology was held between

[77] MC Register A, fo 8r, my translation; extracts from the college register relating to royal visits to the college in the founder's lifetime are printed in Macray, *Register of the Presidents and Other Members of Magdalen College Oxford: New Series – Fellows 1458–1915*, 8 vols, Oxford 1894–1915, ii, 9–13.

[78] *Epistolae Academicae Oxon* ii, 446; see above 64.

[79] C. Ross, *Richard III*, 1982, 148.

[80] *Ibid.*, 132.

Master John Taylor, professor of sacred theology and Master William
Groceyn respondent. . .[81]

Richard generously rewarded those taking part and in addition, gave money to
President Mayew to provide wine for all. Although on that evening it must have
seemed unlikely that Waynflete, now in his eighties, would outlive the king,
that was what was to happen. Waynflete's hopes that his college had found a
royal patron and protector for the future must have been dashed with Richard's
defeat at Bosworth.

These years were ones of great uncertainty in England and the future security
of Magdalen College must have been in Waynflete's mind. A letter to Waynflete
from John Gygour,[82] fellow of Merton College and warden of Tattershall college
in Lincolnshire with which Waynflete was involved, dated 19 April 1483,
emphasised the uncertain position of Tattershall college now that the king was
dead and his successor was not known. Gygour advised Waynflete to '. . . nowe
ys a good tyme and acceptable both to spede your maters and utterli conclude
them that concern your worshippful colege of Oxenford as wel as of Eton and
pore Tateshale.'[83]

Waynflete presumably hoped that Richard's visit to Oxford in 1483 would
secure the future position of his foundation. Although the transference of
property from the bishop to his college which began in 1481 made it considerably more independent financially the founder was still relied on for money to
finance the building works.

Waynflete also remained final arbiter in cases of dispute within the college;
Mayew as his appointee could turn to him for support if he met with opposition within the college. A letter addressed to the college from Waynflete from
his manor at Waltham in April 1482 shows that the bishop still played an active
part in the direction of the internal affairs of the college. The tone of the letter is
stern, beginning, 'It is come to oure knowlache and to owre displeasure . . .'
Apparently a dispute had arisen within the college concerning the elections of
university proctors. Waynflete's response was to act in a ruthless manner against
those whom he described as '. . . sedycyous, wylfull and non conformable to the
advyse and the gyding of yow and the more party of the maisters of oure seid
college . . .'. On the grounds that such people '. . . wolbe troubelous and fulle
onprofitable for my seid college . . .', Waynflete ordered president Mayew to
'discharge suche persons' who opposed the decision of the majority.[84] The
bishop also continued to play a part in the election of members of the college,
overriding if necessary the statutory limitations on numbers or geographical
origins. In a letter sent to the college on 15 March 1485 he ordered that
William Hewlis, a college chaplain, be elected:

[81] MC Register A, fo 27v, my translation.
[82] *BRUO*, 840.
[83] MC Ms 367, no. 4; printed in Richmond, 'A letter from John Gigur', 116.
[84] MC Register A, fo 9r; printed in Chandler, *Life*, appendix xxii, 366.

... at oure next election among other and before all other, the seid Master William be elected unto the more and the greter number, contrary statutes made by us notwithstanding.[85]

The visit of 1483 was the last recorded one by Waynflete to his foundation. Physically he may have been failing – one document of 1484 was signed in what has been described as a weak and feeble hand.[86] His itinerary shows his perambulations to be less frequent and less extensive, he restricted his movements to the manors at Southwark, Esher and Waltham in the last years of his life and he spent several months at a time in each one rather than merely weeks in each place. He continued to be preoccupied with the endowment of the college, both the amassing of further properties for it and transferring lands already collected to it. By 1484 the bulk of the collection of lands had been completed and was slowly being conveyed to the college. During this period Waynflete's main link with the college seems to have been through visits to him made by president Mayew. The collegiate accounts record frequent visits being made to Waynflete at his manors in Hampshire and Surrey.[87] At the same time valuable goods including chalices and other ornaments for the college chapel were sent at intervals from the bishop's household to Oxford:[88] experience had taught Waynflete that to leave directions in a testament for the disposal of goods might not be enough to ensure the college received the stipulated items.

From the early spring of 1486 when he seems to have become ill, Waynflete was increasingly feeble. He no longer left his manor at Bishop's Waltham. President Mayew can increasingly be found acting for the college on occasions where once the founder would have represented them, as for example, at the coronation of Henry VII from which Waynflete was absent.[89] Waynflete continued to oversee the transaction of business relating to his college until the very end of his life; his last recorded grant of manors was made on 20 May 1486[90] but visits from Mayew continued until August, the month of Waynflete's death.

[85] *Ibid.*, appendix xxix, 389.

[86] MC Deeds, Henton 48a; the description is Macray's in his calendar of the deeds of Norfolk but the same could be said of the signature on Waynflete's will written in March 1486, MC *Chartae Regiae* 43.

[87] MC *Liber Computi* i, fos 99v–100r; in 1486 alone Mayew visited Waynflete at Bishop's Waltham six times between January and August.

[88] E.g. 'Proveccione xvi ymaginum cum panno rubio et cum libro a Waltham ad collegium, iiiis . . .' Macray, *Register of Magdalen*, i, 6.

[89] Mayew attended the coronation by order of Waynflete, *Liber Computi* i, fo 99v.

[90] MC Deeds, Henton 36a. As late as 11 July along with co-feoffees Waynflete was receiving grants of land destined for Magdalen, MC Deeds Ashurst & Lancing 4.

IV

Collegiate Statutes and Educational Innovations

Much of what is known about the constitution and organisation of medieval academic colleges is drawn from the statutes provided by their founders to regulate the activities of the institution.[1] Late medieval English academic secular colleges tended to take the form of self-governing communities of fellows. The statutes which controlled their activities were detailed in their provision for the distribution of power and authority amongst the fellows. The statutes were concerned with regulating all aspects of collegiate life. They can be divided into a number of categories – organisation of authority, eligibility and election of fellows, regulation of daily affairs, visitations and visitors, the care of muniments and control of endowments.

The statutes provide a picture of the ideals of a founder for his or her college; they often reflect ambitious and pious hopes which the reality of inadequate endowments might prevent from being achieved. The statutes of Gonville College Cambridge for example state that twenty fellows were to be maintained; in fact there seem normally to have been no more than four at any one time. According to the statutes of the eight Cambridge colleges in the fourteenth century, a total of 137 fellows were to be supported by these institutions. The reality was that only about 80 fellows were actually supported at any one time.[2]

The foundation of New College Oxford by William Wykeham in 1379[3] marked a new departure in the scale of academic collegiate foundations. It was Wykeham's clearly stated intention to provide an institution which would train an intellectual and administrative elite. Wykeham not only had ambitious intentions but with the resources of the see of Winchester behind him and considerable political influence, he also managed to carry them out. The sheer size of his college, with a normal complement of seventy scholars, meant that it

---

1 See V. Davis, 'The Making of English Collegiate Statutes in the Later Middle Ages', *History of Universities* xiii, 1993, 1–23.

2 A. Cobban, *The Medieval English Universities: Oxford and Cambridge to c.1500*, Aldershot 1988, 121–2.

3 J. Buxton and P. Williams, *New College Oxford 1379–1979*, Oxford 1979.

was home for many figures at fifteenth century Oxford. Of the circle of bishops surrounding Henry VI, both Henry Chichele and Thomas Beckington had attended Winchester College and then New College Oxford. The statutes of Winchester and New College were innovative in their sheer scale and depth of detail; subsequently when founders in the fifteenth century were looking for a model, they frequently looked to those of New College.[4]

The fifteenth century also saw the foundation of a considerable number of colleges of secular clerks. Some were of chantry priests only, others of the chantry-priest type also incorporated a grammar or song school. Many were founded by lay men and women and the new lay interest in education in the fifteenth century meant that some bequests placed emphasis on the educational aspects of the foundation as well as the chantry-priest element. Simon Eyre, a draper of London who died in 1459 left in his will a large sum of money for founding a college for a master, five priests, six clerks and two choristers with three masters for grammar, writing and song.[5] Archbishop Chichele's foundation at Higham Ferrers was for a college with eight chaplains and eight clerks of whom one was to teach grammar and another was to be choir master.[6] These institutions did not have the longevity that the Oxford and Cambridge academic colleges had and statutes do not always survive for them. When they do, they are less elaborate than those of the academic colleges. However, they too give us an idea of the priorities and concerns of the founders. Waynflete was involved with the drawing up of statutes for one college of this type, that of Ralph Lord Cromwell at Tattershall in Lincolnshire. The statutes for that institution are another expression of the interest of Bishop Waynflete in education and grammar teaching and thus will be considered in this chapter as well.

Early Eton Statutes

Henry VI's foundation of two colleges, one in Eton and one in Cambridge not long after he had attained his majority meant that he had two colleges in need of statutes. This was hardly a job he would be capable of himself, despite his evident interest and thus commissioners were appointed led by senior episcopal and administrative figures. The commissioners appointed to draw up statutes for his college of St Mary and Nicholas in Cambridge were William Alnwick Bishop of Lincoln, William Ayscough, bishop of Salisbury, William Lyndewode, keeper of the Privy Seal, John Somerset the chancellor and John Langton, chancellor of the university of Cambridge. They were discharged,

---

[4] The statutes of a number of the Oxford colleges founded in the fifteenth century drew on the very detailed provisions of those made by William of Wykeham. These included All Souls College and Lincoln College.

[5] D. Knowles and R.N. Hadcock, *Medieval Religious Houses in England and Wales*, 2nd edn 1971, 431.

[6] E.F. Jacob, *Archbishop Henry Chichele*, 1967.

presumably having completed their duty, on 10 July 1443 when William Millington was appointed provost of King's College. The position regarding the early Eton statutes is rather more confused. The names of the men who drew up the original statutes of Eton college have not survived but it is likely that Waynflete as Provost and as a man with first hand experience of the workings of Wykeham's system at Winchester college would have been consulted.

The first reference to Eton statutes occurs in a notarial instrument[7] which describes the formal swearing in of Waynflete as Provost on 21 December 1443. This instrument also cites earlier statutes now repealed concerning incomplete buildings. Presumably these were some form of interim statutes which provided for the workings of the embryonic college. The statutes referred to in December 1443 may well be those of which there is an incomplete draft. Eton College MS 300 is a copy of the statutes with multiple interlineations and corrections which certainly predates July 1446, the date at which the archbishop of Canterbury was involved in the visitation procedure as metropolitan. The statutes which have been printed by Heywood and Wright[8] therefore are at least the third recension of the statutes; they postdate Waynflete's elevation to the bishopric of Winchester, perhaps dating from 1452–3.[9]

This confused situation makes it difficult to define precisely William Waynflete's role in the drawing up of the early statutes of the college. What is clear, however, from a close comparison of the printed text with the text of the Wykeham's statutes for Winchester College is that they are very similar, the main changes being made in the phrasing in order to fit in with the founder's royal status.

In 1455 Waynflete was appointed by Henry VI together with the ex-provost of King's College, John Chedworth, now bishop of Lincoln, to reform the statutes of both the colleges of Eton and King's. The letters patent which set out their commission refer to practical defects which needed to be removed. The wording of their authority to reform suggests that what was required was not major alterations but rather slight changes to ease the daily running of both colleges and to remove anomalies which had arisen.[10] The main changes were the affirmation of the fact that statutes ought not to be altered by successive provosts; that the provost may hold ecclesiastical benefices and spiritual offices singly or plurally providing they do not involve residence or cure of souls; arrangements were made for punishments for those who damaged or alienated possessions or property of the college.[11] The changes made in 1455 seem to have solved the problems for the present and despite his later involvements in

7   ECR 39/30.
8   J. Heywood and T. Wright, eds, *Ancient Laws*, 1850.
9   Lyte, *Eton College*, 18, n. 3.
10 *CPR 1452–61*, 241; the letter is printed in full in *Ancient Laws*, 624–5 but there it is wrongly ascribed to 1445.
11 Heywood and Wright, *Ancient Laws*, 624–5.

building works at Eton College in the 1470s, William Waynflete's involvement with the statutes of Henry's foundation ended in the 1450s.

Tattershall College

Eton College did not provide Waynflete's only experience of formulating collegiate statutes. He was deeply involved in the drawing up of statutes for the collegiate community at Tattershall, a task which arose out of his responsibilities as executor to Ralph, Lord Cromwell. In his capacity as bishop Waynflete was frequently called upon to act either as a feoffee to use or an executor, or both, to many members of the gentry and nobility. Within his home county of Lincolnshire Waynflete's prime involvement of this sort was with Ralph, Lord Cromwell, soldier and administrator under both Henry V and Henry VI, who by the time of his death in 1456 was one of the richest men in England.

The use of profits acquired during a career as a soldier for charitable and religious purposes was common in the fifteenth century. Towards the end of the 1430s Ralph Lord Cromwell planned a collegiate church at his newly-built castle at Tattershall in Lincolnshire. In November 1440 he issued a foundation charter.[12] 'Henry bishop of Winchester and cardinal' headed the list of patrons and it is not therefore surprising that after Beaufort's death in 1447, the new bishop of Winchester, born less than fifteen miles from Tattershall and with continuing family connections there, should replace his predecessor among those involved with Cromwell's projected college.

Waynflete's involvement began in 1454 when he acted as a feoffee to use together with a number of other bishops and magnates.[13] He was sole representative of the episcopate among Cromwell's executors.[14] His role was more than notional. One of his major duties as Cromwell's executor was to ensure the completion of the embryonic foundation at Tattershall.[15] Cromwell was, of course, very familiar with Waynflete's experience at Eton College and may have chosen him deliberately with this in mind. For the next thirty years Waynflete played an active and personal role in supervising the welfare of Tattershall College. The day-to-day running and maintenance of the college was in the

---

[12] *Report on the Manuscripts of the Lord de L'Isle and Dudley Preserved at Penthurst Place*, Hist Mss Com 1925, i, 172; the other patrons were listed as Sir John Scrope, Sir Walter Hungerford, Walter Tailboys and William Paston.

[13] *CPR 1452–61*, 199–200, 1 November 1454.

[14] The other executors were Sir John Fortescue, Sir Thomas Tirell, Robert Beaumont, John Tailboys, William Venour, John Saucheverell, William Stanlowe, John Leynton and William Grille, *Early Lincoln Wills*, ed. A. Gibbons, Lincoln 1888, 138. On Cromwell's will see R.L. Friedrichs, 'The Two Last Wills of Ralph, Lord Cromwell', *Nottingham Medieval Studies* xxxiv, 1990, 93–112.

[15] The survival of the building accounts for Tattershall have ensured that the works there are well known, *The Building Accounts of Tattershall Castle 1434–1472*, ed. W.D. Simpson, Lincolnshire Record Society lv, 1960.

hands of a warden.[16] John Leynton, another of the executors and a lawyer from Lincoln's Inn dealt with the bulk of the legal affairs of the college while others of the executors, especially Sir Thomas Tirell took an active interest. The bishop of Winchester remained the guiding figure and was frequently turned to for advice.

Two periods stand out as times when Waynflete was particularly involved with the affairs of Tattershall. The first is from Cromwell's death in 1456 until c.1460 when the statutes of the college were drawn up; the second is the late 1470s and 1480s. A number of letters written by John Gygour, warden of the College, to Waynflete survive for this latter period although since there appears to be no reason why Tattershall should be particularly in contact with the leading executor at this time a false impression may be being created by the change survival of letters from this period.[17] Occasional references at other times suggest that Waynflete was concerned with the affairs of the college on a regular basis from 1456.[18] The first period of activity, that which succeeded Cromwell's death in January 1456[19] concluded with the statutes which were proclaimed in the late 1450s.[20] These were drawn up by Waynflete, Sir John Fortescue and Sir Thomas Tirell but were partly based on Cromwell's own ideas which survive in a memorandum dated c.1450, 'Articles touching the foundation of the college of Tattershall.'[21] This document is in the form of questions addressed to the founder together with his answers. It included a scale of fees and salaries for the master and priests. The college was to consist of seven chaplains, including the master, six secular clerks, six choristers and an almshouse for thirteen poor men, male or female. Essentially it was a chantry for the souls of Henry VI, Lord Cromwell and his wife Maud, but one section of the statutes reflects Waynflete's own particular interest. 'The master shall hire a clerk or priest to teach grammar to the choristers and to all the sons of the tenants of the lordship of Tattershall and of the college without charge. . . .'[22] This emphasis on the teaching of grammar, not only to the choristers but to boys from the surrounding neighbourhood is a hallmark of the other statutes with which Waynflete was involved, both for his own foundation in Wainfleet

---

[16] The first warden was William More whose name occurs in the early accounts relating to the college, *De L'Isle Manuscripts*, 173, 190–1. In 1458 he was succeeded by John Gygour who was also master of Merton College Oxford. Gygour held the position until his death in 1504, *BRUO* 841.

[17] MC MS 367, nos 4, 5, 6; MC deeds, East Bridgeford 10, 25.

[18] *De L'Isle Manuscripts* i, 174–5 is a quitclaim by Cromwell's feoffees (including Waynflete) of all rights in certain manors, 4 August 1468; MC deeds Candlesby 50A is a release from Lady Willoughby to Waynflete of all rights to Cromwell's estates.

[19] E. Myatt-Price, 'Ralph, Lord Cromwell', *The Lincolnshire Historian* ii, 1957, 10.

[20] *De L'Isle Manuscripts* i, 179–86; the statutes have been assigned to c.1460, but name William More as warden. They therefore must date from before 1458 when John Gygour succeeded More in this post.

[21] *Ibid.*, 179.

[22] *Ibid.*, 182.

and at Eton College which in 1446 had been granted a monopoly for teaching of grammar within a ten mile radius of the college.[23]

Magdalen College, Oxford: Statutes and Educational Provisions

The statutes provided by Waynflete for his foundation of Magdalen College in Oxford are the most interesting of all the statutes with which he was involved for they provide real insight into his mature ideas about education and teaching. They date from the end of his life; it was not until 1480, more than twenty years after the re-foundation, that Waynflete issued any statutes for Magdalen College. Prior to that, the internal administration of the college must have been governed by President Tibard along lines directed verbally by the bishop and subject to Tibard's discretion. The non-provision of statutes which left the bishop as founder in the position of final arbiter in any matters of dispute, was in accord with Waynflete's policy towards the endowment of the college. Thus in matters both financial and administrative Waynflete retained a close control over the affairs of his foundation and was slow to give it autonomy.

The most pressing reason which led Waynflete finally to issue statutes in 1480 must have been his own advanced age; by then he was over eighty. His lifestyle was becoming increasingly sedentary although he remained physically active for several more years. By 1480 he must have felt that the time had come to present the college with a code of statutes which would order the direction of its affairs after his death. A precipitating factor may have been the desire of the president of the college, William Tibard, who had been appointed in 1458, to retire. With a change of headship it must have seemed a good moment to draw up statutes to be implemented by Richard Mayew the new president.

The composition of collegiate statutes was a lengthy process and must have been carried out by Waynflete in consultation with Tibard and other college officers. The need for such discussions may have been behind Waynflete's visit to Oxford in 1479, on which occasion he stayed not in the college but at his episcopal manor of Witney. The code of statutes now known as the founder's statutes was not presented to the college in its completed form all at once. Some were brought to the college by Mayew in 1480,[24] others were added in 1482 and when Waynflete visited the college in 1483[25] while minor changes may have been made from time to time before Waynflete's death. Two contemporary manuscripts of the statutes exist. The complete code of statutes including Waynflete's later emendations survives as Bodleian MS Rawl Q.c.14. The second manuscript remains in the college archives, MS 277 which was also written

---

[23] Leach, *Educational Charters*, 413.

[24] The college register begins with a description of Mayew's arrival in the college in August 1480 with letters from Waynflete and statutes relating to the governing of the college, MC Register A fos 1r–2v.

[25] *Ibid.*, fo 15r.

in the 1480s. This copy contains emendations made by Waynflete in July and November 1483. Writing on the final folio has been attributed to Waynflete and certainly appears similar to other known examples of his handwriting. This may be the volume of statutes for which 16d was paid for binding in the accounts for 1483–4.[26]

When complete the corpus of statutes[27] can be taken to represent the mature reflections of Waynflete, based on widespread personal experience, on both the administration of a collegiate body and on its educational function. They were the product of a lifetime of experience in Winchester College, Eton College and Magdalen College itself spanning more than half a century.

The arrival of the Richard Mayew at Magdalen in August 1480 with the statutes provided by Bishop Waynflete for his college was clearly seen as the beginning of a new, more permanent phase in the institution's history. Magdalen College Register A begins with a description of Mayew's arrival in the college. He preached a sermon on the theme 'Bear ye one another's burdens' (Galatians VI, 2) to the assembled community before being sworn in as president. Mayew then produced letters from Bishop Waynflete and the statutes and the vice-president and the bursar were swore their oaths. However, matters did not all proceed smoothly for some of the masters refused to take an oath to obey the statutes. Mayew reacted by depriving them of their commons until they complied. The reason for this refusal of ten masters to take an oath to observe the statutes and obey the president is not given; possibly they resented the imposition of Mayew and had favoured one of their own number to follow Tibard. They may also have seen the arrival of a code of statutes as indicative of a new stricter regime and it may be that in the last years of Tibard's presidency discipline had become lax.

In their provisions for the administration of the college Waynflete's statutes follow those issued by William Wykeham at the beginning of the century for the use of New College Oxford, which had become the template for collegiate statutes in the fifteenth century. Waynflete's innovations came in the educational provisions of the statutes, in particular with the division of members of the foundation into demys and fellows and the arrangement for lectureships. The college was to consist of ninety-nine members in all – a president, forty scholars, thirty demys, four priests, eight clerks and sixteen choristers. The main body of scholars thus numbered seventy, the same size as in New College and Eton College. The majority of the fellows were to study theology, with two or three only being selected to study law (civil or canon) and the same small number to study medicine.[28] Most founders of colleges expressed similar

---

[26] Macray, *Register of Magdalen* i, 13.

[27] The printed copy of the statutes was taken from Bodleian MS Rawl.Q.c.14, with corrupt passages corrected by collation with BL Harl. MS 1235 and BL Hargrave MS 148, *Statutes of the Colleges of Oxford*, 3 vols, 1853–6, ii, 5–91.

[28] *De numero scholarium*, *Magdalen Statutes*, 5–6.

preferences and these were often, as in Waynflete's case, based on their own educational experiences.

Waynflete showed that he conceived his foundation as being constructed along similar principles to those of Wykeham, not only in drawing on New College's administrative statutes but also in the restriction of the choice of a president for Magdalen College to fellows or ex-fellows of either Magdalen itself, or of Wykeham's foundations.[29] A selection of suitable men was to be drawn up by the body of fellows but the final choice of president was restricted to the seven senior fellows. During his own lifetime Waynflete exercised his founder's prerogative in personally selecting the president, although Mayew was in fact a fellow of New College. The statutes were designed for the future, after the bishop's death.

The fellows of Magdalen were to be chosen in a manner similar to that used at New College, but in honour of the patron saint of the college the elections were to take place on the feast day of Mary Magdalen.[30] The geographical composition of the body of scholars reflected Waynflete's own experiences for he had connections with each of the areas from which he stipulated that members of the college were to be drawn. Five were to come from Winchester, seven from Lincolnshire (some of whom would come from the grammar school he founded in Wainfleet), four from Oxford and four from Norwich (reflecting the endowment Waynflete had just succeeded in securing for his college from the Fastolf inheritance), three from Berkshire (where a number of his episcopal manors were situated) and two each from Chichester (where John Waynflete was Dean of the cathedral chapter), Gloucester and Warwick.[31] In addition a bequest from Thomas Ingeldew stipulated that two scholars in theology were to be drawn from Northern England, preferably from York or Durham.[32] A continuing commitment to the idea that a college was a religious not a secular body can be seen in the statute which stated that every fellow must be ordained within a year of achieving his M.A. and that each was to preach and celebrate mass regularly in the college.[33] Within his own episcopal household were a handful of educated laymen but most of the men in his service were clerics, even men filling positions such as that of episcopal supervisor of lands.[34]

Although Waynflete was a bachelor of theology this was only one aspect of a

[29] *Ibid.*, 7.
[30] *De electione scholarium, ibid.*, 16.
[31] *Ibid.*, 22–23; why Gloucestershire and Warwickshire were chosen is unknown; the college does not seem to have acquired Warwickshire land from Waynflete although they did hold property in Gloucester which the bishop had acquired from the earl of Nottingham as well as some from the estates of Ralph, Lord Cromwell; it is possible that the acquisition of some of this land might have carried a stipulation that scholars would be drawn from these areas.
[32] *De electione scholarium, ibid.*, 17.
[33] *De tempore assumendi sacros ordines, ibid.*, 34.
[34] Stephen Tyler, *BRUO* 1922, filled this position throughout the later part of Waynflete's episcopate; he seems to have been as much part of the bishop's household as he was of

man of wider interests. In accordance with this, despite his extensive provision for men studying theology, he made an effort to ensure that his college would not be excessively dominated by theologians. Two of the three deans who were to be in charge of the educational side of the college were to be masters of arts not theologians.[35] A respect for education and training rather than mere longevity can be seen in his stipulation that seniority among the fellows was to be determined by their academic achievements not by the length of time they had spent as fellows of the college. Waynflete classed the degrees in the order of Doctors of Theology, Doctors of Canon Law, Doctors of Civil Law, Doctors of Medicine, Bachelors of Theology and Masters of Arts.[36]

It was in his provisions for education within the college that Waynflete was particularly careful, detailed and innovatory. The scholars' day was carefully divided up. Disputations were to take place twice a week during full term in the main hall of the college. One of these weekly sessions was to deal with a problem or matter of doubt; the other with an issue relating to the solving of doubts. In the nave of the chapel was to be held a weekly discussion of theological controversies. During the vacation period from 7 July – 1 August an arts disputation was to be conducted weekly.[37] Disputations were the commonest method of teaching and practising in the late medieval universities. Waynflete's major innovation in the sphere of teaching was his provision of three lecturers whose lectures were to be open to all students, whether of Magdalen College or from elsewhere in the university. One lecturer was to teach on natural philosophy, one on moral philosophy and one on theology.[38] Their lectures were to take place daily (excepting feast days) from 9 October – 1 August. The educational day was to begin at 6 a.m. with the lecture on natural philosophy; at 9 a.m. came the lecture on theology and finally at 1 p.m. that on moral and metaphysical philosophy. These lectures were designed for the benefit of the forty full scholars and other members of the university who wished to attend.

Waynflete's second innovation was in the legislation he made for the junior scholars or demys. These demys were young men who, not yet having taken their degrees, would concentrate on the study of grammar, sophistry and logic until they could demonstrate a firm grounding in these subjects. Separate provision was made for them. The statute relating to their position, especially the clause which prohibited boys from proceeding to further study without a proper elementary grounding in grammar, has the ring of experience about it;

the structure of manorial administration; many of his duties involved the rapidly growing endowment for Magdalen College.

35 *De decanorum officio et eorum electione, Magdalen Statutes*, 24–5.
36 *De senioritate sociorum, ibid.*, 27–28.
37 *De disputatione sociorum et scholarium faciendis, ibid.*, 27–8.
38 *De officiis lectorum, ibid.*, 47–8.

Particularly, since a weak foundation undermines the whole building, as experience shows, and as we discovered that in recent times some of our thirty scholars, once they had been adequately trained in grammar, which is known to be the mother and foundation of all sciences, are accustomed to turn too soon to logical and sophistical studies; . . . we ordain that none of them is henceforth to be admitted to sophistry, logic or any other science, unless first he is found fit and able to do so by the judgement of the President and master in grammar and by one of the Deans of the said college.[39]

In addition the stipulation that some of the demys should devote their efforts to '. . . grammar and poetry and other humane arts . . .' in order to be able to instruct others, looked back to the era in which Waynflete himself had taught, the 1430s and 1440s, when there was serious concern about the absence of grammar teachers and adequate training for them; a concern which had led to the foundation of God's House in Cambridge in 1439 as a place where teachers could be trained.[40] The importance of teachers continued to be stressed in educational circles of the fifteenth and early sixteenth centuries:

> It is an honest labor to teche, and suche a labor that a man ma both please God in and do muche good to the commonewelth, for tully seith what gretter or better gyfte ma we bryng to a comenwelth than if we teche and informe yong men, and especially now in owre tymes in the wyche all yong men for te most part gyve them-selfe more to pleasur than to learnyng.[41]

The bishop's personal concern with the teaching of grammar was also reflected in his foundation of two grammar schools which would both act as 'feeder' schools for the college and be open to all comers. One was situated in Wainfleet in Lincolnshire,[42] the other was in Oxford, attached to the college itself. Stipulations governing the financing and organisation of both schools were laid down in the Magdalen College statutes.

When exactly Magdalen College school came into existence as an adjunct to the college is not clear but it was functioning by the time the statutes were drawn up in the 1480s. The building of a school-house, complete with upper

---

[39] *De electione scholarium vocatorum Demys, ibid.*, 16. Echoes of examinations in grammar can be found in some vernacular Oxford schoolbooks suviving from the early sixteenth century: 'Ther were viii of owre scole felose takyn from vs the last weke wich had ben at gramare iii or iiii yere and were judged able to go to sophistice, and I shold haue gone to sophistir too if my creanser wold a byn content but he wold fayne haue me to here a lityn more gramer ar I be taken from hense', BL MS Royal 12 B.xx, fo 39r, c.1512–27, edited by N. Orme, 'An Early-Tudor Oxford Schoolbook' in his *Education and Society in Medieval and Renaissance England*, 1989, 138.
[40] Leach, *Educational Charters*, 402–03.
[41] Orme, *Education and Society*, 140.
[42] This is discussed more fully below, pp. 84, 112.

rooms and a kitchen, was begun in August 1480. The entry in the contemporary college register relating to this is ambiguous:

> Nevertheless, before [August 1480] all and each were freely instructed in grammar at the expense of the lord founder by one master and an assistant and this for a half year before, namely from the previous Easter, in a certain lower hall in the college on the southern chapel in an ancient building . . .[43]

It is left unclear whether the teaching had only been going on from mid–1479 or whether the school had been longer established but only situated in the lower hall mentioned since the previous Easter. This latter explanation seems more likely, especially in view of the fact that the companion school in Lincolnshire had been in existence since the mid 1460s.[44] Within the founder's lifetime the school was evidently closely connected with the college and it may have been difficult to distinguish clearly the line between the two institutions. It was situated, according to the statutes, 'next to our college'. The master of the school was responsible to the president of the college – it did not, like Winchester College, have its own warden or head – and was to get a room and weekly commons on the same terms as the collegiate fellows. While many of the pupils must have come from Oxford and the surrounding area, for the school was to be open to all,[45] some of the demys are likely to have also been amongst the pupils for they were not permitted to proceed to the study of logic or sophistry until they were fully conversant with grammar. The grammar master was to join with the president in examining their competence in grammar.[46]

Magdalen College school differed from its counterpart in Wainfleet which, while also a grammar school open to all, was more traditional in conception, for it incorporated a chantry element and its master had to be a priest.[47] Magdalen College school was the larger of the two, with both a master and an usher; the master there did not have to be in priest's orders and in fact the first recorded master, John Anwykyll was a married man.[48] While the school in Wainfleet was never more than a country school, within a decade of its foundation Magdalen College school had become one of the leading grammar schools of England and was foremost in the introduction of the new humanistic grammar teaching being developed on the continent. Finally Waynflete adopted a practice found in the Cambridge college of King's Hall from the 1430s[49] but not as yet

[43] MC Register A fo 3r; see also Stanier, *Magdalen School*, OHS iii, 1940, 12–14.
[44] The first recorded master, John Marshall, was paid in 1466, when he was described in the Lincolnshire Receiver's Account Roll for Holland and Lindsey as 'clerk and master of the grammar scholars in Wainfleet', MC EP 165/6, cited in B. Parry-Jones, *Five Hundred Years of Magdalen College School Wainfleet 1484–1984*, Wainfleet 1984, 6.
[45] *De magistro seu informatore grammaticorum*, Magdalen Statutes, 76.
[46] *De electione scholarium vocatum Demys*, *ibid.*, 1.
[47] *De magistro seu informatore grammaticorum*, *ibid.*, 77.
[48] *BRUO* 39.
[49] Cobban, *The King's Hall*, 71–2; see also A.B. Cobban, 'Colleges and Halls 1380–1500',

elsewhere. Twenty sons of noble and powerful personages were permitted to attend the college at their own expense.[50] This astute provision meant that the college could attract the interest and support of powerful friends, while at the same time it catered for the growing demand for education in the humanities by both by those who might go on follow a clerical career and those who did not intend to enter the church. It was another step in the move towards the secularisation of education; in this, as in his provision of lectureships, William Waynflete looked forward to developments in the next century.

These statutes must have been compiled by the bishop with the aid and advice of Tibard, perhaps Mayew and of legal experts in his own household. They are, however, very much Waynflete's own statutes reflecting his past career, his own beliefs and interests in education and especially his idea that education should be open to a wider group than merely the small circle of men who were privileged to be members of the college foundation.

Educational Innovation: Patronage of Grammar

The manifestation of humanism in England during the second half of the fifteenth century took a very different form from that seen in contemporary Italy, where classical values and the cult of the antique predominated. In England the approach was more practical – humanistic ideas were not seen as ends in themselves but were applied, especially within the universities, to further scholasticism. Ideas were drawn from Italy to further theology, philosophy or diplomacy. Humanism was a medium for improving and enriching other studies, not the sole object of study.

A major landmark in the spread of practical humanism was the introduction of Greek as a subject in Oxford and Cambridge but this development was preceded by a revolution in the teaching of Latin. Although the first half of the fifteenth century saw a renewed interest in and concern about the teaching of grammar and ecclesiastics and laymen alike founded schools to provide education at a popular level, methods changed little; texts such as Donatus and the *Doctrinale* of Alexander which had been the staple grammar works since the late twelfth century were still in use, though accompanied by commentaries; boys being taught in the 1470s would have used books and exercises similar to those being used by Waynflete teaching in Winchester College a half century earlier. In the early 1480s a 'revolution' in grammar teaching began, partly based on books by contemporary Italian grammarians and spread by means of the

in *Late Medieval Oxford: The History of the University of Oxford II*, ed. J.I. Catto and R. Evans, Oxford 1992, 619–20.

[50] *De extraneis non introducendis ad onus collegii, Magdalen Statutes*, 60. These students were to be known as 'creancers' which meant creditor. The word was also used in the late fifteenth century in the sense of tutor or guardian – the Paston letters contain a reference to 'my creansyr master Thomas' [at Eton], 1478, *OED*.

printing press. This revolution was led by Magdalen College school and actively encouraged by William Waynflete.

Printing was crucial for the dissemination of the early works of the Magdalen grammarians. A press existed in Oxford from 1478; by 1479 Theodoric Rood, from Cologne, the town's first printer was living in a tenement rented from Magdalen College.[51] Thus Rood had from the first a connection with Waynflete's college and it is not therefore surprising that his press played such an important role in publishing works which helped to spread continental ideas about the teaching of grammar in England.

The first of three grammar books printed in Waynflete's lifetime, the *Longe Parvula*[52] has survived only as an anonymous fragment. It has been attributed to John Stanbridge subsequently usher and then master at Magdalen College School who was later the author of a number of grammatical textbooks but in 1479 however, Stanbridge was aged only twelve and was still a pupil at Winchester College.[53] It may have been the work of John Anwykyll, headmaster of Magdalen College School.[54] Little is known of Anwykyll personally beyond the fact that he was a layman, not a clerk and held a degree as master of grammar from Cambridge. In 1474–5 he was granted permission at Cambridge to incept in grammar in two years time and then in 1475–6 he was fined 13s 4d for not incepting.[55] He may have come to Oxford shortly after this although he is not referred to headmaster at Magdalen College School until 1483.

Anwykyll was certainly responsible for the second and most important of these early grammatical works emanating from Magdalen, the *Compendium totius grammaticae*. Two editions of this, neither of which survives in full, were printed in Oxford in 1483.[56] One of these editions also included the *Vulgaria quedam abs Terencio in Anglicam linguam traducta* which Rood also produced separately in these years.[57] The *Vulgaria* was a short work – its thirty-two leaves consisted of sentences derived in the style of the plays of Terence together with English translations. It was in effect a phrase book of classical Latin which would be useful for general conversations such as those of schoolchildren or young students including such sentences as – 'All odyr thyngys left or sett asyde I muste giff me to my book'; 'Scolers shuld love togyder lyke as thei were bredys'; 'It is better to holde chylder undir with shame and gentillnes, sofnes or

51 *Cart St John* iii, 272, 276 Rood was from Cologne and is described as 'Dyryke Douche-man' or Dyryke Rood' in the rentals; for details of his career see H. Carter, *Oxford University Press: a History*, Oxford 1975, 6–7.
52 F. Maddan, *The Early Oxford Press 1468–1640*, Oxford 1895, 3, 257.
53 *BRUO*, 1754–5.
54 *BRUC*, 39.
55 *Grace Book A 1454–88*, ed. S.M. Leathes, Cambridge 1897, 106–11.
56 G. Duff, *Fifteenth Century English Books*, Oxford 1917, nos 28, 29.
57 *Ibid.*, nos 29, 30, 31; *Oxford University Press: a History*, 8. The *Vulgaria* may possibly also have been the work of Anwykyll although it is not credited to him, see N. Orme, 'Early School Notebooks', in *Education and Society*, 77–8.

esyness than be fere or drede'; 'The condicyon or disposicyon of wymen is whan a man will thei will not and whan a man will not than thei desyre moste'; 'Com hydere that I may strooke thyn hede'.[58]

The full title of Anwykyll's grammatical work is significant in indicating its continental pedigree – *Compendium totius grammaticae ex variis autoribus, Laurentio, Servio, Perotto, diligenter collectum et versibus cum eorum interpretatione conscriptum, totius barbariei destructorum et latine lingue ornamentum non minus preceptoribus quam pueris nece necessarium.* Anwykyll could have become familiar with the works of the Latin authors mentioned in Oxford. Perotti's own grammar, which had only been printed in Italy in 1473, was amongst the books in the library of John Nele, Waynflete's chaplain.[59] Valla's treatise *Elegantiae* was in the libraries of both Lincoln College and Balliol College.[60] That Magdalen College appointed a man familiar with these humanist grammarians, no doubt with Waynflete's approval in view of the founder's concern with the proper teaching of grammar reiterated in the collegiate statutes,[61] suggests that the college and the bishop were open and welcoming to ideas and influences from contemporary Italy.

William Waynflete was personally connected with this revolution in the teaching of grammar, not just as the founder of the body which played such a leading role in these changes, but as the direct patron of the *Compendium totius grammaticae*. The earliest surviving complete edition of Anwykyll's work, printed at Deventer in 1489,[62] contains a dedicatory preface composed by Pietro Carmeliano, an Italian who assisted first Rood and later Caxton with editorial work before becoming Latin secretary to Henry VII.[63] This dedication unequivocally praised Waynflete as patron of the work.

> Fame will sing such great praises of you,
> William, most celebrated father,
> who are now bishop of the church of Winchester,
> and will celebrate you for as long as the steady polestar
> is in its stable axis.
> For the author John wrote this book at your persuasion,
> whence your fame will be for ever.[64]

[58] From Anwykyll's *Vulgaria*, quoted in Stanier, *Magdalen College School*, 32.

[59] J. Fletcher, 'A Fifteenth Century Benefaction to Magdalen College Library', *Bodleian Library Record* ix, 1974, 271.

[60] *Humanism in England in the Fifteenth Century*, 94, 168 – Lincoln Coll MS 60; Balliol Coll MS 233.

[61] *Magdalen Statutes* 16.

[62] *Fifteenth Century English Books*, no. 30. Anwykyll, *Compendium Totius Grammaticae*, Deventer 1489, 1.

[63] For Carmeliano, see W. Nelson, *John Skelton, Laureate*, Columbia 1939, 20–21; *BRUO*, 358.

[64]   *Te Gulielme pater multum celebrissimus qui nunc*
    Ecclesie presul vintoniensis ades
    Fama canet tantos et te celebrabit ad annos

Carmeliano himself was intimately connected with the business of publishing textbooks for the study of grammar and rhetoric. Anwykyll's work was the first of a flood of grammatical works which were to appear in print during the reign of Henry VII, partly encouraged by royal patronage. Grammars were prepared for the presses of Caxton and Pynson. A poem by the Frenchman Bernard Andre, tutor to Prince Arthur, prefaces one of the earliest grammars printed in England, *Introductiorum Lingue Latine*.[65]

The tradition of grammatical innovation established by Waynflete at Magdalen was continued after the bishop's death. In June 1487 an agreement was drawn up between Anwykyll and the college under which Magdalen was to pay to him an annual pension of £10.

> . . . on account of the excellent knowledge and of all the merits by the said John and for the common utility, continuation and profit of the said school and scholars, having thoroughly considered the many virtues and works which the same master John about the new and very useful form of learning for the same school being conceived and written down by the same, a certain yearly pension of £10.[66]

The wording of the agreement suggests that it followed his wishes; the president and fellows swore to uphold the mind of the founder.

The foremost grammarians of the early sixteenth century, John Stanbridge and William Lily were both products of this Oxford tradition. Lily probably entered Magdalen College in 1486 although he also studied both Latin and Greek in Italy at a later date.[67] The first teacher of Greek in the University of Oxford, William Groceyn, was also intimately connected with Magdalen College as reader in divinity there between 1483–88. Groceyn featured prominently in the disputation arranged by Bishop Waynflete and the College for the entertainment of Richard III when he paid a visit to the college in 1483.[68]

No evidence suggests that Richard Mayew, president of Magdalen College between 1480 and 1508, had any special interest in grammar. This reinforces the importance of the founder in establishing a strong grammatical tradition. Waynflete's involvement in the introduction of the new learning is reflected in the sixteenth century tradition that he introduced the study of Greek into the college.[69] Although unfounded and erroneous, the very existence of such a

---

Dum fuerit stabili firmis in ace polus
Hoc opus auctor enim te persuadente joannes [Anwykyll]
Edidit unde tibi fama perennis erit.
Anwykyll, *Compendium Totius Grammaticae*, 1.

[65] *Fifteenth Century English Books*, no. 31.

[66] MC Register A fo 54v; Latin text printed in Bloxam, *Register of Magdalen* iii, 7,8.

[67] *BRUO*, 1147, 1754–5.

[68] MC Register A, fo 27v; '. . . facta est alia solempnis disputatio theologica, etiam in praesentia regis, per . . . magistrum Willelmum Groceyn responsalem . . .'; printed in Macray, *Register of Magdalen* i, 11–12.

tradition reflects the bishop's prominent position in the new developments as seen by his immediate successors.

For William Waynflete the foundation of a collegiate community in Oxford was high among his priorities as is evidenced by the rapidity with which he set the foundation in motion after he had become bishop of Winchester. It remained a dominant interest; a project to which he devoted a huge amount of his time, energy and resources for the remainder of his life. Almost unflaggingly from its foundation in 1448 until his death in 1486, despite his commitments elsewhere, Waynflete kept Magdalen College and its needs and welfare in the forefront of his mind. Waynflete's training as a schoolmaster dominated his life. His success as provost of Eton College made possible his promotion to the episcopate. The resources – financial, political and administrative – at his disposal as bishop of Winchester were ploughed back into education. Magdalen College with its particular emphasis on the teaching of grammar and the provision of a solid educational grounding, was a fitting memorial to the lasting interest of a man who had begun his career teaching Donatus to schoolboys at Winchester College.

[69] L. Humphridus, *Epistola de Graecis Literis et Homeri Lectione*, Basle 1558; cited in H.L. Gray, 'Greek Visitors to England 1455–1456', *Anniversary Essays in Medieval History by Students of C.H. Haskins*, ed. C.H. Taylor and J.L. LaMonte, Boston 1929, 111.

V

Patronage: Books and Buildings

Books

The fifteenth century was one during which England was open to extensive continental influences in the field of scholarship. This was not a new development; there had been extensive contact in the fourteenth century particularly within the world of the schools and universities[1] but these links continued to be important in promoting new intellectual developments and interchange. Both churchmen and lay figures had intellectual connections both in Northern Europe and in Italy. Some members of the English episcopate, men such as Bishop Fleming (Lincoln 1420–31) and Bishop Gray (Lincoln 1431–36), travelled to Italy and forged close connections with Italian scholars. Waynflete did not have these personal connections and neither did he have Italian scribes in his household or maintain regular correspondence with contemporary Italian humanists as Cardinal Beaufort, his predecessor had done. In Waynflete however, can be seen a mingling of the old and the new. He promoted the teaching of grammar in Oxford reflecting his own training as a schoolmaster but using new continental-style texts; although 'humanist' texts have not survived among his books we know that he appreciated the value of the new printing presses. Above all he was open-minded when faced with new ideas and developments.

Waynflete's patronage of early printed grammatical works produced in Oxford has already been discussed. His interest in the new method of disseminating information was not confined to works designed for teaching. He also appreciated its usefulness for religious purposes. The earliest known printed indulgence to be issued by a member of the English episcopate was that issued by Waynflete in conjunction with the bishops of Ely, Norwich and Chichester in the early 1480s. Earlier printed indulgences have survived which had been addressed to people in England by Pope Sixtus IV and the earliest document printed in England by William Caxton was an indulgence which was issued by the abbot of Abingdon in December 1476.[2] Yet clearly Waynflete was in the vanguard of this development. The fifteenth century saw extensive use of

---

[1] See W.J. Courtenay, *Schools and Scholars in Fourteenth Century England*, Princeton, NJ, 1987.
[2] G. Duff, *Fifteenth Century English Books*, nos 209, 210; PRO E 135/6/56.

indulgences and they increased in popularity. Waynflete's own episcopal register contains details of indulgences available for a range of acts of almsgiving.[3] The use of printing as a means of dissemination undoubtedly extended the potential range of these instruments of the church. The fragmentary nature of the printed indulgence issued by Waynflete gives no clue as to the purpose for which this particular indulgence was issued. It begins:

> Whosoever being in the state of grace thei devoutly wil say the psalter of oure lady in the worship of the xv grete passions whiche oure Lord suffered before his death. And in the worship of the xv joyes of his blessed modir and lady specially in remembrance of the same passion. . . .[4]

The indulgence was printed in Westminster by Wynkyn de Worde at some time between 1479–83, the only period in which these four bishops acting together could have issued it. Of the four bishops concerned Waynflete was the oldest: Goldwell and Morton were relatively young men and both had explicit interests in humanistic developments on the continent. Story, bishop of Chichester was also considerably younger. Waynflete's name appears as the first of the four named in the indulgence. That a man in his eighties should take advantage of the opportunities offered by new mechanical developments suggests that he was forward looking and open-minded to the end of his life, aware of the potential of new developments.

In view of his other patronage of the printing press we might expect to find that Waynflete had in his own library a number of printed works. This was certainly true of members of his household; his chaplain John Nele had an extensive library which he left to Magdalen College.[5] Libraries are often valuable sources for information concerning for the humanistic and cultural leanings of many of the members of the episcopate. Unfortunately while Waynflete is known to have possessed a large number of books we know the titles of very few of them. Wills often provide valuable glimpses of the contents of individuals' libraries or of an individual's most treasured books but Waynflete appears to have disposed of all his books before April 1486; his will drawn up in that in that month does not mention any books or indeed any personal possessions, the bequests being restricted to varying sums of money.[6] The most probable explanation is that most of his books must have been transferred to Magdalen College prior to that, most probably in 1483 when he sent cart-loads of

---

[3] These indulgences were primarily issued for the support of works of charity and piety both within his own diocese of Winchester and elsewhere in England, e.g. those issued for the repair of Farnham bridge, Reg Waynflete i, fo 15*r and to raise contributions for the building of a chapel in the church of St George Southwark, *ibid.*, ii fo 160r.

[4] Lambeth Library, Maitland fragment 5.

[5] J. Fletcher, 'A Fifteenth Century Benefaction to Magdalen College Library', *Bodleian Library Record* ix, 1974, 271.

[6] MC *Chartae Regiae*, 43.

muniments and eight hundred books to Oxford.[7] Some works may also have been transferred directly from the episcopal palace at Bishop's Waltham to President Mayew during the latter's visits to Waynflete in the last months of the bishop's life.[8]

Magdalen College Library today contains 146 incunabula, many of which had been acquired by 1500.[9] In addition many of those in the library in the late fifteenth century have since been lost.[10] None are known to have belonged to Waynflete but a number could possibly have done so. The college certainly possessed a number of printed books in Waynflete's lifetime, including Alexander de Hales, *Exposition sur tres libris Aristotelis* which was printed in Oxford by Theodoric Rood in October 1481 and purchased by the College in the same year.[11]

As is so often the case, many of the books bequeathed to Magdalen College by medieval benefactors can no longer be traced in its library. Some may be there but without distinguishing marks of ownership or *ex dono* notes; others may have been lost, stolen or sold. Only three of the manuscripts in the college library are noted as being of the gift of the founder[12] and none of the incunabula can be attributed to his possession, although in view of his encouragement of printing, it is likely that he possessed some early printed works. However, a short list of the books which were at one time or another in Waynflete's possession can be compiled from a variety of sources.

Albertus Magnus, *Libri Octo* and *Opera Physica*[13] are two of the Magdalen College manuscripts which contain notes stating that they were of the gift of the founder. Together they contain the complete works of the thirteenth century Dominican friar Albertus Magnus on natural philosophy, including both Albertus' interpretations and explanations of Aristotelian ideas and his own additions. Although the writing of Albertus spanned all of Aristotle's ideas, Waynflete is not known to have possessed any of his other works. His owner-

---

7   MC Register A, fo 7v; eight hundred is a round number but clearly it indicates an enormous number of items being transferred to the college; it is possible that the figure may include separate items of deeds and charters which would reduce the number of actual books destined for the library – the register merely refers to '. . . diversos libros quamplurimos pro nova libraria . . .'.

8   MC *Liber Computi*, i, fos 99v–100r.

9   D. Rhodes, *A Catalogue of Oxford Incunabula Outside the Bodleian*, Oxford 1982, pp. xxiii–xxiv.

10 Many of the books we know to have been bequeathed to the library in this period, those, for example, of Waynflete's chaplain John Nele, are no longer in the college's collection.

11 *Catalogue of Oxford Incunabula*, no. 55c; in 1485–6 the College paid 12d to have an edition of Antonius Andrea bound. This volume had been printed in London in 1480 and had been the gift of Thomas Rushdall, *ibid*, no. 80.

12 Details of manuscripts in the college library can be found in H.O. Coxe, *Catalogus Codicum Mss. qui in Collegiis Aulisque Oxoniensibus Hodie Adervantur*, 2 vols, Oxford 1852, ii.

13 MC MS Latin 85, MS Latin 174.

ship of these particular manuscripts which contained information central to the study of natural philosophy in the fifteenth century, fits in well with his interests as reflected in his foundation of a lectureship in that subject at Magdalen College. That natural philosophy was seen as the most important of the philosophies in the fifteenth centuries can be seen from collegiate statutes in general and university graces at Oxford and Cambridge. However, scholarship in the subject was firmly based on medieval texts, particularly Aquinas' *Super physicam* and the works of Albertus Magnus.[14]

Liber Collectionum[15] is the third manuscript Waynflete is known to have given to the college library. It is unexceptional in type, being a collection of sermons drawing heavily on the writings of St Augustine which were intended to be read aloud during Lent.

At first sight the manuscript of Jacobus de Cressolis, *De Ludo Scacchorum* seems to indicate more definite links with the ideas of continental humanism. Written by one of Waynflete's notaries Simon Aylward in 1456,[16] it is in a firmly humanistic hand which belies the traditional nature of its contents. Aylward had been a fellow of King's College Cambridge before becoming a member of Waynflete's household. He may have written *De Ludo Scacchorum* at the bishop's behest for it subsequently came into his hands as a note, 'Winton episcopi', on its front flyleaf attests. While the script is humanistic in style, however, the book is far from being in such a category. It was a moral tale dating from the thirteenth century which used the pieces of a chess set in an allegorical manner to describe the duties of various sections of society. It was known among English humanists in the fifteenth and early sixteenth century; the educationalist Sir Thomas Elyot recommended it in *The Governor* (1531).[17] Its popularity in England in the later fifteenth century led William Caxton to print an English translation of the work taken from a French text in 1474.[18]

A number of the other books which are known to have belonged to Waynflete came to him by means of bequests from people for whom he acted as executor. Into this category falls a Bible said to have belonged to St Louis of France and later to John Stanbury, confessor to Henry VI and bishop of Hereford. Waynflete acted as one of Stanbury's executors after his death in 1474 and this bible was bequeathed to him.[19] The St Louis bible is the only book mentioned in Stanbury's will; Waynflete's fellow executors were left sums of

[14] D. Leader, 'Philosophy at Oxford and Cambridge in the Fifteenth Century', *History of Universities* iv, 1984, 25–46.

[15] MC MS Latin 231.

[16] MC MS Latin 12; Aylward's hand as seen in this manuscript is illustrated in [A.C. de La Mere] *Duke Humphrey and English Humanism in the Fifteenth Century*, Catalogue of an exhibition held in the Bodleian Library Oxford 1970, 54–5, plate xxi. On Aylward see *BRUC*, 12.

[17] I am grateful to Nicholas Orme for drawing this to my attention.

[18] *Fifteenth Century English Books*, no. 81.

[19] *Registrum Johannis Stanbury Episcopi Herefordensis*, ed. A.T. Bannister, Canterbury & York Society xxv, 1919, ix.

money rather than goods. Waynflete obtained one of Sir John Fastolf's books in a similar manner; a Magdalen College manuscript which contains the *Imago Mundi* of Henry of Huntingdon, Isidore of Seville's *Originum Libri* and two short anonymous chronicles, has a note on the final folio which describes it as having come from Waynflete, 'de testamento' Fastolf.[20]

Two further works came to Waynflete as gifts from Fastolf's secretary, William Worcester. The first was Boccaccio's *De Casibus Virorum Illustrium*,[21] a didactic work retelling stories of famous people whose pride brought them to unhappy ends; the other, *De Sacramentis Ecclesiae sive de Conveniento Veteris et Novi Testamenti* was presented to Waynflete by Worcester in memory of Fastolf on 16 December 1473.[22] The inscription marking this occasion is interesting for its reflection of Worcester's eclectic interests as an antiquary[23] although there is no evidence that Waynflete shared these interests:

> To his most reverend lord master William of Wichester, bishop of the cathedral see of St Swithun of Winchester which was once before the consecration of the said church, called 'Templus Dagon' in the time of the pagans.[24]

These gifts were an attempt by Worcester in the wake of John Fastolf's death, to attract the patronage of Waynflete. Later the same year he presented the bishop with another volume, this time an English version of Cicero's *De Senectute* which he claimed to have translated himself from the French version by Laurence de Premierfait.[25] This text may have been based on a copy belonging to John Paston II which occurs in an inventory of his library in the early 1470s. Worcester's attempt to benefit from the patronage of Waynflete was unsuccessful, for he laments in his account of this visit to the episcopal palace at Esher, 'But I got no reward from the bishop.'[26]

Waynflete also possessed at least one book which was directly relevant to his pastoral work as bishop, a copy of Richard Rotherham's series of lectures on

[20] MC MS Latin 8.

[21] MC MS Latin 198.

[22] MC MS Latin 26.

[23] On Worcester's antiquarianism see K.B. McFarlane, 'William Worcester – a Preliminary Survey', *England in the Fifteenth Century: Collected Essays*, 1981, 199–224.

[24] '. . . suo domino colendissimo magistro Willelmo Waynfleete; sedis ecclesie cathedralis sancti Swythun Wintoniensis episcopo, que olim ante temporus consecracionis dicte ecclesie Templum Dagon vocabatur, tempore Paganorum gencium . . .' Coxe, *Catalogus*, ii, 18.

[25] *PL*, no. 316, an inventory of the library of John Paston II; many of the works listed are romances and most were in the vernacular but it included, 'Tully, de Senetute' and 'Tull or Cypio de Ami . . . leffte wyth william Worcester valet . . .'

[26] *Itineraries of William Worcester*, ed. J.H. Harvey, Oxford 1969, 253. This was the text subsequently printed and revised by Caxton in 1481 as *Tullius of Olde Age*, N. Davis, 'The Epistolary Uses of William Worcester', in D. Pearsall and R.A. Waldron, eds, *Medieval Literature and Civilisation*, 1969, 251–3.

pluralism, *De pluralitate beneficiorum*.[27] Essentially a practical work, the four lectures dealt with pluralism and its evils, the problems of dispensations and unlicensed absences. Clearly it was used, either by Waynflete or by a member of his household for parts are annotated in a contemporary hand. Rotherham had been Master of Balliol College in 1420 and Chancellor of the University of Oxford in 1439–40.[28] Rotherham was a canon of Hereford cathedral and it is likely that the lectures, which refer to a pluralism scandal there in the 1430s, were written at Hereford although they may have been originally given at Oxford. This copy was written and bound c.1453 and was probably a presentation copy, with the arms of the see of Winchester in the first initial.[29]

This list of Waynflete's books is a short one; the number of items on it which can be considered as being of his own choice is further reduced by the number of books which were acquired as gifts or bequests. A number of manuscripts in Magdalen College Library whose provenance is unknown may also have belonged to him. In view of Waynflete's personal devotion to Mary Magdalen Magdalen College MS Latin 139, may well have come from his library although it has no distinguishing marks. This is a fifteenth century manuscript of the life of Mary Magdalen ascribed to Rabanus Maurus.[30] It is unfortunate that there is no surviving fifteenth century inventory of the college library, such as those which exist for other collegiate libraries, which might enable us to pinpoint more accurately a larger number of Waynflete's books.

Waynflete, or perhaps a member of his household, may also have been the first owner and thus the initial compiler of a manuscript containing a variety of material, now British Library Additional MS 60577.[31] Its earliest leaves contain Middle English verse and prose, some recorded elsewhere, some unique, including sermons, treatises, verse alphabets, medical recipes, astrological notes and a lapidary. The provenance of the manuscript is clear from about 1500 from whence it had a succession of owners who were Winchester clergy; before that the situation is less clear although there are strong indications from the contents and binding, that it originated in Winchester, probably before the early 1470s.[32]

---

[27] BL Egerton MS 2892; it consists of four lectures but is incomplete, breaking off in the middle of the fourth lecture. A complete copy, containing five lectures can be found in Balliol College MS 80.

[28] *BRUO*, 1593.

[29] The binding of this work is discussed by G. Pollard, 'The Names of Some Fifteenth Century English Binders', *The Library* 5th series, xxv, 1970, 193–218.

[30] This work is wrongly ascribed to Rabanus Maurus although the real author is unknown, H.M. Garth, *Saint Mary Magdalene in Medieval Literature*, Baltimore 1950, 12.

[31] The manuscript [BL Add MS 60577] is edited by I. Fenlon and E. Wilson as *The Winchester Anthology*, 1981. Its contents and provenance are discussed in I. Fenlon, 'Instrumental Music, Songs and Verse from Sixteenth Century Winchester, BL Add Ms 60577', in Fenlon, ed., *Music in Medieval and Early Modern Europe*, Cambridge 1981, 93–116. See also E. Wilson, 'A Poem Presented to William Waynflete as Bishop of Winchester', in *Middle English Studies Presented to Norman Davis*, ed. E.G. Stanley and D. Gray, Oxford 1983, 127–51.

[32] Fenlon, 'Instrumental Songs and Music', 95–6. It was bound by the Winchester Virgin

The inclusion within it not only a poem addressed to Waynflete as bishop of Winchester[33] but also bidding prayers for a bishop of Winchester and some texts relating to school life, including a Latin-English *vulgaria* indicate strongly that it may have been in the bishop's collection.

Information about too few of the books owned by Waynflete has survived to enable a judgement of his intellectural tastes to be made. However, the manuscripts of Albertus Magnus combined with the endowment of the natural philosophy lectureship at Magdalen College suggests a genuine interest in the subject. This, the moralising *De Ludo Scacchorum* and the Lenten sermons all suggest that his reading lay within the accepted traditions of medieval scholarship.

Among the men who surrounded Waynflete on a daily basis, few seem to have had a specific interest in the 'new learning'. Waynflete himself never left England, not even to make his *ad limina* visit to Rome.[34] He would have been aware of contemporary continental developments however, both through his fellow members of the episcopate and through the men who were in Italy as his proctors at the papal curia from time to time. His patronage of art as displayed in the wall paintings in Eton College chapel and in the iconography of the glazing at Tattershall College Chapel, both discussed below, shows an awareness of Flemish developments in this field.

Waynflete's household was composed primarily of conventionally educated university men rather than exceptional intellectual figures. A determining factor in this may well have been the bishop's own intellectual training. He after all had received a conventional theological training in earlier part of the fifteenth century and his educational interests lay in the realm of grammar teaching.

Among his chaplains, Thomas Chaundler, chaplain and simultaneously warden of New College Oxford had a wide interest in learning and educational developments. His own writings were written from a rigidly medieval standpoint however, despite his liking for quotations from Greek authors and the influence of Cicero on their style. He aimed to write like a humanist but he saw the new learning primarily as a tool to improve the old. Despite the conservatism of his writings, especially the *Allocutiones* and *Collocutiones*, Chandler had a prestigious reputation in Oxford and when the Italian scholar Cornelio Vitelli

and Child binder, whose bindings cover manuscripts and books with imprints between 1474–1497, see M. Foot, 'English Decorated Bookbindings', in J. Griffith and D. Pearsall, eds, *Book Production and Publishing in Britain*, Cambridge 1989, 72. For more detail on the Virgin and Child binder see N. Ker, 'The Virgin and Child Binder and William Horman', *The Library* v series, xvii, 1962, 77–85.

33 This circumstances surrounding the compositon of this poem are unclear; it may have been composed for the ceremony of the installation of the bishop in his cathedral in 1449, see E. Wilson, 'A Poem Presented to William Waynflete as Bishop of Winchester'.

34 *CPL*, 1458–71, 782.

delivered a Latin oration in Oxford c.1491, it was Chaundler who replied in kind.[35]

Of all the men linked with his household, Chaundler was perhaps the most firmly connected with humanist learning in Oxford. Some indication of the literary interests of Waynflete's other chaplains and other household members can be determined from their bequests to Magdalen College. Richard Bernys,[36] vice-president of the college, left it a fifteenth century copy of the psalms but this was hardly more than a normal working book. A copy of the commentary of Thomas Aquinas on Aristotle's Nichomachean Ethics came from master Thomas Halle, dean of Waynflete's chapel.[37] John Nele, chaplain to Waynflete from 1460 until his death, left a substantial number of both manuscripts and printed books to the college in 1491 though their contents were primarily theological and devotional.[38] Among the notaries who served Waynflete, Simon Aylward wrote a humanistic hand, but as his copying of De Ludo Scacchorum already mentioned above shows, an ability to write humanistic scripts is not in itself indicative of humanistic intellectual interest. Thomas Danvers, Waynflete's right-hand man for almost thirty years read Cicero and Ovid.[39]

Waynflete was recognised by his contemporaries as a person of importance in English humanistic circles of the period. He was highly complemented as a patron of learning in the 1480s when Lorenzo da Savona dedicated a work to him. Lorenzo, an Italian franciscan, had studied in Padua and Bologna before coming to England where he lectured in theology at Cambridge University.[40] Lorenzo was not only familiar with continental educational developments but was the leading Italian rhetorician in England in the 1470s and 1480s. In 1478 in Cambridge Lorenzo completed his Rhetorica, a work inspired by classical models.[41] His choice of Waynflete as dedicatee of the second of his works written during his sojourn in England, Triumphus Amoris Jesus Christi, indicates that, despite his advanced age, the bishop was considered an important patron of learning.

The Triumphus Amoris Jesus Christi is a devotional poem which has as a preface a lengthy dedicatory epistle addressed to Waynflete.[42] The language is distinctively neo-classical and while the references to Waynflete are couched in classical allusions, it is clear that Lorenzo saw the foundation of Magdalen College as Waynflete's major contribution to humanistic study in England. The work survives in the autograph manuscript written for presentation to

[35] BRUO, 398–9; Weiss, Humanism in England in the Fifteenth Century, 132–7.
[36] Bernys was not actually a member of the bishop's household but had close ties with Waynflete in his position of vice-president of Magdalen College.
[37] BRUO, 853.
[38] Fletcher, 'A Fifteenth Century English Benefactor', 169.
[39] PL no. 745.
[40] Humanism in England in the Fifteenth Century, 162–3, 199; A.G. Little, The Grey Friars in Oxford, OHS xx, 1892, 265–6.
[41] Humanism in England in the Fifteenth Century, 162.
[42] Lambeth MS 450, fo 2r.

Waynflete. It is beautifully written in a careful humanistic script with the bishop's arms with their distinctive lilies forming part of the illuminated 'O', the first letter of the epistle. Although compared to some of his fellow bishops Waynflete seems almost divorced from the 'new learning', Lorenzo's praise and eulogy provides a useful corrective to an impression which is clearly misleading.

Waynflete's role as a patron can also be seen in the area of book-binding. The great ecclesiastical as well as lay lords tended to be natural patrons of such developments. The second half of the fifteenth century saw substantial changes in book-binding practices.[43] Tanned leather with stamped designs begin to be fashionable in England from the late 1450s. The ancient bound treasures of Winchester cathedral played a role in this development; an important source of design stamps were derived from a series of twelfth century Romanesque bindings to be found in Winchester, bound in polished calf and elaborately tooled. The stamps of the binding of *De pluralitate beneficiorum*[44] which was bound by an Oxford binder Thomas Hopkyns were derived from these rare Winchester models. Two other Oxford bindings dating from c.1482, possibly by the University Stationer, Thomas Hunt, were tooled to similar Romanesque style designs.[45] Who was the arbiter of taste in Oxford bookbinding, with Winchester connections, who could have known about and encouraged imitation of Romanesque book binding? William Waynflete is the strongest candidate for this position which fits in well with his interest in books and education. His influence in Oxford it seems, was not just restricted to the foundation of a college but also extended to the patronage of influential Oxford bookbinders.

The development of much music in the fifteenth century was inextricably linked with the church; indeed it has been suggested that much of the church's promotion of music was the consequence of obligation not of patronage, with the need to expand polyphony for the choral purposes.[46] For many composers of the fifteenth and early sixteenth century, as later, composition was a sideline for men whose primary duty was as singers or masters of choristers. While Waynflete does not appear to have made any particular feature of music within his episcopal household, his involvements with the schools of Eton and Winchester and with Magdalen College Oxford, involved him with supporting the new trends in polyphony. At Eton, it was intended that the choristers should gather each evening in front of the image of the Virgin in the antechapel

---

[43] This paragraph is largely based on G. Pollard, 'The Names of Some Fifteenth Century English Binders', *The Library* v series, xxv, 1970, 193–218.

[44] BL Egerton MS 2892.

[45] In the Oxford bindery work from the 1450s used six imitation romanesque tools; at least thirty-five bindings can be identified as originating from this bindery and can be attributed to three known binders, Thomas Hopkyns 1438–65), John More (1439–72) and Thomas Hut (1473–92), see M. Foot, 'English Decorated Bookbindings', 70.

[46] R. Bowers, 'Obligation, Agency and Laisser-Faire: the Promotion of Polyphonic Composition for the Church in Fifteenth Century England', in I. Fenlon, ed., *Music in Medieval and Early Modern Europe*, Cambridge 1981, 2–3.

to sing Marian antiphons.[47] The Eton musical tradition is represented by the production of what has been described as the finest surviving English musical manuscript of the period, written between c.1490–1502, the Eton Choir-book.[48] Waynflete himself, took active steps to promote a musical tradition in his foundation in Oxford, establishing the post of a master of the choristers who was to instruct the choristers in plainsong and other music.[49]

Buildings

Many bishops, with considerable resources at their disposal and without direct heirs to inherit their wealth, invested a substantial amount of their income in building works which could remain as monuments to posterity. Had William Waynflete left no other monuments to his episcopate, he would still deserve to be remembered as an important patron of building. He was the earliest of the episcopal builders in brick whose works were to dominate Tudor architecture. The second half of the fifteenth century saw two important contrasts in English architectural style; on the one hand buildings such as the magnificent chapel of King's College Cambridge, begun by Henry VI and completed by Henry VII, marked the pinnacle of the perpendicular gothic style in England; on the other, these latter years of the century saw the gradual influx of brick as a popular building material. Used at first primarily for dressing stone buildings, by the early years of the Tudors it was coming to transform the appearance of English domestic buildings.[50]

Waynflete's building projects in brick and stone show him to have been an active patron of building – he extended the Winchester episcopal palaces at Farnham and Esher and constructed a grammar school in Wainfleet. In his cathedral church at Winchester he had constructed a lavish chantry and he may also have been the patron of the magnificent Great Screen of the cathedral. The nucleus of Magdalen College Oxford was designed and completed in his life-time, under his watchful eye. In addition Waynflete played a major part over-seeing the completion of two projects begun by other patrons – Eton College chapel and Tattershall College in Lincolnshire.[51] Waynflete was not merely the paymaster, employing architects, masons and leaving them to 'get on with it'; what little documentary evidence survives demonstrates that he was personally

---

47 *Ibid.*, 12.
48 *The Eton Choirbook*, ed. F.L. Harrison, 3 vols, 1956–8; on the development of sacred music in general see F.L. Harrison, *Music in Medieval Britain*, 1958.
49 *De numero presbyterorum et aliorum mistirorum deservientium in capella; de officiis, servitiis et stipendiis eorum, Magdalen Statutes*, 23.
50 For the growing importance of brick in English architecture see J. Wight, *Brick Building in England from the Middle Ages down to 1550*, 1972; A. Clifton-Taylor, *English Brick-work*, 1979; N.J. Moore, 'Brick', in *English Medieval Industries*, ed. J. Blair and N. Ramsay, 1991, 211–36.

involved, specifying features of the design and making contracts with masons and carpenters.

Waynflete's earliest involvement with building works occurred more by accident than by personal choice. As provost of Eton College during its early years when Henry VI was pouring money into the construction of the church and the other collegiate buildings, Waynflete became acquainted with the practical details of building – the employment of masons and carpenters, the drawing up of contracts and the payment of labourers. This experience was to stand him in good stead when he became a patron of such works himself.

It was not until the second half of his episcopate, from the mid 1460s that Waynflete undertook major building projects. Only then, having shed his political commitments, did he have the necessary leisure to apply himself to these building works. In these as in so many of his activities he displays a desire to be closely involved with the details. In the twenty years which remained of his episcopate he was to show himself a lavish and up-to-date patron of architecture.

Two of the buildings with which Waynflete was associated had been initiated by others and he was only involved with them by virtue of his responsibilities as an executor. At Eton College Waynflete's prime concern was to complete the chapel envisaged by Henry VI although this was done on a smaller scale than the king had planned, dictated by the reduced funds available for the job. Similarly Waynflete's involvement in the completion of the buildings of Tattershall chapel, the central building of Lord Cromwell's collegiate foundation, was also in an executive capacity. As already seen Waynflete as chief executor, carried through the foundation of Cromwell's desired college of bedesmen there. In a codicil to his will Cromwell had left directions for the sale of manors, the proceeds of which were to be applied to the construction of the church and the other collegiate buildings. While the building accounts show that the domestic buildings were in the process of reconstruction from the late 1450s[52] it was not until the early 1470s that work on the church began, under the direction of John Cowper, a master mason from Winchester.[53] Cowper and a skilled carpenter, Henry Alresbroke also worked at other buildings which were constructed under Waynflete's control including the great grammar school at Wainfleet. At Tattershall, John Gygour, warden of the college, was in charge of the day-to-day progress of the works but Waynflete was involved in a consultative

51 It has been suggested that Waynflete was also intimately involved with building works at King's College Cambridge, both during Henry VI's reign and in the 1460s, F. Woodman, *The Architectural History of King's College Chapel*, 1986, 36, 94. No evidence is cited to support these suggestions. On the circumstances surrounding the building of the chapel at King's College, see W. Leedy, 'King's College, Cambridge: Observations on its Context and Foundation', in E. Fernie and P. Crossley, eds, *Medieval Architecture and its Intellectual Context: Studies in Honour of Peter Kidson*, 1990, 209–17.

52 *The Building Accounts of Tattershall Castle 1434–72*, ed. W.D. Simpson, Lincolnshire Record Society lv, 1960.

53 Harvey, *English Medieval Architects*, 77.

capacity and clearly felt that he had contributed to the construction extensively enough to justify having his episcopal arms carved in stone over the north porch entrance to the chapel. His arms were also incorporated in some panels of the nave glass.[54]

Waynflete may well have been involved with the overall plan for the design of the great glass windows in Tattershall collegiate church which were its most noteworthy feature. These windows did not survive the Reformation except in fragments but a reconstruction of their subject matter demonstrates its complexity. The scenes covered most of the elements of Christian belief including the life of Christ along with parallels from the Old Testament, lives of saints and the catechism. This sophisticated iconography was based on a Netherlandish block book which had only recently made its appearance on the continent.[55] It was unlikely to have been the property of a glazier and it seems likely that whoever selected the iconographical scheme also provided the template for the designs. The block book may well have belonged either to Waynflete or perhaps to John Gygour. The names of a number of the glaziers are known but cannot be directly connected with Waynflete; it is unfortunate that nothing more is known of the bishop's own glazier whom we know was involved with the production of the windows of Eton College church, in particular with the great east window there which depicted the Annunciation.[56]

Northern European influence is to be seen also in a further major piece of art work known to have been carried out under the patronage of Bishop Waynflete, the remarkable grisaille illustrations on the walls above the choir stalls in Eton College chapel. Again a model such as the Netherlandish block book used at Tattershall must have been supplied either by Waynflete or by a senior member of his household.

These grisaille frescoes depict scenes from the miracles of the Virgin and each scene is divided from the next by a single figure painted in imitation of sculpture. The style is Flemish, resembling the work of contemporary artists such as Dirk Bouts and Hugo van der Goes. Almost nothing is known of the artists employed at Eton College beyond three names which appear in the college audit rolls, those of William Baker, Gilbert and Richard, 'pictor'.[57] In

54 Waynflete's central role in the building works at Tattershall is stressed in R.C. Marks, *The Stained Glass of the Collegiate Church of the Holy Trinity, Tattershall*, Courtauld Ph.D. 1975; published London & New York 1984, especially 18–25, 240.

55 The iconography of the glazing scheme has been carefully reconstructed in R. Marks, 'The Glazing of the Collegiate Church of the Holy Trinity Tattershall: a Study of Late Fifteenth Century Glass Painting Workshops', *Archaeologia* cvi, 1979, 133–56. The block book on which the designs were based was the Netherlandish *Biblia Pauperum*.

56 Willis and Clark, *Architectural History* i, 409; this window is no longer extant.

57 Gilbert is mentioned in the audit roll for 1485–6, ECR 61/AR/F/1, m4; Richard Seywell is referred to, together with four un-named painters in 1477, ECR 61/BR/K/6, m2; William Baker does not occur until 1488, ECR 61/AR/F/2, m3. The frescoes are illustrated in G. Agnew, 'Pictures', in *Treasures of Eton*, ed. J. McConnell, 1967. See also M.R. James and E.W. Tristram, *The Frescoes of Eton College*, 1907 and by the same

addition the Eton college audit rolls refer to an unnamed priest, described as 'master of the painters', who supervised the work.[58] The artists are not mentioned in the lists of the members of the gild of St Luke at Bruges[59] and nothing is known of either their nationality or training although their names do suggest that they may have been Englishmen while the style of their work suggests that they trained in Flanders or at least were familiar with the latest developments there. The priest-master may, as has been suggested, have come from Waynflete's household[60] but no one with such skills or with connections in Flanders has been identified within the household.

It is clear that Waynflete was responsible for the major cost of these paintings which were carried out between 1477 and 1488; not until after his death in 1486 did the full cost of those still to be completed fall on the college. The audit rolls for 1486–7 lists pigments being paid for by the college for the first time.[61] The employment of artists to carry out these works indicates both originality of ideas and a willingness on the part of Waynflete to patronise contemporary and up-to-date fashions in painting.

Waynflete's Oxford foundation began its life in rented buildings and after its re-foundation in 1458 it was housed in buildings which had belonged to the Augustinian hospital of St John the Baptist. This was to be only a temporary situation: According to a late sixteenth century president of the college:

> All the edifices of the saide hospitall weare in a manner defaced and utterly rased in the Founder's tyme, one chappell only except, wherein we kepe diverse lectures and exercises of learninge; and under the sayde chappel a stonie vault verie lowe under the grownde, and therby unholesome, which since in common reporte hath borne the name of the allmeshouse bycause (as we take it) that only remayned of the ruines of the sayde hospitall.[62]

Rebuilding commenced in 1468 although between this date and the early 1470s the main achievement was the construction of a wall and ditch which defined the college site.[63] Construction of the collegiate buildings proper began formally on 5 May 1474 with a ceremony during which Robert Tully, bishop of St David's blessed the foundation stone before it was laid in the centre of the high altar by William Tibard, president of the college.[64]

authors, 'The Wall Paintings in Eton College Chapel and in the Lady Chapel of Winchester Cathedral', *The Walpole Society* xvii, 1928–9, 1–43.
58 '. . . presbyter magister pictorum . . .', ECR 61/AR/D/1.
59 *Les Liggenen et Autures Archives de la Guilde de Saint Luc*, ed. P. Rombout, Antwerp 1872.
60 Marks, 'The Glazing of the Collegiate Church of the Holy Trinity Tattershall', 147.
61 ECR 61/AR/F/2, m2.
62 *Cart St John* ii, 463.
63 *VCH Oxford* iii, 203.
64 Bloxam, *Register of Magdalen College* ii, 227. It is not clear why it was Tully (bishop of St David's 1460–81) who carried out this ceremony. He is not known to have had any particular link with either Waynflete or Oxford.

Magdalen College, as built in the bishop's lifetime did not depart in any radical way from the contemporary norm of Oxford collegiate architecture. In part, its plan, the central element of which was the long building made up of the chapel and great hall backing onto one another, had been pioneered like so much else in fifteenth century foundations, at New College. Like that of New College, Waynflete's chapel had a transeptal ante-chapel similar to that built at All Souls college in the 1430s.[65] Essentially Magdalen College was designed and built along the lines of its fifteenth century predecessors. Except in minor details such as the bay window in the great hall which was the earliest bay window in Oxford[66] it was not a particularly innovative building, rather it was a substantial and practical college building, built with little apparent regard to the cost. The fact that the whole college was provided with battlements from the start signifies its ostentation. The buildings of Magdalen College represent an early form of what is commonly called Tudor Gothic, an enrichment of English architecture, influenced by the highly developed 'flamboyant' style of the Low Countries.[67]

Accounts for the early building works predate the keeping of formal college accounts. The first surviving accounts show vast quantities of stone being quarried from Oxfordshire quarries and brought to the college together with fuel for the kilns, scaffolding and tools. This was for the construction of the chapel and adjoining hall which together formed the south side of a great quadrangle; the accounts later show payments for the making of windows in the nave and the chancel of the church and the insertion of an oratory in the wall next to the altar. Once begun the work proceeded quickly; shortly afterwards the construction of chambers around the other sides of the great quadrangle above the monastic style cloister began. This cloister-chamber arrangement was new to collegiate architecture. A tower was being constructed in these early years for carpenters and slaters were paid for work on its roof although the accounts do not make clear whether this was the founder's tower or the gate-house tower, probably the former.

It was Waynflete rather than the president and fellows of the college who controlled the progress of the building. Money for the works was allocated directly from the episcopal exchequer at Wolvesey to Richard Bernys, the vice-president, who had to account directly back to the bishop for his expenditure.[68] While Bernys dealt with the administrative and financial side of the building project, filling the position of a clerk of the works, the chief architect-mason was William Orchard, a well-known Oxford mason and quarry-owner.[69]

---

[65] Willis and Clark, *Architectural History*, iii, 269.

[66] M. Wood, *The English Medieval House*, 1965, 59.

[67] See J.H. Harvey, 'Architecture in Oxford 1350–1500', in J.I. Catto and R. Evans, eds, *Late Medieval Oxford: The History of the University of Oxford II*, Oxford 1992, 764–7.

[68] This is made clear in the opening phrases of the early building accounts, MC CP/2/67/1.

[69] Harvey, *English Medieval Architects*, 199–200. Baron was Bernys' chief assistant in the supervision of the works.

Plate 4 Founder's Tower, Magdalen College, Oxford

On occasion Bernys would only make the initial payment for a contract and the remainder of the money had to be obtained from the hands of the bishop by William Orchard who was in direct personal contact with him. Sometimes, Orchard, accompanied by Richard Baron, one of the fellows and Bernys' chief assistant in the supervision of the works, rode to London to consult Waynflete in person and if necessary rode to one or other of his episcopal manors to find him. It would have been on such occasions that Orchard and Waynflete discussed the plans for the buildings and drew up contracts.

A handful of building contracts made by Waynflete have survived from the late 1470s. The first, of September 1475 dealt with the construction of 'a window of seven lights' at the western end of the chapel; in addition agreements were made for cloister windows with buttresses and doors for the chambers required to be as good or better than those at All Souls and also for a window for the library.[70] In January 1479 a further contract was made, this time for battlements and buttresses for the church, the great hall, the library and two towers and the cloister chambers[71] while in April of the same year Waynflete contracted with Orchard for a 'vise' or spiral staircase in the tower and agreed payments for the finishing touches on buildings already constructed – pinnacles for the church, hall and two towers.[72]

Among the finishing touches must have been the five statues which were placed over the entrance to the college chapel. These partly encapusalate the founder's interests or debts with regard to his college. One was of St John the Baptist, a reference to the Hospital of St John the Baptist which had been suppressed in order to permit the founding of the college and whose possessions provided the core of the endowment put together for Magdalen College. A second statue was of Mary Magdalen, the dedicatee of the college and Waynflete's own personal patron saint and a third was of St Swithun, a reference to the see of Winchester. The five were completed by a diplomatically chosen statue of Edward IV and one of Waynflete himself.

Unlike Wykeham who never visited his foundation at New College,[73] Waynflete paid a number of visits to his college. The first of the visits for which there is a detailed description took place in the autumn of 1481 and the account explicitly states that the founder came, '. . . to supervise the state of his college and the new buildings.'[74] By this date a substantial part of the collegiate buildings had been completed and he could safely bring cartloads of books and muniments to give to the college. The muniment tower which would contain them was carefully constructed to the instructions laid down in the statutes; in the highest room of the tower annexed to the chapel were to be chests to keep

---

[70] MC deeds Misc. 349, no. 1.
[71] *Ibid.*, no. 3.
[72] *Ibid.*, no. 4.
[73] G. Jackson-Stops, 'The Building of the Medieval College', in *New College Oxford 1379–1979*, 157.
[74] MC Register A, fo 7v.

the muniments relating to the college. The common seal and common chests were to be kept in the room next to the main hall, probably a reference to the hall of the president's lodgings. The muniment tower was on two floors; the room on the lower floor held the valuables, plate which was not used on a regular basis and money saved out of daily expenditure which was to be kept for use in law suits and for the purchase of estates. The upper floor was used to store other monies and the muniments with the originals and copies being kept in separate chests.[75]

The traditional burial place for a bishop of Winchester was, of course, within the precincts of his cathedral church. The lengthy nave and chancel of Winchester cathedral is filled with the lavish tombs of past prelates, many of them expressing in miniature the prevalent architectural styles of their eras. The only documentary reference to the existence of Waynflete's tomb and chantry in Winchester Cathedral during his lifetime occurs in his will made shortly before his death where he requested that his body be buried in the chapel dedicated to St Mary Magdalen which he had constructed in his cathedral church.[76] No accounts exist relating to its construction and little is known of either the architect or the sculptors or of its date of construction. It seems likely that it may have been completed about the mid 1470s, at the same time as the great screen of the cathedral.[77] This chantry chapel is situated at the eastern end of the nave of the cathedral opposite that of Cardinal Beaufort which was clearly the model for it.[78]

The chantry chapel is enclosed between two pillars by stone screens which are carved as a series of open arches, surmounted by elaborate pinnacle work, with a canopied niche at each end. The floor is of Purbeck marble. The vaulted ceiling has in the central division a boss carved as a demi-angel holding a shield of the bishop's arms. The walls have niches for statues which no longer exist.[79]

---

[75] *Magdalen Statutes*, 40, *De custodia, librorum, ornamentum, jocalium et aliorum bonorum Collegii*, 48, *De evidentiis, munimentis et aliis scriptis secrete et secure conservandis.*

[76] Chandler, *Life*, appendix xxix, 380–1; on the chantry see W. Leedy, *Fan Vaulting*, 1980 and G.H. Cook, *Medieval Chantries and Chantry Chapels*, 1947.

[77] P. Lindley, 'The Great Screen of Winchester Cathedral II: Style and Date', in *Burlington Magazine*, forthcoming. I am grateful to Dr Lindley for a pre-publication copy of this article and for discussing the issues with me.

[78] W.H. St John Hope suggests, in a report prepared for Magdalen College Oxford, that the two tombs may have been the work of the same architect or mason, *Report on Bishop Waynflete's Chapel in Winchester College*, privately printed, Burlington House, 1898, available in Society of Antiquaries Library TR 237*. I am grateful to Dr Christopher Wilson for this reference.

[79] Some of the missing sculptures for these niches may be amongst the large quantity of late medieval sculpture fragments to be found in the transept galleries and the crypt. In particular, two figures – one a nun with a wimple and one a monk – have been suggested as having once belonged to Waynflete's chantry chapel, P. Lindley, 'Figure-Sculpture at Winchester in the Fifteenth Century; a New Chronology', in D. Williams, ed., *England in the Fifteenth Century: Proceedings of the 1986 Harlaxton Symposium*, Woodbridge 1987, 166. On the quality of the architectural sculpture of Waynflete's

Most of the area within the chantry is occupied by the bishop's tomb. It consists of a purbeck marble plinth with projecting bases at the corners for twisted marble shafts which carry the upper marble slab. Between the plinth and the upper slab on each side are stone panels which are carved with tracery enclosing in the centre of each a transverse scroll, behind which rises a long-stalked lily. The tomb effigy is life-size and highly coloured; its colours were described at the end of the nineteenth century.

> . . . the bishop in grey amys, amice with broad blue apparel with gold border, white albe without apparels, red stole with widened ends, red fanon with gilt edging, and a glue chasuble without orphreys and bordered with gold. On the hands are white gloves with jewelled backs and wrist bands with rings painted over them. Beneath the gloves the small buttons of an underdress are visible on the underside of each forearm. On his head the bishop has a blue mitre, originally decorated with spraywork in imitation of pearl embroidery, with bold jewelled circlet and orphreys. Under the left arm is a gold crosier with head of very unusual form, from which depends a long red napkin. Under the bishop's head are two pillows, the upper of blue, the lower of red with gold tassels. The feet which are encased in black shoes with red edges to the soles, rest against a demi-angel holding a shield of the bishop's arms.[80]

Around the edge of the tomb slab is a narrow band with rivet holes for a brass fillet, now missing, which would have carried an inscription. When newly constructed and freshly painted, the whole would have have been a vivid representation of a rich and successful bishop, the lilies on his arms and scattered throughout the chapel a reminder of his links with the royal college of Eton.

Only a tiny fraction of the original medieval figure sculture is still *in situ* on the Great Sceen in Winchester cathedral, but some of the cathedral's sculptural fragments can be assigned to the original programme. The great screen's archtiectural repertoire is not dissimilar to that of Waynflete's chantry and recent work on stylistic and documentary evidence suggest that the great screen was complete by 1476, when the translation of the relics of St Swithun took place. Thus it is likely that it can be associated with the patronage of Wayflete (or, less probably the patronage of St Swithun's priory during this period), despite the absence of direct documentary evidence for this. Stylistic comparisons suggest that the sculture may well be the work of a Netherlandish sculptor.[81]

---

chantry chapel see Lindley, 'The Great Screen of Winchester Cathedral II: Style and Date', n. 78.

[80] St. John Hope *Report*, 5; he concludes that the colouring which he describes is quite recent but it is 'probably a more or less correct repainting of the original decoration. With the exception of the upper part of the bishop's mitre [an eighteenth century restoration] the whole monument is original and in excellent order'.

[81] P. Lindley, 'The Great Screen of Winchester Cathedral II: Style and Date', in *Burlington Magazine*, forthcoming.

William Waynflete in 1479 also paid for the construction of a tomb in Chichester Cathedral for his brother John who had been dean there. This tomb has not, however, survived but it was built, somewhat unusually, of brick, as the funeral accounts testify.[82]

The choice of brick for his brother's tomb fits in well with what is known of Waynflete's other building patronage. Before 1440 few buildings were constructed entirely in brick; more commonly it was only one material of several and was primarily used for dressings on stone-built buildings. The key decades for the influx of brick into England were the 1440s and 1450s when Flemish and German craftsmen came to work in England. Brick-making was not as yet a widely-practised native English skill. Henry VI employed William Vesey, a German brick-maker in the 1440s while Lord Cromwell imported brickmakers from the same area for his works at Tattershall.[83] Despite the growing availability of bricks only a handful of brick buildings were constructed over the next quarter century – Caister castle (1430s), Tattershall castle (1440/50s), Hurstmonceaux castle (1440s). Continental influence was important in the introduction of more extensive brick building into England in the first half of the fifteenth century; most of the patrons of early brick buildings had themselves been abroad.[84] Brick was to become popular among episcopal builders in the last fifteen years or so of the century when men such as Morton, Fox and Rotherham built or extended episcopal palaces using brick, but it was relatively little exploited in this way prior to the late 1480s. Thus in his extensive use of brick in his episcopal palaces at Esher, Farnham and for Wainfleet school William Waynflete was ahead of his peers.

Waynflete's choice of brick must have been influenced by the fact that he was familiar with at least two of the three major brick buildings referred to above, Caister and Tattershall. In addition brick had been used to a limited extent at Eton College during his provostship.[85] He was thus familiar with the advantages of building in brick – since bricks could be made on the site the cost of transportation of materials was considerably reduced; it was suitable for 'domestic' buildings yet could provide defensive positions; it could be moulded with relative ease where necessary. The dates of Waynflete's works at Esher in the 1460s and at Farnham in the 1470s make him the earliest of the great episcopal builders and his activities were to be very influential. A recent discussion of the development of brick building in England commented that, 'there seems to be only one coherent, identifiable group of fifteenth century people who stimulated the simultaneous fashions for brick, domesticity and comfort; that is the bishops.'[86] His successors in the bishopric of Winchester, Fox, Langton and

[82] MC CP/2/55.
[83] *Brick Building in England*, 30–52.
[84] T.P. Smith, *The Medieval Brickmaking Industry in England 1400–1450*, British Archaeological Reports cxxxviii, 1988, 7, 19.
[85] *Ibid.*, 116–32.
[86] *Brick Building in England*, 137.

Plate 5 Waynflete's Tower at Esher Palace, Surrey

Wolsey together with Alcock (Ely), Morton (Canterbury and Ely) and Rotherham (York) were the foremost brick builders in the early Tudor period.

The most important of the episcopal palaces in the diocese of Winchester
had been built in the twelfth century by Henry of Blois – Esher, Farnham and
Bishop's Waltham. His constructions determined the basic form in which they
were to remain for several centuries. Some alterations and repairs had of course
been made over the intervening period but Waynflete clearly found a number of
them unsatisfactory in terms of standards of comfort. He rebuilt extensively at
Esher and Farnham, two of the places where he was frequently in residence.

Less is known of Waynflete's buildings at Esher than at Farnham or Wainfleet
because no building accounts have survived there. Beginning in the mid 1460s
however, much of the manorial living accommodation at Esher was rebuilt.[87]
Of this rebuilding only the gate house has survived but a plan dating from 1606
indicates clearly the form of the reconstructed palace. The plan shows a substantial gate-house through which lay a large courtyard, where the church and a
number of domestic buildings were situated. The main residential buildings lay
across the courtyard on the right, backing onto the river Mote. Exactly how
much of this complex can be attributed to Waynflete is uncertain but at the
least he was certainly responsible for the great hall, part of the living quarters
and the gate-house, all of which were constructed entirely in brick. The gate-
house contained some living quarters as was common in many fifteenth century
constructions. The tower-house '. . . was among the supreme examples of its
type, being in a way more typical of a renaissance intellect than the formality
which Henry VIII imposed on his palaces in the name of the Renaissance.'[88]

Considerably more is known about the building of Farnham for much of the
expenditure on it is detailed in the manorial accounts for the 1470s.[89] Here
Waynflete faced the same problems as at Esher of an old palace in need of
repair. The site was still dominated by the twelfth century keep and motte
although numerous additions and alterations had been made in the ensuing
centuries. Waynflete's contribution consisted of the replacement of a bridge and
earlier gate-house by a brick gate-house which could provide domestic accommodation.

Brick making commenced on the site in 1469; the brick makers seem, like
those employed for the construction of Tattershall Castle some thirty years
earlier, to have been from the Netherlands – their names Cornelius, Florence
and Jacob are not commonly found in England in this period.[90] Work on the

[87] J.K. Floyer, 'The Ancient Manor House of the Bishops of Winchester at Esher Place',
Proceedings of the Society of Antiquaries xxxii, 1920, 69–79; G. Lambert, *Esher Place*,
1884.

[88] N. Pevsner and I. Nairn, *Surrey*, 1963, 200.

[89] M.W. Thompson, 'The Date of "Fox's Tower", Farnham Castle, Surrey', *Surrey Archaeological Collections* lxx, 1960, 85–92.

[90] 'The Date of "Fox's Tower" ', 88; in 1470 alone 240,000 bricks are recorded as having
been made at the 'breakplace'. This was the first year of building works there but for the

Plate 6 Brick gatehouse, Farnham Castle, Surrey

tower did not begin in earnest until the following year when an older wooden hall was dismantled and the foundations for the new brick tower were dug. Work continued throughout the 1470s; the accounts are primarily concerned with detailing labour costs and materials but they do refer to the hall, kitchen and buttery of the new tower[91] which indicates that the tower was intended to be a complete residential building. The ground floor was divided into two rooms, while above there were two stories, each containing suites of rooms. Not only did it provide comfortable living quarters, it was also a building which expressed in its imposing form the exalted position of the bishop of Winchester. In it stylish renaissance brickwork was combined with a formidable facade which included false machicolations, turrets and a portcullis. Pevsner has described it as 'extra-ordinarily sophisticated – it makes Hampton Court (begun 1514 in the same idiom), look like nouveau-riche ostentation.'[92]

The other major brick construction erected under Waynflete's patronage lay outside the boundaries of his diocese, in his Lincolnshire birthplace. This was the building designed to house Waynflete's grammar school in Wainfleet and it was conceived on a monumental scale dominating the town. A schoolmaster – John Marshall, clerk – was in post in January 1466[93] but it was not until the early 1480s that work began on the school buildings. The statutes drawn up for Magdalen College at the beginning of the decade ensured the school's income of £10 a year from the Lincolnshire lands held by the college.[94] The school was built entirely in brick and was an imposing building with the west front flanked by two three storey towers. The familiar diaper pattern which is a mark of Waynflete's brick buildings and which is to be found at Esher and Farnham, reappears here also.

The extent of Waynflete's personal interest in the construction of the building at Wainfleet is better documented than for his works at Esher or Farnham. Two documents survive to demonstrate his active involvement with both the design and the work itself. The first of these is a letter from John Gygour, warden of Tattershall College, who acted generally as the bishop's agent in his native county. The letter began by referring to a recent discussion Gygour had had with Waynflete and continued,

> I was with master Gotoft and John Robenson to let them witt how your lordship trusted up on them to help you, they might have a house and they

remainder of the decade there was a substantial output of bricks, ranging from 30,000 to 128,000 annually.

[91] Pevsner and Nairn, *Surrey*, 201; 'The Date of "Fox's Tower" ', 85–89.

[92] Pevsner and Nairn, *Surrey*, 200.

[93] Parry-Jones, *Five Hundred Years of Magdalen College School Wainfleet 1484–1984*, 6–7. Marshall was a fellow of Magdalen College and subsequently became rector of Wainfleet All Saints (1498–1505). He was succeeded as schoolmaster by Thomas Whetley, c.1479–80; then Thomas Bocher (1480–82), William Hode (1483–91), William Dobyll (1493–5), *ibid.*, 8.

[94] MC deeds, Multon 157; *Magdalen Statutes*, 77.

say thay can have none that the timber would be secure to continue in time to come but they think that there must be ordained for a new roof if your lordship so will be pleased . . .

Gygour then explained that he had sent Henry Alresbroke, the carpenter to speak to Waynflete personally because,

> . . . ye lorschip can best undertstond whether his petrycion be reasonably, I beseche you to commune rypli with hym and to express the measurements . . .

Clearly Gygour was familiar with Waynflete's other building projects, for he concluded the letter by suggesting that Waynflete should show Alresbroke Esher, '. . . that may be example to hym.'[95] Waynflete seems to have followed this suggestion for the indenture subsequently concluded with Alresbroke on 25 April 1484 was for a roof, floor, stairs, desks, reredoses and other necessary carpentry work in the building

> . . . after the patron and facyon of the flore of the chambyr in the towre over the gate of the manor of Essher . . .[96]

The survival of these documents demonstrates Waynflete's concern with the details of his building projects. He must have been equally involved with the works at Esher and Farnham which were amongst the episcopal manors he visited most regularly. Relatively little is known of the men who were employed on the various building works of which Waynflete was the patron. It is not clear whether he followed the example of his predecessor William Wykeham who kept a regular team of builders and craftsmen almost constantly in his employment.[97] However the little that is known of Waynflete's masons and architects suggests that this might well have been the case for master craftsmen at least. Few contracts naming craftsmen have survived and this lack of information is exacerbated by the fact that the bulk of the payments for building works seem to have come directly from the central episcopal exchequer at Wolvesey and were not recorded on the manorial account rolls which are the only surviving accounts for Waynflete's episcopate.

The man who can be seen to have been most closely involved with a number of the bishop's building projects was William Orchard.[98] From the late 1460s until Waynflete's death he acted as architect and chief mason at Magdalen College. The bishop provided him with a livery and paid him for his services, not only as architect-mason but also as supervisor and paymaster of the other

---

[95] MC deeds, Candlesby 20, printed in full in Chandler, *Life*, appendix xxiii, 367–9.
[96] MC deeds, Candlesby 16, printed in *ibid.*, appendix xxiv, 370.
[97] 'The Building of the Medieval College', in *New College Oxford 1379–1979*, 151, 163.
[98] *English Medieval Architects*, 199–200.

A View of WAINFLETE's SCHOOL, at WAINFLETE Lincolnshire.

Plate 7 Wainfleet School, Lincolnshire

workmen on the site.[99] Orchard was a designer as well as a mason; one of the few surviving contracts stated that he was to build the western window of the chapel, '. . . according to the purtrature made and delyverd to the said Reverend fader . . .'[100] Orchard also leased a quarry from which he sent stone not only to the works at Magdalen College but also to Eton College for the completion of the chapel there.

A second mason John Cowper may also have worked on several of Waynflete's projects. A man of this name who worked at Tattershall college in the 1470s has been identified as the same man who worked at Winchester College in the 1450s and whose son worked at Eton College in the same decade.[101] A John Cowper, 'mason of Winchester' was employed by Waynflete in April 1477 to repair Bamber bridge in Sussex[102] but it is not possible identify him conclusively with the John Cowper who worked at Tattershall and built a brick castle at Kirkby Muxloe for Lord Hastings, particularly since it is not an uncommon name. Harvey asserts, without citing his evidence, that Cowper was Waynflete's architect for the buildings. It is not certain that the same man acted as architect for both of these brick buildings, for despite a superficial similarity between them created by the use of a diaper pattern common to both, they differ considerably in style.[103]

Henry Alresbroke, a Lincolnshire carpenter, was employed at both of Waynflete's projects within that country – Wainfleet and Tattershall but again there is no evidence for Harvey's assertion that Alresbroke was the carpenter at Esher.[104] In fact this is most unlikely in view of the phrasing of Gygour's letter to Waynflete cited above in which he recommended that Waynflete show Alresbroke, '. . . sum maner house in your nobly place of Ascher that may be example to hym . . .'[105] Waynflete is known to have employed at least two other carpenters. David Orton worked on Witney manor in Oxfordshire on a number of small projects – the roof of the manor chapel, the grange and the great kitchen – in the period 1462–72.[106] The second carpenter, Walter Nicholl was from Southwark, possibly from the bishop's manor there.[107] Nicholl was also responsible for the construction of the rood loft in Eton College chapel.[108] On two occasions in 1476, while working on Eton College chapel, Walter Nicholl

99 MC MS CP/2/67/1, fo 18v.
100 MC deeds, Misc. 349, no. 3.
101 *English Medieval Architects*, 77.
102 L. Salzman, *Building in England Down to 1540*, 1952, 538–9.
103 'The design [of Farnham] has no close equivalent . . . the obvious place to look is Esher but the character of this is quite different . . .', Pevsner and Nairn, *Surrey*, 201.
104 *English Medieval Architects*, 20.
105 MC deeds, Candlesby 20.
106 *English Medieval Architects*, 201.
107 There is no real evidence for Harvey's assertion that Walter Nicholl may have been a foreigner. The assertion is based on the fact that Nicholl may be the same man as 'Watkyn Kerver' who was living in St Thomas' hospital, Southwark in 1478.
108 *Ibid.*, 179; ECR 38/309.

visited the Bishop of Winchester, presumably to discuss the progress of the work.

It is regretable that more is not known of the men who were responsible for designing and building Waynflete's brick buildings. What is clear however, is that the men employed by Waynflete were extremely talented in their use of brick; in the half century after Waynflete's death their original ideas were to be followed by a number of episcopal builders, in the diocese of Winchester and elsewhere.[109]

Waynflete was a generous patron to the building trade in the third quarter of the fifteenth century; the range and scale of his works surpass those of his contemporaries. Of particular importance was his role in the dissemination of the use of brick to areas both north and south-west of the area in which hitherto it had been in popular use. Although the 1450s had seen a fairly widespread introduction of brick, outside the eastern counties of England which had the closest links with the Netherlands and northern Europe it was not commonly used, except for facade dressings and crenellations. All of Waynflete's brick buildings were built on the periphery of the area where brick was common. He set a pattern for later renaissance use of brick for domestic purposes in England which was to be extremely influential. The very fact that his buildings at Esher and Farnham were commonly attributed to his successors in the see – known as 'Wolsey's tower' and 'Fox's tower' respectively – indicates how much he was ahead of his contemporaries with his preference for and active patronage of building in brick.

---

[109] See above, note 44.

VI

Episcopal Income and
Educational Expenditure[1]

Income

A bishop was not only the spiritual head of a diocese but also a temporal lord, often a very wealthy one, who drew revenues from and had jurisdiction over wide areas of land. These lands not only gave the bishop status as a landowner but also provided him with the income necessary to maintain his household and his position as one of the foremost lords of the realm.

The estates attached to the see of Winchester were some fifty in number, scattered over the southern counties of England. The bulk lay in Hampshire, the heartland of the see but there were also lands in Surrey, also part of the diocese, Wiltshire, Somerset, Berkshire, Oxfordshire and Buckinghamshire. The geographic situation of these estates helps to account for the position of the bishop of Winchester as the richest of England's prelates. The see was wealthier than that of Canterbury where the annual value of the estates during the fifteenth and early sixteenth century was £3178.[2] In addition to supplying revenues to support the bishop and his household, some manors were the sites of important residential seats. Those at Southwark, Wolvesey, Farnham, Esher and Bishop's Waltham were regularly frequented by Waynflete and his household. Other manors, particularly those outside his diocese, featured only occasionally on his itinerary. The dual sources of a bishop's income reflected his position as both diocesan and landowner. Dues and fees collected for the performance of his pastoral work, from institutions, consecrations, probate cases and visitations – made up his spiritual revenues. The total sum derived from this source provided a very small portion of his gross income, although to the individuals paying the fees they must often have appeared heavy. In 1535 the spiritualities of Winchester provided only £154 4s 3d out of a total income

---

[1] The substantial section of this chapter which deals with the gathering together by Waynflete of a landed endowment for Magdalen College is largely based on an unpublished Oxford B.Litt. thesis by J.F. Mills, 'The Foundation, Endowment and Early Administration of Magdalen College Oxford', Oxford 1978. I am grateful to Mr Mills who has most generously permitted me to draw extensively on his work.

[2] F.R.H. DuBoulay, *The Lordship of Canterbury*, 1966, 323–4.

of just over £4000.[3] This is likely to be a considerable underestimate; the sources for calculating the spiritualities are at best patchy and incomplete. It is likely that the spiritualities of the diocese of Winchester are at least double the figure given in the *Valor Ecclesiasticus*, perhaps near to £300 a year.[4]

For Winchester, as for the other sees of England, there are two sources for its medieval income, the *Taxatio* of Pope Nicholas of 1291 and the *Valor Ecclesiasticus* compiled by Henry VIII's commissioners in 1535. £2977 15s 10d was the estimated value of the Winchester episcopal estates in 1291, by 1535 this sum had risen by just over a third to £4037 19s 11d.[5] This increase was considerably less than that of some other episcopal estates – those of Bath and Wells increased from £511 to £1939 in the same period – and must reflect the fact that Winchester was an old and well-established see which had benefited from the generosity of early medieval kings. A late fifteenth century estimate of the income of the bishopric gives the total income as £4354 with arrears owing to a total of £587.[6] In addition to these records of clerical wealth which are available for all the English dioceses, the survival of a lengthy run of ministers' accounts for the temporal estates of the bishopric of Winchester mean that the episcopal revenues are exceptionally well documented.

The ministers' accounts for the episcopal estates of Winchester are extant from 1208. With their detailed coverage of many aspects of manorial life they have been widely used, particularly by agrarian historians.[7] The basic article which has been written on their dating is misleading in that it gives the impression that this run of accounts ceases to exist in 1453.[8] Twenty five of these accounts survive covering the whole span of Waynflete's episcopate.[9] In fact 1454 marks a dramatic change in the physical form of the accounts, but a change of form not content: from Michaelmas of that year onwards the accounts were bound into volumes, still with large pages and closely written on

---

3   *Valor Ecclesiasticus*, 6 vols, 1810–34.
4   Recent work by R.N. Swanson indicates the inadequacy of the *Valor Ecclesiasticaus* for calculating the true value of episcpal income from spiritualities, see R.N. Swanson, 'Episcopal Income from Spiritualities in Later Medieval England: the Evidence for the Diocese of Coventry and Lichfield', *Midland History* xiv, 1988, 1–20 and R.N. Swanson, 'Episcopal Income from Spiritualities in the Diocese of Exeter in the Early Sixteenth Century', *JEH* xxxix, 1988, 520–30.
5   *Taxatio Ecclesiastica 1291*, 1802; *Valor Ecclesiasticus* ii, 2.
6   HRO EC/2/1595159/30, Box 157. It has been calculated that Cardinal Beaufort's annual revenue from the episcopal estates of Winchester was approximately £3,700 Harriss, *Cardinal Beaufort*, appendix iii.
7   See for example, A.E. Levett, *The Black Death on the Estates of the See of Winchester*, Oxford 1916; J.Z. Titow, *Winchester Yields*, Cambridge 1972; W. Beveridge, 'Wages on the Winchester Manors', *EcHR* viii, 1936, 22–43.
8   H. Hall, 'A List of the Rent Rolls of the Bishopric of Winchester', *Economica* x, 1924, 52–61.
9   HRO EC/2/159438–44 and EC/2/155827–45. There are no accounts for the years 1450, 1455, 1456, 1458, 1459, 1464, 1468, 1469, 1471, 1482, 1485, 1486 and that for 1481 consists only of a few loose gatherings.

both sides but now in book form with a soft vellum cover. This alteration would have greatly facilitated consultation of the accounts. The change from roll form to book form in itself was not a new idea; episcopal registers were originally kept on rolls but they had made the transition to books in the thirteenth century. In making this change in the manorial accounts the diocese of Winchester was ahead of many other lordships; the accounts of the Duke of Clarence for 1479, for example, were still being enrolled on large membranes.[10]

Each pipe roll or volume covers a single year and contains a transcript of the accounts for each manor, borough or liberty for that year. These accounts were rendered to the bishop's receiver-general 'the Treasurer of Wolvesey' at the episcopal exchequer in Wolvesey Palace in Winchester. The accounts provide a mass of information – about rents of assize, leases, farm stock, grain prices, costs of demesne management and building works – but they do not provide a straightforward answer to the question, what was the annual income of the bishop of Winchester? No *proficium maneriorum* account is extant for the bishopric and in no way can the manorial accounts be regarded as a profit and loss account. They were not intended to show the total manorial surplus but rather to record the charges and discharges of the receiver, to establish his liability.[11] An additional problem in using these accounts to estimate bishop Waynflete's income is that by the fifteenth century the form of the accounts which had been established in the thirteenth century had become stereotyped and had not altered as agricultural practices had changed. Frequently 'dead' sums were recorded under receipts and then subtracted under allowances.

The most accurate indication of the quantity of disposable income actually available to Waynflete as bishop of Winchester is to be found in the sums of money surplus to manorial requirements which were paid over to the central episcopal exchequer at Wolvesey.[12] These occur in the accounts for each manor under the heading *liberacio denarii*. This represents the 'profit' remaining after the payment of manorial running costs, wages to officials and other fixed expenses such as fees and pensions. This was the money available to William Waynflete which he could use to meet other commitments. When estimating his income in this manner it is also necessary to include the sums of money paid

[10] R. Hilton, *The Ministers' Accounts of the Warwickshire Estates of the Duke of Clarence*, Dugdale Society 1952, lx, n. 1.

[11] On some of the problems of dealing with manorial accounts see, F. Heal, *Of Prelates and Princes*, Cambridge 1980, 51; A.E. Levett, 'The Financial Organisation of the Manor', *EcHR* i, 1927, 65–86; N. Denholm-Young, *Seigniorial Administration in England*, Oxford 1937, chapter 4; Hilton, *The Ministers' Accounts of the Warwickshire Estates of the Duke of Clarence*.

[12] This is a far more useful figure for the purposes of estimating the amounts of money available to Waynflete than the figures described as *summa totalis cum arreragiis* which bear little relation to the sums of money actually at his disposal and which are particularly inflated in the fifteenth century by accumulated arrears. In 1480 for example, the total plus arrears for Downton manor was £294, manorial expenses totalled £41, arrears were £118 and only £135 was actually paid over to the treasurer of Wolvesey.

out by manorial officials directly to Magdalen College or to the Treasurer of the episcopal household and authorised by letters under the episcopal signet seal. These sums were not for manorial expenditure and must be added in with his disposable income.

One other source of income which Waynflete had in the latter part of his episcopate was not derived from this episcopal revenues. That was the income from the substantial endowment he collected for Magdalen College but which he only handed over to his college in a slow and piecemeal fashion in the last years of his life. This may have amounted to another £500 per year.[13]

The sums of disposable income varied slightly from year to year but totalled between £2000 – £3700 per annum. When other costs such as manorial expenses, stipend for manorial officials and domestic building costs are taken into consideration, this figure accords reasonably well with that estimated for the episcopal income of Winchester derived from other sources. Gross receipts from individual estates could be affected by the incidence of poor harvests, outbreaks of disease among either humans and animals or other localised problems. The cash deliveries made to Waynflete's exchequer might also be substantially reduced if a major building or maintenance programme was being undertaken. In 1470, for example the manor of Marwell in Hampshire, produced only £12 in cash instead of its more usual sum which was in excess of £30. This abrupt drop was due to the fact that £25 had been spent in that year on repairs of the manor and of the chapel attached to it, thus increasing the total manorial expenses for the year from the normal £13–£20 to £44. By 1472, however, the building works were more or less finished and £33 was paid to the episcopal treasurer in that year.[14]

The administration of the temporal estates of the bishopric was carried on at two distinct levels, local and central. Locally each manor was managed by a reeve while groups of manors were overseen by bailiffs. The real direction of affairs and ultimate responsibility remained with the central administration: the bishop's council and the officials with specific financial responsibilities. The *consilium domini* of bishop Waynflete, although frequently mentioned in the ministers' accounts remains a shadowy body. What is known of its composition elsewhere can be assumed to apply to Winchester; it must have been composed of the main estate officials and legal advisors and also included prominent local landowners. The advice of local men about the customs and conditions affecting manorial administration would be especially valuable to a bishop who had come into the diocese as a newcomer and would not be familiar with local practices. Its role was primarily advisory, its actions were mainly manorial and territorial, although it must be remembered that this picture may be distorted by the fact that the sources of information concerning the activities of

---

[13] This is discussed in more detail later in this chapter.

[14] HRO EC/2/155835; EC/2/155836. The same substantial drop in income can be seen in the accounts for Farnham manor in the early 1470s when a major reconstruction of the castle in brick was undertaken, EC/2/155835–41.

Waynflete's council come primarily from manorial accounts. Certainly Cardinal Beaufort's council apparently acted for the bishop in matters not concerning the bishopric.[15] For advice in other spheres of his interests, however, especially his primary concern – Magdalen College – it seems that Waynflete turned to men within his immediate household, his chancellor, chaplains and the important figure of the treasurer of Wolvesey, the receiver-general of the diocese of Winchester who took his name from the episcopal palace in Winchester which was the seat of the bishop's exchequer. The treasurer of Wolvesey was the man who controlled the cash flow into and out of the bishop's exchequer; in his hands lay overall responsibility for the episcopal revenues, the receipt of cash and rents and the payment of officials. He also authorised payments to the treasurer of the bishop's household for daily expenses. He can be equated in terms of rank and importance with the chancellor of the household or the diocesan vicar-general.

All the men who served Waynflete as treasurers of Wolvesey were laymen;[16] part of the growing body of lay administrators and bureaucrats which was rapidly developing in England in the course of the fifteenth century.[17] The treasurer acted as confidant and adviser to the bishop, as his paymaster and,on occasion, as the purchaser of lands for the future endowment of Magdalen College. The treasurer of Wolvesey formed the single most important and consistent link between the bishop and the men who managed his temporal estates. His duties however, extended beyond the boundaries of the diocese; due to his position as bishop's treasurer he was involved in all of his master's activities, which in Waynflete's case meant particularly his educational foundations

Although the administration of the temporal estates of the diocese of Winchester, like the ecclesiastical administration of the diocese, could be carried out on a day-to-day basis without his direct participation, its smooth and efficient running was important to Waynflete if maximum income was to be gleaned from his lands. These estates produced the revenues necessary not only to maintain his household and comfortable lifestyle but also to carry out projects dear to his heart – the foundation of Magdalen College and building works at Eton College and elsewhere. Waynflete clearly took a personal interest in the estate administration; during his episcopate a professional auditor was introduced and the form of accounting was changed to make it easier to handle. A single professional auditor, Nicholas Sharpe, was first appointed to carry out the annual audit in 1448. Sharpe had been auditor of the accounts of Eton

---

[15] E. Swift, 'The Machinery of Manorial Administration with Special Reference to the Lands of the Bishopric of Winchester 1208–1454', unpublished London M.A. thesis 1930, 15.

[16] The treasurers of Wolvesey under William Waynflete were – from Beaufort's episcopate to 1454 William Porte; 1454–61 Hugh Pakenham; 1461–69 Thomas Gyan; 1468–78 Thomas Pounde; 1478–86 Thomas Danvers.

[17] Storey, 'Gentlemen Bureaucrats', in C.H. Clough, ed., *Profession, Vocation and Culture*, 90–129.

College in 1446 when Waynflete was still provost there. His appointment appears in the episcopal register dated October 1451 but Sharpe must have come directly from Eton College to the diocese with Waynflete for he appears in the ministers' accounts as early as 1448, '16d for the expenses of Nicholas Sharpe, the lord's auditor, riding from London to Winchester for the minsters' accounts'.[18]

The change in the physical form of the accounts of the diocese of Winchester in 1454 coincided with the replacement of William Porte, who had served Beaufort, by Hugh Pakenham as treasurer of Wolvesey. Pakenham was Waynflete's choice and while there is no direct evidence for the change in accounting forms being the result of the bishop's initiative it must have had his sanction. Since he can elsewhere be seen to be personally concerned in all affairs touching his interests as bishop, it is reasonable to assume that he was the instigator of the new-style accounts or at least approved and encouraged the change.

The same characteristic of a desire to be involved personally in all matters relating to his diocese can be seen in the temporal as well as the ecclesiastical administration of Winchester during his episcopate. Thus Waynflete's temporal administration was both efficient and subject to close personal supervision by the bishop although a slight upward trend in his receipts in the latter part of his episcopate must have been due as much to the general upturn in the economy as to any particular aspect of his temporal administration. What is clear, however, is that bishop Waynflete had a substantial amount of surplus cash throughout his episcopate which could be used to support projects in which he was interested. This is true even for the beginning of his episcopate despite the fact the middle years of the century are usually considered to have been the nadir of the fifteenth century English economy. The sheer scale of his temporal lands and the diversity of his income from them insulated him from the worst effects of this depression.

Expenditure I: General

The ministers' accounts with their largely stereotyped format are not very helpful in elucidating the level of episcopal expenditure. They are concerned primarily with recording the day-to-day running expenses of the individual manors. Payments to bailiffs and other officials directly involved with the temporal administration are recorded but references to non-manorial officials are rare. No payments, for example, are referred to for the lawyers who must have been retained by Waynflete; similarly pensions being paid to men unconnected with the minutiae of daily administration also go unrecorded. Payments

---

[18] Swift, 'The Machinery of Manorial Administration', 59ff; HRO EC/2/159439 fo 22v. In Canterbury a succession of professional auditors can be traced from c.1412, F.R.H. Du Boulay, *The Lordship of Canterbury*, 273.

of this kind must have been made directly from the central episcopal exchequer at Wolvesey. Unfortunately no household accounts or accounts of the treasurer of Wolvesey are extant. Occasional references confirm that such payments were made directly, as for example, the grant of an annual pension to William Lord Hastings in 1461, the terms of which state that £10 was to be paid to him directly by the treasurer of Wolvesey.[19] The building accounts of Magdalen College also record the receipt of money directly from the episcopal exchequer at Wolvesey.[20] In a few particular instances money was paid directly from manors to an individual or institution under the authorisation of the bishop's signet. These payments were recorded in the accounts under the heading *Solucio per warranto* and relate primarily to money being paid to Magdalen College and to a lesser extent, Eton College.[21] Money was also paid by manorial officials to the treasurer of the household to meet household expenses. The running expenses of his household was one major charge on the bishop's income. In addition to the major household officials there were also numerous lesser servants. The prestigious position of the bishop of Winchester demanded that he maintain a substantial retinue. In his declining years as bishop of Winchester, Waynflete's successor Richard Fox was said to have had about two hundred servants and retainers.[22] Some idea of the size of Waynflete's household can be gathered from a lengthy codicil to his will which instructed payments to be made to one hundred and twenty-five persons, servants and chaplains, at a total cost of more than £270.[23]

In the absence of household accounts the cost of feeding his extended household can only be surmised. In addition to food and drink, cloth for liveries and the cost of fuel were major household expenses. It has been estimated that in the early sixteenth century bishops were generally spending something between one-quarter and one-third of their income on food and maintenance. Southwark, where Waynflete spent much of his time, as a suburb of London was acknowledged as being an expensive place in which to live.[24] In view of Waynflete's obligations as one of England's foremost prelates and his frequent sojourns in London, it can reasonably be assumed that he was spending towards the upper end of this scale and he may therefore have been spending up to £1000 per annum on his household. Some of the necessary supplies could be drawn directly from the episcopal manors although the transportation costs of bulky, heavy goods could be high. The episcopal household may well, however, have been an important outlet for these manors.

Major costs must have been incurred at the beginning of his episcopate by

---

[19] Reg Waynflete ii, fo 32(2v).
[20] MC Archives CP/2/67 (1, 2).
[21] For example, in the account for 1451 an episcopal warrant ordered £28 to be paid from the manor of Adderbury to Eton College, HRO EC/2/15942.
[22] Heal, *Of Prelates and Princes*, 75.
[23] MC Archives Chartae Regiae 43, printed in Chandler, *Life*, 379–88.
[24] Heal, *Of Prelates and Princes*, 83.

Waynflete when hospitality within the diocese on his first visit to it, celebrations of his consecration, common services and petty services paid to the papacy and payments to the king on his promotion all had to be covered.[25] However the length of time that Waynflete remained bishop of Winchester enabled him to recoup these sums; bishops who were translated from see to see frequently often suffered badly from the initial costs.[26] Financial demands from the crown continued, of course, throughout his episcopate – both directly as taxation and indirectly, as the bishop absorbed the costs of being involved in royal government, as a justice of the peace, as a tax collector. Loans to the crown could also be a drain on his resources, with repayment being both slow and uncertain.[27]

His own family was another possible object of expenditure although the fact that Waynflete seems only to have had a single brother, also in the church, minimised such expenses. However, the substantial alabaster tomb, now in Magdalen College chapel but once in the church of Wainfleet All Saints, which was erected for his father, was probably paid for by Waynflete. Accounts have survived for the funeral expenses of John Waynflete, Dean of Chichester who died in 1479 showing that Waynflete paid over £110 for the funeral arrangements for his brother.[28]

The main areas to which Waynflete directed his attention and which must have absorbed the major proportion of his disposable income were two-fold – his educational projects and his building works which took place both on his manors and in connection with his foundations. Waynflete's main area of expenditure was for Magdalen College. While the endowment worth £600 per annum which he gathered together for the college was largely obtained at favourable prices it did not come cheap. Building works at the college were a further drain on his resources. They were paid for partly by money sent directly to Oxford by the treasurer of Wolvesey and partly by payments made to Richard Bernys, supervisor of the building works, from four manors in or near Oxfordshire. These payments were made by the bishop's warrant.[29] In the years 1467–85 the manors of Witney, Adderbury, Harwell and Brightwell

---

25 Waynflete paid 14000 florins into the Papal treasury after his elevation to the episcopate, W.E. Lunt, *Financial Relations of the Papacy with England 1327–1534*, Cambridge Mass. 1962, 830. This was the equivalent of approximately £2000.

26 Heal, *Of Prelates and Princes*, 93 discusses the strain placed on the resources of many of the early Tudor episcopate by such costs.

27 £100 was lent in 1449, *Issues of the Exchequer*, 465; £300 in 1451, *CPR 1446–52*, 452; £87 in 1453, PRO E404/69/163 towards the cost of the expedition to Gascony; £220 in November 1457, PRO E404/71/2/68; £40 in April 1470, PRO E404/74/3/6. Two letters in the Magdalen College archives relate to a further loan made to the king in the 1480s. One from Waynflete's servant John Legh states that Legh has paid over 300 marks as a loan from the bishop to the king; the second from John Woode, the under-treasurer of the exchequer, acknowledged receipt of 300 marks and promised that the 200 marks would be repaid the following Easter, MC MS 367 nos 9, 10.

28 MC Archives CP/2/55.

29 Sums paid in this way were recorded in the manorial accounts and thus can be traced even when building accounts have not survived.

contributed a total of £2,328 to the works, an average of £120 per annum. In addition surviving building accounts show that approximately 30% of the money for which Bernys was accounting came directly from the treasurer of Wolvesey.[30] It has been estimated that between 1467–85 at least £220–230 a year,was being spent on building works in Oxford by Waynflete, a sum which represents about 9% of his net income. This is a minimum figure; he may well have been spending more.

At the same time he was contributing towards the costs of building works at Eton College and *ad hoc* payments for these works were recorded in the manorial accounts. To these major projects must be added the costs of his building works at Wainfleet in Lincolnshire. The fact that so much of Waynflete's expenditure was done through the episcopal treasurer – a process which enabled him to monitor it closely – makes it impossible to calculate his total outgoings on particular projects. What is clear however, is that after the household expenses had been covered the bulk of his remaining disposable income was being used for the benefit of Magdalen College and his building works. In particular, from the late 1460s when a number of projects were under way at the same time his resources must have been almost fully expended. His will which contains numerous small bequests does not contain any major ones;[31] it is clear from the level of his expenditure throughout his episcopate that he cannot have been hording money to disperse on his death but rather spent it lavishly, although under his close direction, during his lifetime.

Expenditure II: The Endowment of Magdalen College

Between 1455 and 1486 Waynflete purchased or acquired property worth about £600 a year which was destined for the endowment of Magdalen College.[32] This was in addition to the property of the Hospital of St John the Baptist which formed the nucleus of the collegiate endowment and which itself was worth about £75 a year. It was not, however, until the last years of his life that Waynflete passed most of this land to his foundation, only about 20% of this property had been conveyed to the college by 1480. Between 1480 and

---

[30] The accounts only survive for the period 1467–1474, MC Archives CP/2/67 1, 2.

[31] They added up of course to a substantial sum; it is difficult to calculate it precisely because it included bequests to each monk in a number of monasteries without stipulating the number of people involved. If, however, we take as a minimum that these houses would have had at least as many monks as were recorded in 1534, Waynflete's bequests totalled in the region of £600, including the £271 bequeathed to members of his household.

[32] Details of Waynflete's individual transactions in land which later passed to the College are set out in Appendix 1. Except where stated, all values are based on average net annual values in the period 1489–98. Full details of the college revenues from land can be found in Mills, 'The Foundation, Endowment and Early Administration of Magdalen College Oxford', chapter 2.

1483 the ownership of a further 40% had been transferred but by the time of Waynflete's death in 1486 only about 83% of the total was in the hands of the president and fellows. The conveyance of the remaining 17% was left to his trustees – of this about 5% was received by the college in 1488, 11% in 1498 and the balance in 1501.

Waynflete acquired most of this property in three distinct phases. The first phase was from 1455, two years before the refoundation of Magdalen Hall as Magdalen College, until 1459, two years after. The Hospital of St John the Baptist and about 30% of the eventual total was acquired in these four years. The second phase came in the two years 1469–70 during which he acquired another 25%, although this total included the reversion of the valuable manor of Candlesby, Lincolnshire which the College did not actually gain possession of until 1498. The third and final phase was from 1479 until Waynflete's death and in this period a further 40% was gathered together of which over half was acquired in 1484 alone.[33]

The acquisition of this property was not a haphazard operation but it is clear that Waynflete found that good land was difficult to come by. He bought virtually no land which did not come from people with whom he or his close connections or officials were demonstrably familiar. Likewise he bought property in areas he knew, even when this meant the estates were not necessarily conveniently placed from the point of view of the college. Waynflete was a shrewd business man and his particular emphasis on familiarity with both vendor and location was the best way of ensuring that titles were secure. In the tangled web of fifteenth century property rights it made little sense to buy land from strangers in unknown parts of the country where an unsuspecting purchaser could easily be faced with a claim of an entail. Such action carried with it considerable risk and in addition, no real mechanism existed for buying land without local knowledge. Waynflete's cautious policy was to pay off. There was little substance to the few challenges to the tenure of certain estates which Magdalen faced in the years after the bishop's death.[34]

The need for the college to be assured of secure titles after his death was clearly an important reason why Waynflete obtained over one third (34%) of the total endowment for Magdalen via his role as executor for two wealthy magnates, Sir John Fastolf and Ralph, Lord Cromwell.[35] His privileged position as executor gave him an unequalled opportunity to investigate closely the history of each property in a way which he could never have done had he been simply a casual buyer. The two executorships also allowed Waynflete to obtain

33 Mills, *op. cit.*, 34.
34 For details of the few challenges faced by the college, see Mills, *op. cit.*, chapter 5, 175ff.
35 Cromwell died in 1456, Fastolf in 1459. Waynflete's involvements with the property of both men in his role as an executor continued for several decades; it was the mid-1470s before he had finally concluded the problems provoked by Fastolf's nuncupative will and he was still involved in disputes relating to the Cromwell inheritance in the early 1480s. His activities as executor are dealt with below.

land in a number of large blocks. Appropriated religious houses were the source of a further 25% of the endowment. Such property was similarly a 'safe' buy. The property of religious houses was the least open to claim and its titles, perhaps, the best recorded. Furthermore it was cheap and, an important consideration, it was already amortised.[36] In addition to the Hospital of St John, the College received property from Sele and Selborne priories, hospitals at Romney, Brackley and Aynho and a chapel at Wanborough. The market value of this amount of land would have been anything up to £4,500 and although Waynflete incurred a wide variety of costs and charges, including those of arrangements at the papal curia in Rome, the costs were hardly great in proportion to this sum. The family and associates of Thomas Danvers, Waynflete's treasurer and principal adviser provided a further 20% of Magdalen's endowment while most of the remaining 20% was acquired from other people with whom Waynflete or his officials were familiar or related to or in areas where they had connections.

Waynflete made only one purchase of land before the foundation of Magdalen College in 1458 but during this period he also obtained two smaller grants of property. His first purchase, in May 1455, was from John Audley, eldest son of James, Lord Audley.[37] In later years Audley prospered, becoming Lord Treasurer under Richard III, but in 1455 he was in acute need of ready cash and Waynflete was able to exploit Audley's discomfort to secure a good bargain. Audley had to raise cash to meet an obligation falling due on 1 November 1455. His original price was apparently £300, but Waynflete secured a discount by paying him £200 in advance of completion to enable him to pay his debt on time. For this sum Waynflete obtained two manors in Hampshire, at King's Somborne, ten miles west of Winchester in the Test valley and at Enham, three miles north of Andover; and a quarter acre block of tenements near Temple Bar on the edge of the city of London. The Hampshire estates together were worth about £28 per annum net and the Temple Bar estate about £14.[38] The latter, however, was in poor condition and both Waynflete and the College needed to invest heavily there in new buildings and renovations.[39] Nevertheless a purchase rate of less than five years' value was a bargain by any standard and the location of the Hampshire property was conveniently near Winchester.

Waynflete made no more purchases until 10 March 1458, by which time the annexation of the Hospital of St John the Baptist and the refoundation of

---

36 On the immense problems which could arise over obtaining mortmain licences see S. Raban, *Mortmain Legislation and the English Church*, Cambridge 1982. Fastolf himself failed to found a college at Caister because he was unable to obtain a mortmain licence, *PL*, no. 570.

37 MC Enham A.89. The following eight paragraphs are taken from Mills, *op. cit.*, 35–41.

38 MC Enham, B.191; Sombourne Regia A1; Temple Bar 52

39 Mills, *op. cit.*, 51, 88; Between 1472 and 1475 for example, Waynflete invested £120 in repairs at Southwark, MC Receivers Accounts, Box D, nos 11, 17, while between 1491 and 1506 the College spent at least £500 there.

Magdalen Hall as a college had been completed. On that date he bought the manor of Otterbourne, Hampshire from Sir William Fiennes, Lord Say and Sele. Fiennes, like Audley, was in need of the money and this was another good bargain for Waynflete. The manor was worth about £17 per annum clear and Waynflete paid £180, a ten years' purchase rate. He was clearly acting on the advice of Thomas Danvers in this case. Fiennes was Danvers' brother-in-law at the time and he assigned the entire £180 to Danvers in settlement of an undisclosed obligation.[40]

A third purchase, his last until 1468, was made by Waynflete in 1459. On 9 February he bought the reversion of two large estates in north-east Lincolnshire from Sir Gervaise Clifton. These were the manors of Saltfleetby and Multon Hall on the coastal fens about nine miles north-east of Louth. This was a much more substantial purchase than the previous ones for Waynflete paid £800 for the reversion of the property. He had to wait until 1475 to take possession.[41] The lands, which belonged to Sir John Gra, were worth about £50 per annum thus giving a 16 years purchase rate. Evidently Clifton had been lending Gra money for he was granted the second reversion of Saltfleetby by Gra in 1451 and of Multon Hall in 1453, together with annual pensions of £10 from each.[42] Waynflete may have learnt about Multon Hall as Lord Cromwell's executor for there had been a long-running dispute between Cromwell and Gra over this manor.[43] Probably it was this which led him to Clifton or Clifton to him. However, Clifton was no stranger to Waynflete; he had been sheriff of Kent in 1451 and would have been in contact with Waynflete for they were both appointed to the legal commission in that county which followed Cade's rebellion of 1450.[44] This was at the same time that Clifton obtained his interest at Saltfleetby. There cannot have been many buyers around for the reversion of estates in a remote location when the owner and his wife was still alive but it was exactly the kind of place in which Waynflete was interested. From his

<hr/>

40 MC Otterbourne 137, 139; Macnamara, *Memorials of the Danvers Family* 155.
41 MC Multon Hall 48, 77, 98.
42 MC Multon Hall 60, 62, Saltfleetby 3, 37a.
43 MC Multon Hall 10, 70, 136. Gra had mortgaged the manor to Cromwell in the 1430s but the latter retained it despite a claim by Gra that he had repaid the mortgage in full. Cromwell's executors including Waynflete, paid £1000 to Gra in recompense, MC Cromwell Papers 317, 357. Fuller details of Gra's financial activities can be found in C. Richmond, *John Hopton*, Cambridge 1981, 14–21.
44 *CPR* 1444–51 388, 508; Waynflete, however, played little part in the work of the commission. According to King's Bench file 46, presentments were made to commissioners on a number of occasions – at Rochester 20–22 August, Maidstone 16–19 September, Canterbury 22–24 September and Dartford 22 October. R. Virgoe, 'Some Ancient Indictments in the King's Bench Referring to Kent 1450–52', in F.R.H. Du-Boulay, ed., *Kent Records; Documents Illustrative of Medieval Kentish Society*, Ashford 1964, 214–65. The commissioners of *oyer and terminer* in attendance on each occasion were listed at the top of the presentments; these show that Waynflete was never present. On one of the relevant dates, 22 August, he was at Eton College, Reg Waynflete i, fo 37*v.

knowledge of Cromwell's affairs he would have known the history of Multon Hall and if the title was good the College could well afford to wait until the deaths of Sir John and Lady Gra. In these circumstances the sixteen years' purchase price must have been regarded with satisfaction on both sides.

Waynflete also acquired a certain amount of property at this time without having to pay for it. Firstly, in January 1456, Magdalen Hall was granted an annual rent of £6 by a merchant in Colchester, Richard Wethyrmarsh.[45] This was apparently secured through the good offices of Simon Godmanston, the farmer of Brightwell and a fellow of Magdalen Hall and later of the College, whose family came from Essex. Simon Godmanston subsequently became one of bishop Waynflete's chaplains. Simon's father, John Godmanston, had been Waynflete's original agent in the acquisition of land for Magdalen Hall in the late 1440s.[46] A life interest in the rent was reconveyed to Wethyrmarsh and by 1477 at the latest it had reverted to Magdalen.[47] Secondly on 20 September 1457, just before the foundation charter of the college was issued, Waynflete obtained the advowson of a small leper-hospital at Romney, Kent, from Sir John Fray, then Chief Baron of the Exchequer.[48] The patronage of a hospital such as this was of relatively little value to a layman but Waynflete was able to set in hand the hospital's annexation to Magdalen together with its annual income of about £6. This, however, was not done until 1481. Thirdly in November 1458, Waynflete secured for Magdalen the manor of Stainswick, Berkshire, worth about £14 per annum, as a charitable grant. The grantor of this property had originally conveyed it to Waynflete and other trustees to be passed on to Winchester College but this proved abortive since the necessary mortmain licence could not be obtained. A reconveyance to Waynflete allowing any charitable use of the property enabled him eventually to give the manor to Magdalen in 1476.[49]

In the autumn of 1459 Waynflete acquired two more advowsons, those of Sele Priory, Sussex and Dodnash Priory, Suffolk.[50] These came from the Duke of Norfolk; there is no evidence of any payment made to Norfolk for these and perhaps they were in return for some political favour. Waynflete was still Chancellor at this time and thus in a position of considerable influence. They were, however, of considerable value; the estates of Sele Priory were worth about £53 per annum to the College at the end of the fifteenth century while those of Dodnash were estimated in 1459 to be worth about £40. Waynflete clearly obtained them in the expectation that they would be annexed to Magdalen.

[45] MC East New Hall 7, 3.
[46] There are no clues to indicate how Waynflete initially came in contact with this family of minor Essex gentry; the connection made have been made through the Duke of Buckingham for Godmanston was one of the stewards of the central circuit for him, C. Rawcliffe, *The Staffords, Earls of Stafford and Dukes of Buckingham*, Cambridge 1978, 203.
[47] MC Bursary Book 177–80, fo 2r.
[48] MC Romney 9.
[49] MC Stainswyke 4, 19, 44.

Norfolk's licence to the prior of Sele, dated 11 March 1459, spoke of the priory being granted to any abbey or college.[51] Waynflete had sent a scout up to Dodnash to inquire about the priory and its estates a month before his deal with Norfolk was struck.[52] In the event only Sele was annexed to Magdalen, in 1473, and not without some difficulty. It is unclear why Dodnash was not also joined to the College; it survived independently until 1525 when it was suppressed in favour of Cardinal Wolsey's colleges at Oxford and Ipswich.[53]

The acquisitions and annexation of the Hospital of St John had already shown how valuable the patronage of decayed religious houses could be to a collegiate foundation and Waynflete was presumably able to use his influence in 1459 to obtain anything that might be available. He nevertheless relied on the Danvers' family connections to acquire land. Thomas Danvers was not to become treasurer of Wolvesey until 1478 but he had been an intimate member of Waynflete's episcopal household for many years before that, representing the bishop's borough of Downton in the critical parliament of 1459. He also represented Downton in 1470–1, 1472–5, 1478, 1483, 1484 and Hinton in the parliament of 1467–8. The election of the burghal representatives to parliament for both of these boroughs was very much under the control of the bishop of Winchester. Thomas Danvers' hand also emerges in the Romney and Stainswick deals which fall either side of the purchase of Otterbourne from Danvers' brother in law. Sir John Fray was also a brother-in-law of Danvers, through the latter's half sister Agnes while the grant of Stainswick came from Joan Danvers, of the Berkshire branch of the family.[54] In the 1480s Waynflete was again able to utilise Danvers' family connections in order to purchase further significant properties.

Waynflete's gathering together of an endowment for Magdalen College made no further progress between Henry VI's deposition and 1468. He bought nothing in this period. The future of Magdalen must have seemed uncertain. It was not until Waynflete had secured the confirmation of the College's charter of foundation and the Hospital charters from Edward IV in October 1467 that he began again to buy land for his college.

In 1468, three months after obtaining the confirmation, he bought a small estate in Hampshire, worth about £5 per annum for £100.[55] During this time also, the College itself had received two small grants of land from close associates of Waynflete, one in Oxfordshire, the other in Somerset. The Hampshire estate, at Rotherwick near Basingstoke was sold to Waynflete by John Haydock, a member of an established Hampshire landowning family.[56] The small Somerset

50 MC Sele 36A.
51 MC Sele III.
52 MC Arch C.I.2.12 [Letters 1460–1800], fo 13.
53 Knowles and Hadcock, *Medieval Religious Houses: England and Wales*, 156.
54 *Memorials of the Danvers Family*, 143–4, 511–13.
55 MC Cowfold 20.
56 Haydock's father had served on several Hampshire commissions in 1449 alongside Waynflete, *CPR 1446–52*, 299.

property was at Ford, near Taunton, a town dominated by the property of the bishopric of Winchester. It was obtained by the college through the connections of William Darset, one of Waynflete's chaplains and rector of Brightwell whose family came from Taunton.[57] The grant in Oxfordshire at Clifton and Deddington came from a widow living in Banbury[58] and was conveniently near not only the Winchester estates at Adderbury but also existing College properties at Bloxham, South Newington and Nether Worton. The College as well as the bishop of Winchester was a familiar landlord in this part of Oxfordshire and Thomas Danvers too had property at Adderbury.[59]

Acquisitions of this kind, however, were only incidental to Waynflete's principal designs. In sum these three were only worth £11 per annum and with the building of the College now in progress further substantial endowments were urgently needed. By 1469, eighteen months after the building of Magdalen had started, Waynflete turned his attention to the valuable estate of Sir John Fastolf, which had been a subject of acrimonious dispute among rival claimants ever since the old man had died, aged 79 and without heirs, on 6 November 1459.[60]

Waynflete's involvement with Fastolf began in July 1449, not long after his promotion to the episcopate. At that time he was among a group of men who were granted lands by Fastolf as a feoffment to use.[61] This feoffment to use and others like it were made as part of Fastolf's attempt to fulfil the desire which dominated the last decades of his life – the foundation and endowment of a college of seven priests and seven poor men to pray for his soul, at Caister Castle in Norfolk. The fact that he left no heirs of the body doubtless increased his enthusiasm for the project. Fastolf did not content himself with making provision for the establishment of Caister College after his death; throughout the 1450s he made repeated attempts to obtain a licence to amortise land for its endowment in order to set up the foundation under his personal guidance. As chancellor Waynflete was among the people whose aid Fastolf invoked in repeated attempts to obtain the required licence.

> I write now to remember yow agayn to meve my lordes of Caunterbury and Wynchestre for the licence to be opteyned that I myght haue the morteisyng withowte ony grete fyne in recompence for my longe seruice

57 MC Ford and Taunton 2, 7; on Darset see *BRUO* i, 544.
58 MC Clifton and Deddington 24.
59 *VCH Oxford* ix, 16.
60 These disputes over the disposal of Fastolf's inheritance are well documented. Papers relating to the inheritance survive in the Magdalen College archives and in addition the Paston Letters are a major source for the progress of the legal wrangles concerning his substantial property. For Fastolf's wealth and its sources see K.B. McFarlane, 'The Investment of Sir John Fastolf's Profits of War', in *England in the Fifteenth Century: Collected Essays*, 1981, 175–97.
61 *CCR 1447–54*, 228; *CPR 1446–52*, 300.

contyned and doon vnto the Kyng and to his noble fader . . . I pray yow acqueynte me and yow with a chapellyn of . . . my lord Chaunceller; for seyng the Kynges disposicion.[62]

It is unclear why this licence was never forthcoming; perhaps the sum involved was considered too great. Waynflete while chancellor did not succeed in granting this request and does not appear to have made much effort on Fastolf's behalf. Equally, however, there is no evidence that he may have realised the possibilities for Magdalen College at this stage; it is clear from Fastolf's will that he was anxious to be commemmorated in the East Anglia area, even if Caister College was not to be a possibility. Waynflete would have found it difficult to persuade him to change his plans to support an Oxford college which had already been founded. Had Waynflete hoped to seize the land when Fastolf died, it would be reasonable to expect that he would not have let almost twenty years elapse before doing so, even allowing for the uncertain political conditions of these years.[63]

Fastolf died in November 1459 leaving a nuncupative will under which John Paston I was to receive the bulk of his property in Norfolk and Suffolk on condition that he established the chantry-style college at Caister.[64] It seems that Paston expected and was prepared to face some opposition, especially in view of the fact that the nuncupative will superseded a written one made in June of the same year. Within a week of Fastolf's death John Paston's brother William and William Worcester (who had been secretary to Fastolf) arrived in London to discuss the matter with Waynflete who was still chancellor, and the most important of the executors.[65] After this visit Waynflete issued a statement in which he set out his advice to the executors. He seems at this point to have taken upon himself the role of chief executor; as bishop he would have been thoroughly familiar with the procedure relating to the granting of probate while as chancellor he was in a position to authorise the issue of writs.[66] He advised

62 *PL*, no. 570.
63 Mills, *op. cit.*, 44 suggests that Waynflete may have had designs on the Fastolf property as early as 1459 when the problem of the nuncupative will became apparant.
64 Nuncupative wills were not unusual; in the seventeenth century they were restricted by law to be valid only when they concerned property worth less than £30 but no such limit existed in the fifteenth century. According to the *Provinciale* of William Lyndwood such wills were valid if there were at least two honest witnesses, *Register of Henry Chichele 1413–43*, ed. E.F. Jacob, 4 vols, Canterbury and York Society, 1943–7 vol. ii, p. xx.
65 A letter written back to John Paston I described the visit and said of Waynflete 'I fund hym well dysposyd in all thyng and ye shall fynd hym ryth profytabyll to yow. And he desyryd me to wrythe yow a letter in hys name and put trust in yow in gaderyng of the good togeder.' *PL*, no. 86. The other executors were John Paston, Thomas Howes, John Lord Beauchamp, William Yelverton, William Worcester, Friar John Brackley, John Stokes, the abbot of Langley and William Jenney.
66 William Paston had requested the issue of a writ of *Diem clausit extremum*, directed to the escheators in relevant counties ordering an *inquisition post mortem*. *PL*, no. 86.

that the goods be kept in a safe place until the executors 'or the moste part of tho that he put hys grete trust vppon speke wyth me and [make] declaraion to me of hys last wille, to the accomplysshment whereoff I wolle be special gode lord . . .'. He also ordered that Fastolf be buried in accordance with his rank and that alms and rewards to the servants should be paid immediately so the recipients, '. . . be better disposed and to pray for the wellfare of hys soule'.[67]

As yet there is no suggestion that Waynflete even considered having designs on some of Fastolf's estates for the endowment of Magdalen College. That arose later out of the deadlock reached over the administration of the property. After his initial appearance as foremost executor Waynflete faded from the scene and remained aloof from the disputes which arose over the nuncupative will. A letter from the abbot of Langley to his fellow executor John Stokes refers to a meeting of the executors held in London 12 May 1460[68] but no details of its decisions have survived and there is no evidence that Waynflete attended, although he was in London at the time. Fastolf's estates and goods extended beyond the boundaries of the diocese of Norwich thereby coming into the category of *bona notabilia* and thus it fell to the Archbishop's court to grant the probate of his will. Since the will was challenged by William Yelverton and several of the other executors, the matter came before the auditor in the archbishop's Court of Audience at Lambeth. It is referred to as being in the Court of Audience as early as May 1460 and the dispute dragged on there intermittently until 1467 without any satisfactory conclusion having been reached: as the amount of evidence increased so did the confusion, particularly since a number of witnesses swore to totally different stories on different occasions.[69]

The first hint of possible involvement by Waynflete in an attempt to resolve the stalemate reached in the Court of Audience can be seen in a letter of 29 January 1467 written by Thomas Danvers to John Paston II. Unfortunately the letter states, as was often the case, that the messenger has been entrusted with the most important information but Danvers wrote:

> All-so, in asmoche as I vnderstode by yow that money shuld cause you conclusion in youre mater this next terme, and ye wull be at London on Monday at nyght er Tewsday by none I truste I haue studyed such a mene that vp-on surete as ye may make to gete yow an c li. or cc mark to be lante vn-to yow for an halfe yere with-oute any cheuysshaunce or loose of good by yow.[70]

While nowhere is it stated that Danvers' arrangement had been made at the behest of Waynflete, in view of the close relationship between the two men, it is likely that this was the case. No more is heard of Waynflete's involvement for the rest of 1467 but the money, if Danvers' offer was availed of, seems to have

[67] *PL*, no. 887.
[68] *PL*, no. 889.
[69] *PL*, no. 895.
[70] *PL*, no. 745.

achieved its aim. On 26 August 1467 Paston and Thomas Howes were awarded probate of Fastolf's will in accordance with the nuncupative will which named them as chief executors.[71] Two days after this grant was made, on 28 August, Waynflete the archbishop of Canterbury and Lord Beauchamp as feoffees of Fastolf, formally released certain of Fastolf's lands in Norfolk and Suffolk including Caister Castle to John Paston II;[72] an action suggesting that they concurred with the grant of probate. Although Waynflete, Yelverton and other feoffees released many of the disputed manors to Paston in 1468 this settlement did not last. In October of the same year some of the feoffees enfeoffed the Duke of Norfolk with Caister[73] – the nucleus of the Fastolf inheritance. This was the start of another half-decade of disputes which continued until the Duke's death in 1476.

Ten years had passed since Fastolf's death and his hoped-for college was as far away as ever. It is at this stage that Waynflete can be seen taking positive action to bring the disputes to an end and obtaining the property to add to the endowment of his own foundation. Hints of this occur in an undated letter from William Worcester to Margaret Paston, probably written in 1468,

> . . . my lord of Wynchestre ys disposed to found a college yn Oxford for my seid maister to be prayd for, yhyt wyth moch lesse cost he myght make som othyr memoriall also yn Cambrygge, and yt weere of ii clerkys, iii or iiii scolers, founded at leest wyth the value of gode benefices and ryche parsonages that mygh be purchased the aduowsons wyth moch lesses goodes then lordhyppes or maners may.[74]

The first practical step was taken with the granting to Waynflete by Thomas Bourgchier, archbishop of Canterbury of the authority to settle the multiplicity of disputes. On 5 May 1469 the archbishop cited Waynflete and Lord Beauchamp to appear before him on 20 May, 'to take upon them charge of Sir John Fastolf's will if they will do so . . .'[75] The grant of administration was made on 13 February 1470 and Waynflete became the sole executor. This move was in keeping with the archbishop's jurisdiction for he regularly reserved to himself the right to recommit the administration of an estate if the first-appointed administrators failed in their duties. In the instance of Fastolf, Bourgchier was conscious both of Fastolf's own wishes and of the delays in carrying them out, for he had been one of the original feoffees to use.[76] John Paston II approved of this move. By this time he must have been so sick of the disputes and uncertainties which had deprived him of his home at Caister and resulted in the death of at least one member of his household that one gets the impression that he was

[71] MC Chartae Regiae 50.8.ii; *PL*, no. 92 headnote.
[72] MC Norfolk and Suffolk 47.
[73] *PL*, no. 200.
[74] *PL*, no. 727.
[75] *Paston Letters*, ed. J. Gardner, 1904, no. 605, abstract of BL Additional Charter 18, 249.
[76] *CCR 1447–54*, 228; *CPR 1446–52*, 300.

ready to grasp at any hope of a settlement. Worcester on the other hand counselled the Pastons to be wary of Waynflete.[77]

An agreement was signed between Waynflete and Paston in the Priory of St Mary Overy in Southwark on 14 July 1470.[78] The preamble to this set out the bishop's position, reciting Fastolf's intentions and explaining that the issues of the land were wasted due to 'grete variances' having arisen between the feoffees. Waynflete cited four reasons to justify his involvement: (i) Fastolf had placed special trust in him both as feoffee and as an executor; (ii) the other living executors had renounced their rights; (iii) he pitied the unfulfilled charitable intentions of Fastolf (iv) the lands were being wasted and the disputes were very complex. The intention of the agreement was to end the disputes and accomplish at least part of Fastolf's intentions. The lands of Fastolf's estates were carefully divided between John Paston II and the bishop; all the relevant documents, the whereabouts of which had been one of the matters of dispute, were to be stored in the Southwark Priory of St Mary Overy and both parties were to have keys and access at will; finally Waynflete undertook to obtain at his own expense a papal dispensation to move the place of Fastolf's college from Caister and within six months of getting seisin of the lands he was to endow in perpetuity at Magdalen College Oxford, seven priests and seven poor scholars who would pray for Fastolf's soul.

Over the next few months Waynflete can be seen to be actively fulfilling his side of the agreement, in particular relating to the expulsion of the Duke of Norfolk from Caister.[79] Even before he had been officially appointed sole executor Waynflete had set in motion the action necessary to obtain the papal dispensation for Caister College. In January 1470 William Darset, his chaplain, left England to obtain a dispensation from the Holy See. The stature of the messenger indicates the importance Waynflete attached to his mission as does the fact that his destination and the purpose of his journey were kept secret. Publicly Darset was supposed to be on a pilgrimage; he died in Rome and even several years later a number of Waynflete's circle believed that he had died en route to the Holy Land.[80] Darset's visit was successful; several bulls were issued

---

77 Worcester wrote to John Paston II (John Paston I had died 1466 but the case was carried on by his sons) '. . . he wenyth that the Byshop wyll be a-yenst yow, in so myche that [he] auysyd my modyr to counsell yow that ye shold labor to my lord Cardynall that the seyd Byshop shold not be admyttyd to take admynystracyon. *PL*, no. 339; see also *PL*, no. 727.

78 *PL*, no. 252; Waynflete often used the priory of St Mary Overy, which was adjacent to his episcopal palace in Southwark, as the headquarters of his administration whenever he was in London.

79 In December 1470 Waynflete came to an agreement with the Duke of Norfolk who undertook to release Caister to the bishop on payment of 500 marks, *HMC* 4, 461; the Duke's co-operation may have been related to Henry VI's readeption which placed the Duke in a weaker position vis a vis Waynflete. He seized Caister again after Edward's restoration in 1471, *PL*, introduction p. lxxx.

80 MC deeds, Sele 90, 91.

to Waynflete on 13 and 14 April, including a dispensation to permit Magdalen College to appropriate the revenue assigned by Fastolf for his foundation.[81] Once he had obtained the necessary licence it was obviously worth while for Waynflete to reach an amicable agreement with the Paston family as soon as possible.

Among the Fastolf papers at Magdalen College is a document which although undated evidently belongs to this period: a statement about the transfer of Fastolf's foundation to Oxford. While it is largely concerned with Paston's reasons for agreeing to the transfer at the same time it seeks to justify Waynflete's position and it may have been a legal opinion prepared in the bishop's interest.[82] It is self contradictory in places, as if those who drew it up were seeking to answer in advance all possible objections which might be brought against the scheme. It begins by making clear that Waynflete had the right to dispose or lands which came from Fastolf's inheritance, not as a feoffee or executor but a purchaser of lands, 'by a newe bargayn made by-twixt hym and Ser John Paston'. It is careful to emphasise that the charge of founding a college had been laid by Fastolf on Paston personally, not attached to possession of the land. Thus Waynflete is not under an obligation as a result of his acquisition of these lands to undertake the foundation of Caister college. Subsequently it is stated the executors of Fastolf had the power to interpret and determine his wishes in the case of any difficulties and as Waynflete is now sole executor his approval alone is adequate justification for the transference of the foundation to Oxford. In addition it is pointed out that under the 1467 grant of probate, responsibility for the foundation rested with John Paston II alone. Overall the emphasis in the document is on justifying the transfer of Fastolf's endowment to Oxford on all possible grounds. This legal option disregards known facts at least once; the Pastons are exonerated from failing to establish a college at Caister Castle because they could not obtain a mortmain licence 'by any means' despite their efforts. This clearly disregards the fact that in 1464 Edward IV granted to John Paston I,

> . . . to haue licens lawfully mad to make and found a college of vii prestes and vii porefolk at Caster in Flegge in Norfofolk, for the soule of Sir John Fastolff, knyght, thei to be indued with certeyn rent and otherwise aftir th'entent and effect as is specifijd in a bille therof signed by the Kyng;'[83]

The statement set out six 'considerations' concerning the proposed transfer. The first three articles are largely lost through the mutilation of the documents. The fourth stated that the increase of learning of the law of God will be the result of

---

81 *CPL 1458–71*, 341–2.
82 *PL*, no. 914.
83 *PL*, no. 686. The surviving licence is a draft, dated 10 September 1464; it is not clear that it John Paston ever obtained it. The draft goes on to state that the king will assist in having the foundation '. . . inacted and auctorised in the parlement next holden . . .'; this certainly did not happen.

the transfer and this consideration has made the 'claymers and occupiers . . . more tretable and better willed . . .' The fifth suggested that the support of colleges in Oxford was of more merit than many other deeds of piety. This opinion was certainly in accord with Waynflete's own beliefs but not Fastolf's whose will (and the alternatives he laid down to be followed if a college at Caister proved impossible to establish) show that he favoured the older idea of a chantry style college rather than the support of educational foundations which were becoming increasingly popular. The final consideration was a pragmatic one, Magdalen College already possessed a suitable mortmain licence.

No problem appears to have arisen to hinder the transfer of Fastolf's inheritance to Oxford once the requisite papal dispensation had been issued.[84] Due to the absence of collegiate records prior to 1480, it is difficult to be sure exactly when the endowment began to be utilised by the college. There are at least six men, however, who came to the college during the latter half of the 1470s who are referred to as Fastolf fellows.[85] In Waynflete's statutes for the college provision was made for (i) four chaplains and two fellows of the college to say masses for the souls of Fastolf and his wife (ii) a junior fellow in priest's orders to remember them in his masses; (iii) seven senior Demys to pray for them in return for batels of one penny per week. Fastolf's name was included in the general list of collegiate benefactors who were to be prayed for daily.[86]

Waynflete may have achieved his aims by these agreements of 1470 but the Paston family's troubles were far from being over. Waynflete can be seen occasionally trying to help them; suing for the release of lands in chancery and re-negotiating with the duke of Norfolk who was proving obdurate.[87] John Paston II continued to trust in the bishop's aid and in February 1471 he bound himself to fulfil his obligations towards Waynflete as best he could.[88] Other members of his family had less faith in Waynflete's efficacy and good will and several letters of 1472 suggest that Waynflete had never handed over the acquittance of Fastolf's goods.[89] A further amended agreement in 1473 of which few details have survived, seems to have been no more advantageous to the family.[90] The failure of Waynflete's agreement of 1470 to solve the problems of the Pastons and in particular to restore Caister castle to them can be attributed to several factors. The Duke of Norfolk was in an advantageous position since he possessed the force necessary to hold Caister physically while politically he was greatly in favour with Edward IV. The character of John Paston II who 'seems to

---

84 *CPL 1458–71*, 341–2.
85 Edward Lupton, Thomas Brampton, William Bawdry, John Cowper, William Picter and William Nutbeam; they are referred as Fastolf Fellows from 1476 onwards, MC CP/8/49 fo 3r–v.
86 *Magdalen Statutes*, 56–57.
87 *HMC 4*, appendix, 461.
88 *PL*, no. 260.
89 *Ibid.*, nos 216, 270, 271.
90 *Ibid.*, no. 277.

have had little heart for hard bargaining and little competence in it'[91] did not help. Perhaps most important, however was the fact that after the endowment was actually transferred to his foundation Waynflete's own efforts to resolve the disputes were not as energetic as they had been hitherto. On one occasion John Paston II described him as the 'slawe[slow] Bysshope off Wynchester';[92] a good description of the way he acted on behalf of the Pastons after 1470.

What advantage accrued to Waynflete as a result of his activities as executor to Fastolf? As shown, he remained aloof until the controversies and disputes over the various wills attributed to Fastolf had reached stalemate in the court of audience. Once involved however, he moved quickly and shrewdly, obtaining the necessary papal dispensation, being appointed sole executor and coming to terms with John Paston II. Magdalen College was the beneficiary of his efforts but its gain required not only considerable trouble on Waynflete's part but also a substantial financial investment even before necessary repairs on properties were carried out. Waynflete paid out at least £1036 to twelve separate claimants to Fastolf's lands and in addition there were substantial legal costs relating the to acquisition of the papal dispensation.[93]

Waynflete's settlement, however, paid little regard to the observance of John Fastolf's wishes. Throughout the last ten years of his life and in all his feoffments and wills Fastolf continually expressed his desire to found a chantry style college with seven priests and seven poor men. At the same time, he recognised that his executors might be as unsuccessful as he himself had been in attempts to obtain a mortmain licence. Thus he had made provision for an alternative scheme which included the provision of three priests in St Benet's monastery near Caister who would pray for his soul and that of his wife and also the support of priests in several other religious houses in Norfolk.[94] Waynflete knew of this alternative scheme and there appear to have been no particular obstacles hindering it yet it was ignored. Waynflete's use of lands from the Fastolf inheritance for the endowment of his own college in Oxford ran completely contrary to Fastolf's wish that he might be commemorated and prayed for locally in Norfolk by chantry priests.

Waynflete's gradual involvement with the settlement of Fastolf's affairs from 1469 was not undertaken in isolation from his other interests. In October 1469 when he was concerned with the Pastons and their problems, he also secured the reversion of a valuable manor in Lincolnshire which formed part of the estate of Ralph, Lord Cromwell, for whom Waynflete was also an executor.[95]

91 *Ibid.*, p. xlix.
92 *Ibid.*, no. 292.
93 Calculated by Mills, *op. cit.*, 50 from a list in MC Fastolf Paper 97.
94 *CPR 1458–71*, 341–2.
95 Ralph, Lord Cromwell planned to use some of the substantial profits acquired during his career as a soldier and politician, to found a collegiate church at his newly-built castle at Tattershall. He initiated the project towards the end of the 1430s issuing a foundation charter in November 1440. At that date Cardinal Beaufort headed the list of

Also, on 30 September 1469 he had initiated the process for the annexation to Magdalen College of Sele Priory, Sussex, of which he had obtained the patronage in 1459.[96] The timing of this was presumably dictated by his chaplain, William Darset's forthcoming visit to Rome.

Cromwell had died in 1456 richer than Fastolf and with even more claims against his estate. Like Fastolf, Cromwell had a castle, at Tattershall in Lincolnshire and he had also charged his executors with the endowment and construction of a collegiate church there.[97] By the time therefore, that Waynflete was contemplating taking over the administration of Fastolf's estate, he would already have been well aware of the problems and the rewards involved in such a task.

Cromwell had obtained a royal licence for his college during his own lifetime[98] and his executors' main task was to complete the rebuilding of Tattershall Church, already begun by Cromwell and the adjoining college.[99] By April 1469, some £10,000 had been spent on this with an estimated £1200 still needed to finish the work. This had been raised by various disposals of Cromwell's property but the executors' difficulty was compounded by the existence of the two heiresses, Cromwell's nieces. These were Maud and Joan Stanhope, the daughters of Cromwell's sister Maud by Sir Richard Stanhope. Both had married well: Joan to Sir Humphrey Bourgchier, son of Henry, Earl of Essex and Maud, three times – to Robert Lord Willoughby, to Thomas Neville, younger brother of Richard, Earl of Warwick and to Sir Gervaise Clifton, the vendor of Multon Hall to Waynflete. Clifton was executed in 1471 after the battle of Tewskbury and Maud Willoughby was left a wealthy and formidable widow, with whom both Waynflete and the College devoted much time to doing business. It was from her on 16 October 1469 that Waynflete obtained for Magdalen the reversion of her manor of Candlesby, worth about £80 per annum.[100]

patrons and it is not therefore surprising that after Beaufort's death in 1447, that the new bishop of Winchester, born less than fifteen miles from Tattershall and with continuing family connections in Lincolnshire, should replace his predecessor as bishop of Winchester, among those involved with Cromwell's projected college. The first reference to Waynflete's involvement occurs in 1454 when Cromwell received a licence enabling him to grant a substantial parcel of land to a number of feoffees to use, including Waynflete, *CPR 1452–61*, 199–200.

[96] MC Sele 36A.

[97] *Early Lincoln Wills*, 138.

[98] The licence was issued on 14 July 1439, *CPR 1436–41*, 292.

[99] There are two main sources for the settlement of Cromwell's affairs between 1455 and c.1480: The Cromwell papers at Magdalen and *Report on the MSS of Lord de l'Isle and Dudley Preserved at Penthurst Place* i, HMC 1925, 172–212. Cromwell's career and family connections are outlined in *Complete Peerage* iii, 552 and E. Myatt-Price, 'Ralph, Lord Cromwell', *The Lincolnshire Historian* ii, 1957, 4–13. The building accounts for the castle are printed in *The Building Accounts of Tattershall Castle 1434–72*, ed. W.D. Simpson, Lincolnshire Record Society lv, 1960.

[100] MC Candlesby 43a. The remainder of this chapter is taken from Mills, *op. cit.*, 52–79.

Thus in the autumn of 1469, two years after the building of Magdalen had been started and armed with an up-to-date royal pardon Waynflete was simultaneously planning the acquisition of property worth substantial sums – in East Anglia, Lincolnshire and Sussex. Fastolf's Norfolk manors alone were worth some £240 per annum. In Sussex, Waynflete's preoccupation was with the lands of Sele Priory which were worth some £50 per annum. There was particularly good reason at this time for beginning the process of annexing Sele Priory to Magdalen in the early 1470s. In January 1470, as mentioned above, William Darset, Waynflete's chaplain undertook a journey to Rome to obtain the papal licence necessary for the transfer of Fastolf's proposed college to Magdalen. Travel to Rome, and business at the curia once there, was expensive and the more that could be done during one visit the better. While there Darset also obtained a routine bull for Waynflete absolving him from visiting Rome on grounds of age and also briefed Waynflete's lawyer in Rome about the annexation of Sele Priory.[101] Thus when the Sele annexation commission was issued on 30 September 1469; Waynflete was already planning a journey to Rome. While in Rome Darset also obtained the bull of 13 April 1470 on behalf of Eton College which cancelled its merger with St George's Windsor.[102] Despite obtaining the bull in 1470 it was not until July 1474 that Magdalen College was finally able to take possession of the estates of Sele Priory, after a variety of legal difficulties.[103]

This marks the end of the second major phase of Waynflete's land acquisitions. During the next five years he bought only one estate. The construction of the chapel at Magdalen had begun in the summer of 1474 and together with the continuing works at Eton must have occupied much of Waynflete's time. Furthermore, he was still deeply involved in administering the complex affairs of Ralph Cromwell in the East Midlands but not without profit; the one manor which he bought in this five year period had formerly belonged to Cromwell and Waynflete obtained it on very favourable terms.

This was Quinton, Gloucestershire, an estate worth £30 p.a. which had formed part of the settlement made upon Sir Gervaise Clifton and Maud Lady Willoughby in 1462. She sold it to Waynflete on 13 March 1475 for only 400 marks, only nine years' purchase, and its value to the College was naturally enhanced by its relative proximity to Oxford.[104] For the same reason it was of less value to Maud Willoughby, the bulk of whose property was in south eastern Lincolnshire, in the vicinity of Tattershall. She may also have had a more direct motive for the sale, for part of the purchase price was assigned to a London merchant to whom she was in debt.

Maud Willoughby was at the centre of all Waynflete's efforts to wind-up Cromwell's affairs. She was a difficult woman with whom to do business

101 *CPL 1461–84*, 13 April 1470.
102 *Ibid.*, 343, also 13 April 1470.
103 MC Sele 17.
104 MC Quinton 67.

especially since she was firmly convinced that she had not received as much from her uncle's estate as she should have done. On one occasion it was necessary to employ the combined resources of the Lord Chief Justice and William Lord Hastings to persuade her that this was not the case.[105] In the late 1470s and early 1480s there was much work for lawyers to do to ensure that her titles were secure, to convince her to claim no more and to make satisfactory provision for the descent of her property after her death. This process included the arrangements already made in 1469 for her valuable manor of Candlesby to pass to Magdalen when she died. These were confirmed in a series of further agreements between Waynflete and Maud Willoughby, and her final release of the manor to Magdalen in return for an annuity from it of £80 eventually took place in September 1479.[106] When his deal was finally concluded Waynflete felt it was money well spent to reward her with 100 marks.[107]

Having effective control of such a large estate in East Midlands and Lincolnshire over a period of 25 years gave Waynflete much influence in the region. This was enhanced by his own family connections at Wainfleet near the Lincolnshire coast about 17 miles east of Tattershall, the site of the other grammar school which he had founded. Throughout this period Waynflete's influence in the region was principally exercised through John Gygour, the warden of Tattershall College. Gygour had been a foundation fellow of All Souls in 1437 and a fellow of Merton from 1438–1454. From here, possibly under Waynflete's influence, he moved to Eton until in 1458 he was promoted by Waynflete to Tattershall. He retained the wardenship for 46 years, until his death in 1504 and combined it from 1471–83 with the wardenship of Merton College. At Tattershall he received a stipend of £20 per annum plus the profits from a number of benefices in the vicinity.[108] He was something of an intellectual with a notable collection of books bequeathed to his two colleges but he was also a man of business and it was no doubt for this reason that Waynflete offered him the wardenship of Cromwell's college. Five of his letters to Waynflete and Danvers have been preserved at Magdalen.[109] These show that in the 1470s and 1480s Gygour was Waynflete's main intermediary, not only with Maud Willoughby but also with a wide variety of other claimants to a share in Cromwell's riches. He was also responsible to Waynflete for the building of the church and college at Tattershall and for the construction and administration of the grammar school at Wainfleet.

However influential Waynflete and his agents were in the area, they had to take due account of the claims of other influential men there. In the 1470s and until his death in 1483 the most powerful magnate in the East Midlands was

[105] MC East Bridgeford 10.
[106] MC Candlesby 43, 54b.
[107] MC Candlesby 65a.
[108] *Report on the Manuscripts of Lord de l'Isle*, i, 179.
[109] MC East Bridgeford 10, 25; Arch C.I.2.12, fos 4, 5, 6.

William Lord Hastings, Lord Chamberlain to Edward IV.[110] The value of having Hastings' favour and support in business matters comes over strongly in Gygour's letters and other Cromwell papers at Magdalen. Not surprisingly, Hastings was keenly interested in the fate of Cromwell's estates. Some of them he purchased and others he laid claim to in the courts.[111] On one occasion Hastings was at Sleaford with the Lord Chief Justice disputing a title to two of Cromwell's manors claimed also by Maud Willoughby. Hastings, according to John Gygour,

> . . . toke a gret displesur bothe wyth my lady and wyth hur cownseyl in so muche that he wrote he trustyd to God avys to ese his hart up on them that let hym of his purpose. And so on the morrowe ther was take an othyr direccyon more to his plesure.[112]

Despite his local connections and his own wealth, in Lincolnshire Waynflete was far from his own power-base in the south and his influence in that county could never match that of a magnate like Hastings.

One device which Waynflete adopted to smooth the passage of his business with Hastings was to use members of the latter's indentured retinue as his agents in the area. One of these was Sir Gervaise Clifton, son of Maud Willoughby's former husband who was sheriff of Nottinghamshire and Derbyshire three times between 1471 and 1487 and who acted for Waynflete in the former county.[113] Waynflete went further than this; significantly, in the list of Hastings' retainers drawn up in 1474, is the name of Thomas Danvers, Waynflete's closest associate, treasurer and friend.[114] In this case Waynflete was not only using one of Hastings' retainers as his agent but had obviously arranged for his agent to join the list in the first place, for self-evident and sensible reasons. For why would Hastings have wanted to retain Danvers, a cultured country gentleman from Oxfordshire who divided most of his time between London, Oxford and Winchester? Surely for exactly the same reasons as Waynflete considered that Danvers should be associated with Hastings. It was an arrangement of mutual benefit and there was little chance that Danvers would be called on to do battle for his lord.

Apart from Candlesby and Quinton, Waynflete acquired one other property for Magdalen from Cromwell's estate. This was the manor of East Bridgeford near Nottingham, worth about £11 a year, which he obtained in 1481. East Bridgeford belonged to Cromwell through his wife Margaret Deyncourt, who

---

110 On Hastings, see *DNB* 25, 148.
111 *Report on the Manuscripts of the Late RR Hastings Esq*, HMC 1928, i, 118; MC Cromwell Papers 354.
112 MC East Bridgeford 10.
113 W.H. Dunham, 'Lord Hastings' Indentured Retainers 1461–1483', *Transactions of the Connecticut Academy of Arts and Sciences* xxxix, 1955, 130, 1–3; MC East Bridgeford 33.
114 *Ibid.*, 118.

had predeceased him and since his own death in 1455 had been held by Joan Bourgchier, Lady Cromwell, Maud Willoughby's younger sister, although Maud herself had asserted a claim to it. By agreement between Waynflete and his co-executors, Sir John Fortescue and Sir Thomas Tirell, the manor descended to Waynflete on Lady Cromwell's death. However there had already been legal difficulties over Cromwell's title to Deyncourt lands held in right of his wife and Waynflete admitted privately that his title to East Bridgeford was not good.[115] He therefore purchased for 200 marks a release of interest from the surviving branch of the Deyncourt family. This was done on 3 February 1481. Even so, Gygour for one, still did not think the title absolutely secure.[116] In fact it was soon challenged by Francis, Lord Lovell, another man of considerable influence in the East Midlands.[117] Lovell's grandmother, Alice Deyncourt, had been Cromwell's sister-in-law. In 1481 he claimed that the descent of East Bridgeford was entailed to the heirs of the Deyncourt barony, to which he had succeeded on the death of his grandmother in 1474. To back up his claim, on 23 June 1481, he sent a force of men under Sir Robert Markham to take possession of the manor. The news was reported to Waynflete by Sir Gervaise Clifton, who said that he could not eject Lovell's men himself, '. . . considering he is a lorde, I may not soo deale,' he pleaded. Clifton did offer however, to support Waynflete if the latter went to law and suggested that he might well be able to use the Hastings' network to build up support against Lovell, thus ensuring that Hastings himself was favourable. 'I truste to God', Clifton continued, 'to make you bigge ynough to try with him within the shire, with help of such others as ye shall easily have the goode willes of, soo that my lorde Chaumbreleyne take not the contrarie part'.[118] But Lovell was a powerful man, rising and difficult to thwart. In view of his legitimate interest in Cromwell's estates, Gygour feared for the future of Tattershall College itself if Lovell was still around after Waynflete had died.[119] Fortunately that contingency did not arise.

The dispute over East Bridgeford was complicated by a separate agreement which Waynflete had made with Lovell's grandmother, Alice.[120] This was for the endowment of chantry priests on her behalf at Magdalen, an idea which was being canvassed as early as 1457, when Alice, as nurse and governess to Prince Edward of Lancaster would have been in regular contact with Waynflete at court. A satisfactory contract proved difficult to draw up[121] but in due course when Alice died in 1474, her feoffees conveyed to Magdalen the manor of

---

[115] MC East Bridgeford 10.
[116] MC East Bridgeford 14.
[117] MC East Bridgeford 33.
[118] MC East Bridgeford 17.
[119] MC Arch C I.2.12 fo 4.
[120] MC Misc. 148; Cromwell papers 425–6.
[121] MC Arch C.I.2.12, fo 1.
[122] MC Cromwell papers 427.

Doddington, Northampton, worth about £14 a year.[122] In 1481 Francis Lovell now claimed title to Doddington as well, on the same grounds as for East Bridgeford. There is no evidence of the progress of the dispute until a compromise was reached in February 1483, a month after Lovell had been made a viscount and when his influence was reaching its peak under the patronage of Richard, Duke of Gloucester. Under this, the College surrendered Doddington, while Waynflete's title to East Bridgeford was confirmed. Perpetual prayers were to be said at Magdalen for Lovell and his progenitors and in return for this bonus, Lovell granted to Waynflete the patronage of a chantry at Wanborough, Wiltshire.[123] This compromise was satisfactory to both sides: Doddington and East Bridgeford were almost of equal value, while perpetual remembrance in College was a much coveted attainment, of which Lovell fairly soon had need. To Lovell, the patronage of Wanborough chapel must have been next to worthless but when Waynflete had it appropriated to the college, it produced an income of £19 per annum. Lovell clearly took good note of Waynflete's willingness to buy the advowsons of such places, for a year later, on 27 February 1484 he sold him another – the advowson of Brackley Hospital, Northamptonshire. For this Waynflete paid 200 marks; again after its appropriation to the College it was worth about £15 per annum.[124]

Waynflete's efforts to ensure that an adequate endowment was built up for his college continued until the very end of his life. The third and final phase, between 1479 and 1486 was marked by two main features; the acquisition and appropriation to Magdalen of a number of decayed religious houses, including Brackley and Wanborough and the arrangement of several transactions by Thomas Danvers, still treasurer of Wolvesey. Danvers, who had played an important role in the negotiations for collecting Magdalen's endowment since the 1450s, was perhaps even more important to the bishop as Waynflete's health began to fail. The possessions of the five religious houses finally annexed to the college in 1486 were worth about £94 a year and the property acquired by Danvers on Waynflete's behalf about £98. In the same period Waynflete also acquired other property worth about £50, including East Bridgeford.

The final transactions arranged by Danvers concerned the purchase of property from Margaret Leynham, Danvers niece through his half-sister Agnes. The property consisted of the manors of Standlake, Oxfordshire and Tubney in Berkshire, both only about six miles from Oxford. Margaret's husband Sir John Leynham had acquired them in 1464 in part satisfaction of a debt of £600 from a Sir Robert Corbet. Sir John died on 29 September 1479 and on 4 December his widow sold Tubney to Waynflete for £400 plus an annuity of £10 from the manor.[125] She also assigned Standlake to the college for pious use after her death and this was sold by her executors to Waynflete for 400 marks.[126] These were

123 MC East Bridgeford 21.
124 MC Brackley B.207.
125 MC Stanlake 29A; MC Tubney 2, 29.
126 MC Stanlake 14, 8.

high prices. Tubney was worth about £17 a year and Standlake about £11, giving purchase rates of 23 and 24 years respectively,[127] but the price probably reflected the capital value of timber in the extensive woods on the manors. There are a number of references to sales of this wood in the college accounts and the wood which could be brought to Oxford by river could be used by the college itself. None the less it is fair to say that Waynflete was prepared to pay a high price for good land so close to Oxford.

In 1482 Danvers sold to Waynflete a Wiltshire manor, Corton, which he had lately inherited. Corton had belonged to the Hungerford family until 1463 when it was sold to Danvers' great-uncle, Richard Quatremayn, to help pay off debts for the ransom of Robert Hungerford, captured in Aquitaine in 1452. Danvers was his great uncle's principal heir when the latter died in 1477. He sold Corton, worth about £9 a year to Waynflete for 200 marks, a fifteen years purchase price.[128] Also in the early 1480s Waynflete began a series of financial deals with another Oxfordshire landowner, John Barantyne of Chalgrove, to whom Danvers was distantly related. Danvers obtained them from Barantyne who had fallen on hard times. The two manors, Chalgrove and Henton, were soon sold to Waynflete by Danvers for a considerable profit. Calculating from later values he had paid about £500 for Henton and Wynnale combined plus an uncertain amount for a small property at Henton bought in 1481.[129] Waynflete, however, paid him £740 for the lot.[130] Similarly Chalgrove, which had cost Danvers £450 was bought by Waynflete in December 1485 for £560.[131] But it is clear that this was Danvers' agreed reward, for Waynflete himself had financed the loans to Barantyne which had led to the property coming into Danvers hands. It is likely that some finance was raised from the issues of the Winchester manors which it was Danvers' responsibility to collect. But even if Danvers made a good profit on his deals with Barantyne, perhaps as much as £300, Waynflete too obtained a reasonable bargain. He paid £1,300 for secure titles to two estates close to Oxford worth together about £61 annually, a twenty-one times purchase rate.

Between 1481 and 1484 Waynflete obtained several other estates for the college near Winchester and Oxford. In 1481 he paid just under £100 for a property at Skyres, in Wootton St Lawrence near Basingstoke, purchased from a Hampshire landowner, Ingelram More, with whom Waynflete had had dealings before over the purchase of nearby Cowfold in 1468.[132] There is little indication of the value of Skyres at this time but Waynflete perhaps paid a purchase rate of about 30 times. A further high purchase rate was paid by Waynflete in 1482 for

127 MC Tubney 52, Tubney 79.
128 MC Corton 19.
129 MC Henton MC Henton 14c, 44c, 41a, 51c, 56, 56d and Chalgrove 30a, 32a, 31a 9b.
130 MC Henton 3d.
131 MC Chalgrove 34A.
132 MC Skyres 89, 81; as at Tubney the presence of a fair amount of woodland on the estate would have been reflected in the purchase price.

an estate at Beenham Valence, half-way between Reading and Newbury, where Waynflete paid £173 to Robert Strangbone for land whose annual return was only £5.[133]

Nearer Oxford in 1482 Waynflete bought a manor at Harwell where the Bishopric of Winchester already had extensive property. This estate, known as Brown's manor, was bought from John Erley for £209, an exactly computed twenty years' purchase rate. Although this manor was leased in 1486 for £11 annually, its average income from it in the 1490s was only about £8, because of substantial rebuilding and repair work needed there.[134] Petersfield in Hampshire, purchased in January 1484 from Richard Rede for £100 was a better bargain. The property was worth about £13 annually and Waynflete also promised to have Rede and his wife prayed for regularly at Magdalen, a promise not apparently fulfilled. Rede sold for further small parcels of property in Petersfield to Waynflete in July 1486 for £20.[135]

One major feature of the endowment of Magdalen was the annexation to it of six decayed religious houses and two parish churches. This falls principally into the last phase of Waynflete's acquisitions although it is clear that he had recognised the value of such places and their lands considerably earlier. This may well have been as a result of his experience at Eton College for the endowment of which Henry VI utilised extensively the lands of alien priories which had been seized by his father. At his time of the foundation of Magdalen itself apart from taking over the Hospital of St John, Waynflete had also planned to appropriate to the college, Luffield Priory in Northamptonshire, although for unknown reasons this did not succeed. After this he had then acquired the advowsons of Romney Hospital (1457) and Sele Priory (1459) as well as Dodnash Priory in Suffolk (1459). The annexation of Sele had been completed in 1471 and confirmed in Rome in 1473 and of Romney in 1481, although in this case papal consent was not obtained until 1486.

The rest of these places were acquired in the last three years of Waynflete's life. In August 1483 he acquired Wanborough chapel as part of the agreement with Lovell over East Bridgeford and Doddington. Two months later he acquired the Hospital of St James and St John at Aynho, Northamptonshire from William FitzAlan, Earl of Arundel, in return for regular and perpetual prayers before a special altar in the chapel in Magdalen College.[136] This was followed in March 1484 by Waynflete's second deal with Lovell when for 200 marks he bought from him the hospital of St James and St John at Brackley, about six miles from Aynho. The value of these two hospitals was about £19 annually combined but they were of particular value because they were near Oxford and close not only to other property south of Banbury which Magdalen had

133 MC Beenham Valence 3.
134 Mills, 'The Foundation, Endowment and Early Administration of Magdalen College', 68.
135 MC Petersfield 90, 31, 64.
136 MC Aynho 4.

inherited from the Hospital of St John but also to the Winchester episcopal estate at Adderbury. On 16 November 1484 Waynflete was given the advowsons of Slimbridge in Gloucestershire and Findon in Sussex by William Berkeley, Earl of Nottingham, again in return for prayers at Magdalen. Waynflete also gave Berkely in exchange one of the tenements in Southwark which had formerly belonged to Fastolf.[137] These two livings were not appropriated by the college until almost twenty years after Waynflete's death. In the meantime they remained in the hands of Thomas Danvers who made the necessary arrangements for their transfer in 1501.

The patronage of such places must have been of relatively little value to aristocratic patrons like Norfolk and Lovell who might otherwise have had difficulty in finding a willing buyer for a rundown place like Brackley Hospital. On the other hand their value to Waynflete was enhanced because their possessions were already safely amortised and generally held on secure and well-recorded titles.

Considerable moral and physical dilapidation was the main prerequisite for initiating the process of annexing these religious houses to a new vigorous arm of the church in the form of an educational institution like Magdalen College. This was not hard to observe. The revenues at Brackley had been declared insufficient for the Hospital's functions and worship in 1425, long before Waynflete was concerned with it.[138] At Sele Priory there were by 1444 only three monks were left besides the prior; it was in debt to London merchants and its revenues were assigned in advance and there was scarcely any religious observance. The dilapidations there grew worse in the 1460s, assisted by the extravagance of the prior, Richard Aleyne, formerly cellarer at Battle Abbey, where according to his own claim he had been 'as well at ese as eny monk of his degre in England'. By 1466 Aleyne owed £150 to two London cloth merchants and when a warrant for his arrest for non-payment was issued, John Arundel, Bishop of Chichester sequestrated the Priory since its religious functions had ceased.[139] Waynflete had been patron of Sele since 1459 but it was hardly in his interest to interfere in these troubles, for the worse the state of the priory the easier its annexation to Magdalen could be justified. Perhaps the decadent Prior Aleyne, appointed in 1462, was chosen for this very reason.

There was a similar tale at Selborne Priory in East Hampshire which was annexed to the college in 1484 having always been in Waynflete's own patronage as Bishop of Winchester.[140] Waynflete himself had sequestered Selborne in 1463 because of its ruinous condition; by this time there were only four canons

---

[137] MC Slimbridge 26; the college was already entitled to a portion from Findon Rectory by virtue of its appropriation of Sele Priory, MC Sele 55.

[138] *Fourth Report of the Royal Commission on Historical Manuscripts* part 1, 1874, appendix 459.

[139] MC Sele 85, 49, 98.

[140] D. Le Faye, 'Selborne Priory 1233–1486', *Proceedings of the Hampshire Field Club and Archaeological Society* xxx, 1975, 65.

in residence beside the prior. This act gave Waynflete an opportunity to examine the Priory's books and he discovered that its potential net income was about £70 annually.[141]

The process of annexation was straightforward if time-consuming. The patron as plaintiff had to argue his case before a commission of the diocesan bishop and if necessary against the counter-claims of vested interests such as cathedral chapters and archdeacons. Evidence of decay and want of worship was heard and recorded at length and witnesses called to testify. The hearing concerning Selborne for example took place over five working days in 1484 and the record of the proceedings shows that the emphasis was very much on annexation as a last resort, as a means of preserving part of the original intentions of the priories founder, following Waynflete's own vain attempts to improve it.[142]

In the matter of the annexation of Selborne Waynflete was both plaintiff and judge. His commission convened at his manor in Farnham on 6 September and issued its decree of annexation on the following Saturday. Other proceedings seem also to have proceeded easily; at Wanborough chapel for example the bishop of Salisbury's commission convened on 2 September 1483, two weeks after Lovell's grant of the chapel and conducted its business at Waynflete's manor of Waltham rather than in its own diocese. The archdeacon of North Wiltshire was content to leave his interest to the Winchester lawyer who acted also for Magdalen College.[143] Similarly the bishop of Lincoln's commission for Brackley Hospital sat at Waynflete's manor of Esher.[144] Both these commissions took about six weeks to conclude matters and issue decrees of annexation. The bishop of Chichester's commission for Sele Priory was convened on 30 September 1469 but did not issue its decree until 25 June 1471.[145]

There was no obligation upon incumbents to resign their livings once decrees of annexation had been issued by the diocesan bishop and the college's possession could only take effect upon the first vacancy. This often meant a long wait. When Waynflete bought Brackley Hospital from Lovell, for example, he undertook to pay an additional 100 marks – 50% of the purchase price – if the Hospital was void of an incumbent within 14 days of completion but even Lovell could not persuade the old master to resign and Waynflete had to wait eighteen months for the decree to become final.[146] At Selborne he met the same problem. He rushed through the process of annexation in September 1484 at a time, when on his own admission he considered himself close to death but had to wait until August 1485 for the aged prior to resign. He was then granted a pension of £6 13s 4d from the priory's revenues and lived on for another four

---

141 Reg Waynflete i, fo 75*v; *Calendar of Charters and Documents Relating to Selborne and its Priory preserved in the Muniment Room of Magdalen College Oxford*, ed. W.D. Macray, HRS, 1891, 114–15.

142 *Ibid.*, 119–34.

143 MC Wanborough 29A, Appropriations 5.

144 MC Appropriations 8.

145 MC Appropriations 22, 7.

146 MC Brackley B.207, Appropriations 26.

years at Basingstoke Rectory.[147] In 1457 however Richard Vise the Master of the Hospital of St John had been persuaded to resign, tempted by an annual pension of £40 provided to support him until he could be found a comparable benefice.[148]

The prior of Sele was less amenable and fought back against the decree of annexation. The college could do little to move him, the papal bull of 8 February 1473 confirming the annexation, permitted Magdalen to take possession only upon the prior's death.[149] Waynflete's lawyer in Rome fought this, claiming that Aleyne had unlawfully alienated the possessions of the Priory and the Bishop of Chichester refused to listen to the college complaints. This persistence proved successful and on 13 January 1474 the Dean of Chichester was ordered to hold an inquiry.[150] At the same time Waynflete had been gathering support from some of Aleyne's creditors, by repaying some of their money in return for undertakings to continue proceedings for the rest.[151] The Dean's inquiry began on 28 May 1474 and on 11 July Aleyne was duly deposed, partly on the rather specious grounds that he had obtained his post simoniacally whilst still a monk of Battle Abbey.[152] The outcome of the proceedings was hardly surprising for not only did Waynflete have money and influence on his side but also the Dean of Chichester was his brother, John Waynflete. Aleyne was not easily defeated and appealed to Rome but although his case dragged on there until 1480 but succeeded only in obtaining a dispensation to hold a secular benefice in conjunction with another monastic appointment.[153] At the same time, in Sussex, Waynflete isolated him by 'rewarding' a number of local men to give him no support.[154]

To ensure that annexations were not to be challenged in the future it was necessary to follow up the annexation process by obtaining papal confirmation of the proceedings. Much attention was paid to the detailed presentation of a good case to the Curia. William Darset in 1470 had left sufficient funds in Rome to cover the costs of a bull to confirm the Sele annexation which was not issued until 1473.[155]

Confirmations for all the other annexations were sought at the end of 1485. It was not until then that Selborne and Brackley had fallen vacant and the proceedings before the bishop of Lincoln in respect of Aynho had been

---

[147] MC Appropriations 3; 'Selborne Priory', 67.
[148] MC *Chartae Concessae* 63, 58.
[149] *CPL 1458–71*, 1.
[150] *Ibid.*, 356.
[151] MC Sele 58, 59.
[152] MC Appropriations 1a, Sele 1.
[153] *CPL 1458–71*, 13, 493, 725.
[154] MC Sele 77, 109; Shoreham 2.
[155] MC Sele 93 – he left 160 ducats for it, twice the amount spent in 1470 on the bulls for Eton and Caister combined; in the event two-thirds of this was not needed, its cost being almost the same as for Eton – MC Sele 90.

completed.[156] Decrees for Romney and Wanborough had been issued some time before.[157] A lawyer expert in these matters was briefed in London to instruct a colleague in Rome to present the necessary petitions in the curia. Draft bulls were prepared for consideration by papal officials and sufficient funds transmitted from London by the Bardi bank. The petitions seeking confirmation of the annexations dwelt heavily on the dilapidations of the houses in question which had led to the decline or collapse of religious observances. it was also pointed out that the revenues of Magdalen College were insufficient for its needs.[158] The basic fee for a bull of confirmation seems to have been half the annual value of the places in question but because of their rundown condition there was some difficulty in calculating correct values. It was important to be accurate for a future check by a diligent papal agent might well reveal an error. The lawyer's instructions were specifically amended to stress that the values given for the five places were only the best estimates which could be made at the time of their annexation. The estimate given to the lawyer in Rome was £79, probably a slight underestimate. The basic cost of the bulls would therefore be about £40 and it was calculated in some detail that another £22 would be needed to cover miscellaneous expenses and a further £21 was allowed to cover unforseen expenditure. Waynflete already had £12 to his credit at the Bardi's Rome branch. The lawyer, James de Montelato of Pisa, could therefore draw up to £95 but he was clearly told not to hesitate to spend more if necessary for Waynflete would refund him with interest. The urgency of the business was also stressed in the brief. Waynflete was old and ailing. If the matter was not concluded before his death the college would find it difficult to do so by itself, on grounds of cost and lack of friends. The business was concluded in time but only just. Several letters requesting further information passed between Montelato and President Mayew in May and June 1486.[159] The confirmation for Wanborough was granted on 9 May 1486, for Brackley and Aynho on 26 May, for Romney on 30 May and for Selborne on 6 June.[160] Since President Mayew did not receive the news of this until a letter of 16 August from Montelato Waynflete may not have been aware of the success of his Roman negotiations before his death on 11 August of that year.

Amassing suitable property which would provide a substantial endowment for his college in Oxford was clearly a matter which occupied much of Bishop Waynflete's time and money throughout his episcopate. In his dealings with vendors he proved a shrewd businessman; he was also well able to push through the necessary proceedings to allow him to annex moribund religious houses.

[156] MC Appropriations 2.
[157] Romney 5 Dec 1481; Wanborough 14 Oct 1483 – MC Appropriations 6, 5.
[158] MC Appropriations 19 [Draft instructions to lawyer at Rome], printed in *Selbourne Charters*, 136–140.
[159] *Selborne Charters* 143.
[160] *CPL* 1471–82, 165 (Wanboro), 183 (Brackley & Aynho), 175 (Aynho), 126 (Selborne).

The collection of the endowment was an activity which fitted into the other activities of Waynflete's own household – it is his chaplains and other household officials who often witnessed conveyancing deeds. Thomas Danvers, treasurer of Wolvesey, masterminded many of the negotiations. Bishop Waynflete used his friends and his contacts to find possible sources of land and on occasion, he made use of his role as an executor to pursue the interests of his college. The single mindedness with which he built up an endowment for his Oxford foundation clearly demonstrates his commitment to his college and everything that it stood for.

As already seen, the foundation of a collegiate community in Oxford was high among Waynflete's priorities. This is evidenced by the rapidity with which he set the foundation in motion after he had become bishop. It can also be seen in the amount of time, energy and money he expended on gathering together the endowment for his foundation. Throughout his episcopate and especially in the period 1450–59 and 1467 onwards, the amassing of such an endowment was a dominant interest; a project to which he devoted a huge amount of his time, energy and resources. Many members of his household were involved in the land transactions and their names appear again and again in agreements relating to land acquisition. Waynflete was constantly on the lookout for opportunities which he could exploit for the purposes of collecting a significant endowment. He was a shrewd businessman and could be unscrupulous in the hunt for endowments, as seen in his treatment of Fastolf's wishes. The resulting endowment was a most generous one but the college saw little of it during the bishop's lifetme. He was reluctant to relinquish control over the property even though it was destined for the college and it was only in the last few years of his life that Waynflete began to transfer the wealth of land to his Oxford foundation. The transfer was far from being complete on his death and it was not in fact until the beginning of the sixteenth century that the college was finally in full control of the property which had been collected for it in the thirty-five years between 1450 and 1486.

Plate 8   Exterior of Waynflete's chantry, Winchester Cathedral

Conclusion

William Waynflete's last months were a period of physical decline. He returned from his London manor of Southwark to his episcopal palace at Bishop's Waltham for the last time in late December 1485. Earlier in the 1480s, when he himself was reaching his mid-seventies, he seems to have become more aware of impending mortality and he had begun to make arrangements for the future of his beloved Magdalen College. He could no longer travel to oversee his interests, although he continued to receive visitors, in particular Richard Mayew and others connected with Magdalen College Oxford. In April 1486 his condition may have declined further for in that month he drew up his will. It was witnessed at Bishop's Waltham on 11 April 1486. A chantry chapel, dedicated to his spiritual patron, Mary Magdalen was complete and a tomb was waiting to receive his body.

His will was conventional in form.[1] In it he bequeathed his soul to Almighty God, the Virgin Mary, Mary Magdalen and the patrons of his cathedral. He left substantial sums to cover the costs of his funeral and for the celebration of the trental of his obit. The main religious houses of the city of Winchester, the priests serving the city parishes, the fellows and scholars of Winchester College, New College and Magdalen College were all remembered in the will. A lengthy codicil remembered the 126 members of his household. His executors – largely members of his household – were directed to ensure that those properties he had collected which were not part of the temporalities of the see of Winchester were to pass to his Oxford foundation. The residue of his goods were to be used for pious purposes, for masses for the salvation of his soul and those of his families and friends and to relieve the necessities of his college and for relief of the poor.

William Waynflete's death marked the end of a generation; he was the longest-serving surviving member of the episcopal bench dating from Henry VI's first reign.[2] Most bishops by the mid 1480s belonged to a younger generation. Yet despite his advanced age, until the last months of his life Waynflete continued to play an active role within his diocese and was strenuously working for the welfare of his Oxford foundations.

For more than half a century he had been a foremost figure in the world of English education, alert to new developments and ideas, shaping the educational practices which were to predominate in the decades after his death. Of all

---

[1] MC *Chartae Regiae* 43; printed in Chandler, *Life*, appendix xxviii.
[2] Two appointees from Henry VI's reign remained after Waynflete's death; Thomas Kempe, bishop of London since 1448, died in March 1489. John Hales, bishop of Coventry & Lichfield, provided in September 1459, did not die until September 1490.

his diverse educational involvements, the most influential was to be the establishment of Magdalen College and Magdalen College School. Waynflete's Oxford foundations were clear precursors to Colet's St Paul's – founded 1509 and often lauded as a milestone in the arrival of Italian educational ideas in England. Waynflete was an active proponent of the new technology of printing in the cause of education. The teachings of Italian grammarians influenced the methods and materials used at Magdalen College School and many of its earliest pupils were to be important grammarians of the early sixteenth century.

Study of his educational activities illuminates a number of aspects of his character, in particular the enormous energy and enthusiasm which he brought to all of his projects and his open-mindedness which is reflected in his readiness to accept new ideas about the teaching of grammar and the new medium of printing. Above all he excelled as an administrator and it was this aspect of his abilities which originally brought him to the attention of Henry VI and subsequently led Henry to support his elevation as bishop of Winchester. Waynflete's personal loyalty to Henry VI as well as his conscientiousness can be seen in the history of his later relations with Eton College when despite heavy commitments elsewhere he helped to support the college and fulfilled the moral obligation which had been laid upon him by the king in his 'Will'.

Energetic, enthusiastic, open-minded in accepting new developments, conscientious, shrewd in business affairs and perhaps not a little dogmatic in his views, William Waynflete measures up well against his contemporaries on the episcopal bench. His most striking characteristic was his reluctance to relinquish control over any aspect of his affairs and while he did delegate tasks to others, his subordinates were kept on a tight reign. Perhaps most remarkable was the consistent success and range of his interests – diocesan, educational and architectural. The image of the ideal bishop portrayed by St Paul in his epistle to Titus would have been both familiar and accepted in the fifteenth century:

> The bishop must be blameless as the steward of God, not self-willed, not soon angry, not given to wine, not given to filthy lucre but a lover of hospitality, a lover of good men, sober, just, holy, temperate, holding fast the faithful word as he that been taught that he may be able by sound doctrine both to exhort and to convince the gainsayer.[3]

Waynflete did not fill all the criteria; in particular he appears likely to have been self-willed and his vocational interests lead one to feel that he was primarily interested in convincing gainsayers on points of good grammar rather than doctrine, despite his theological training. Yet Waynflete played a valuable role as a member of the episcopate, a conscientious bishop strongly committed to the interests of his diocese and was accepted as such by his contemporaries.

Waynflete's experiences as a schoolmaster dominated his life. His success as provost of Eton College made possible his promotion to the episcopate. The

---

3   Epistle of Paul to Titus, Titus I, 7.

resources – financial, political and administrative – at his disposal as bishop of Winchester were ploughed back into education. His foundations with their particular emphasis on the teaching of grammar and the provision of a solid educational grounding were appropriate memorials to the interests of a man who throughout his career played an outstanding role in the promotion of the education in England.

APPENDIX I

William Waynflete's Land Acquisitions, 1455–1486[1]

The following list contains all the properties bought or otherwise acquired by Waynflete and later conveyed to Magdalen College Oxford.

The figures given for annual values are based on mean annual receipts between 1489–1498, except for Clifton, Oxfordshire, based on 1482–1488 (after when it was included in the general Oxfordshire receipts); Candlesby, based on 1499–1509; and Slimbridge and Findon, based on 1506–1514. Figures for individual properties in Hampshire are based on values recorded in the *Valor* of the College estates prepared at Michaelmas 1485 (LC I, fos 79–89); in the annual accounts receipts from these properties were always grouped together. Values of these properties are given in brackets.

DATE	PROPERTY	£	SOURCE	DATE TO MC
20/5/1455	Enham			12/07/1481
	King's Sombourne	(42)	John Audley	10/05/1481
	Temple Bar			1/10/1482
12/01/1456	Ramsey, Essex	£6	Richard Wethyrmarsh	by 1477
27/10/1456	Hospital of St John	£73	Henry VI	5/07/1457
10/03/1458	Otterbourne	(£17)	Sir John Fray	5/12/1481
27/11/1458	Stainswyke	£14	Joan Danvers	6/07/1476
9/02/1459	Multon Hall			
	Saltfleetby	£49	Sir Gervaise Clifton	17/07/1477
	Somercotes			
3/08/1459	Sele Priory	£53	John, Duke of Norfolk	25/06/1471
11/10/1465	Clifton	£2	John Phippes	11/10/1465
30/10/1465	Ford	£4	John Bishop	12/10/1482
12/01/1468	Cowfold	(£5)	John Haydock	20/02/1481
1/02/1469	Southwark	£16	Exectors of Sir John Fastolf	18/02/1483
16/10/1469	Candlesby	£70	Maud Willoughby	1498
14/07/1470	Lands in Norfolk and Suffolk	£75	John Paston, executor of John Fastolf	4/11/1483

[1] This appendix is taken from Appendix I of Mills, 'The foundation, endowment and early administration of Magdalen College Oxford'. More details relating to their acquisition can be found in chapter 2 of that thesis. I am grateful to Mr Mills for permission to use this material.

DATE	PROPERTY	£	SOURCE	DATE TO MC
2/05/1471	Hartshorne, Southwark		Lawrence Downe	18/02/1483
1/12/1471	Boreshead, Southwark		William Moleneux	18/02/1483
24/03/1473	HighBeerhouse, Southwark		Thomas Buckley	18/02/1483
13/03/1475	Quinton	£30	Maud Willoughby	1/11/1480
1/09/1475	Taunton (value with Ford)		John Bishop	12/10/1482
24/05/1477	Enham		Thomas Hende	12/07/1481
14/04/1479	Hillhampton	£3	Thomas Welles	8/11/1481
4/12/1479	Stanlake	£17	Margaret Leynham	1/10/1482
	Tubney	£11		
10/01/1481	Skyres	(£3)	Ingelram More	
3/02/1481	East Bridgeford	(£11)	Ralph Cromwell's estate	1/10/1482
20/02/1481	Andover (with Enham)		Thomas Harper	12/07/1481
26/02/1482	Beenham Valence	£5	Robert Strangbone	20/10/1482
4/10/1482	Harwell	£8	John Erley	10/06/1484
26/10/1482	Corton	£9	Thomas Danvers	20/01/1483
16/08/1483	Wanborough Chapel	£19	Francis, Viscount Lovell	14/10/1483
1/10/1483	Aynho Hospital (with Brackley)		William, Earl of Arundel	29/08/1485
3/01/1484	Petersfield	(£13)	Richard Rede	22/01/1485
8/01/1484	Skyres (with Skyres)		John Roger	unknown
27/02/1484	Brackley Hospital	£19	Francis, Viscount Lovell	7/05/1484
20/07/1484	Henton	£31	Thomas Danvers	20/05/1486
	Wynnale			
10/09/1484	Selborne Priory	(£50)	Waynflete, as patron	8/08/1485
20/11/1484	Slimbridge	£9	William, Earl of	1/09/1501
	Findon		Nottingham	10/07/1502
10/12/1485	Chalgrove	£30	Thomas Danvers	20/09/1488
6/07/1486	Petersfield (with Petersfield)		Richard Rede	unknown
11/07/1486	Ashurst & Lancing (with Sele)		John Fagger	unknown

APPENDIX II

William Waynflete's Itinerary, 1447–1486

The major source for Waynflete's itinerary is his episcopal register but other information as to his whereabouts has been added where the detail is known. His attendance at parliaments has not generally been noted except for the fairly rare occasions where there is evidence that he was present on a specific day. For the period of his chancellorship the patent and close rolls have proved valuable, dating under the great seal usually being a good indicator of the location of the chancellor on that date.[1] However, this evidence is confused by the number of routine acts dated from Westminster and bishop Waynflete is unlikely to have been present for all of these occasions, for example in November 1459 when acts were dated from Westminster and Coventry on alternate days or even on the same day. In the case of clashes of evidence between the patent and close rolls and the Winchester episcopal registers I have relied more on that of the registers which elsewhere have shown themselves to be a reliable guide to the bishop's whereabouts; these clashes are not common; usually the different sources compliment each other.

ABBREVIATIONS PECULIAR TO THE ITINERARY

CCR	*Calendar of Close Rolls*
CPR	*Calendar of Patent Rolls*
Gx	*Register of the Common Seal*, ed. J. Greatrex
OG	*Register of the Most Noble Order of the Garter*, ed. J. Anstis
Southwark/Wmin	implies the bishop is recorded at both Southwark where he had an episcopal manor and at Westminster in this period.
Bp's Waltham	Bishop's Waltham

1447		
Southwark	7, 28 Oct.; 4 Nov.	I fo 1r
Westminster	11 Nov.	PRO C81/1546
Southwark	20, 27 Nov.; 2, 19 Dec.	I fo 1v
Eton	23 Dec.	I fo Ar
Southwark	30 Dec.	I fo 2r

1448		
Southwark	5 Jan.	I fo 2r
Canterbury	8 Jan.	I fo 1*r
Eton	11 Jan.	I fo 1*r
Southwark	17, 19, 26 Jan.	I fo 2r–v
Westminster	27, 30 Jan.	PRO C81/1456

---

[1] Wolffe, *Henry VI* 361.

Southwark	5 Feb.	I fo 3r
Eton	7 Feb.	ECR39/75
Southwark	12, 21, 26, 27; 15, 30, 31 Mar.	I fos 3r–v, 1*v
Esher	3 Apr.	I fo 4r
Southwark	8, 24 Apr.; 17, 21, 26 May	I fo 4r–v
Southwark	5, 6, 11 Jun.; 8, 10, 11, 20 Jul.	I fos 5r–6v
Farnham	31 Jul.	I fo 6v
Eton	16 Aug.	I fo 6v
Farnham	21, 23 Aug.	I fo s6v–7r
Marwell	20, 21 Sep.; 2 Oct.	I fos 7r, Av
Southwark	21, 23 Oct.; 18 Nov.	I fo 8r; Reg Bek 389
Westminster	19 Nov.	PRO C81/1546
Southwark	22 Nov.; 2, 5, 15 Dec.	I fos 8r–9r
Esher	21 Dec.	I fo 9r

1449

Winchester	Jan. [dates unknown]	WCM 22992
Southwark	12, 15 Feb.	I fos 9r, 2*r
Westminster	3 Mar.	PRO C81/1546
Southwark	6, 8, 15, 17, 20, 22, 28, 29 Mar.; 2 Apr.	I fos 9*v, 2*v, Bv; EHD IV, p. 206
Eton	8 Apr.	I fo 10r
Winchester	29 Apr.; 1, 2, 4 May	I fos 10v, 12r, 14v, 2*v
Southwark	9, 17, 18, 20, 27, 28, 30 May	I fos 14v, 15v, 2*v, 2*v, p. 471; Bek Reg 420

Eton	3 Jun.	I fo 15v
Winchester	11 Jun.	I fo 5*r
Southwark	12 Jun.	I fo 15v
Winchester	24, 25, 28, 30 Jun.	PRO C81/1546; I fos 4*v–5*r
Taunton	7 Aug.	I fo 16r
Southwark	16 Aug.	I fo 15v
Farnham	26 Aug.	I fo 16r
Southwark	29 Aug.	I fo 17r
Westminster	4 Sep.	PRO E28/79
Southwark	18 Sep.	I fo Cv
Farnham	22 Sep.	I fo Cv
Winchester	27 Sep.; 2, 5, 12, 23 Oct.	I fos 5*v–6*r
Southwark	5, 13, 21 Nov.	I fos 6*r–v, 17r
Westminster	26 Nov.	PRO E28/79
Southwark	1, 2, 3, 4, 5, 12, 13, 17, 19, 20 Dec.	I fos 6*v–7*r, Bv, 17v; PRO E28/79

1450

Southwark	20 Jan.	I fo 7*r
Westminster	21, 31 Jan.	CCR 1447–52 p. 194; I fo 7*r
Southwark	20, 21, 26, 28 Feb.; 1, 3, 5, 9, 11, 14, 17 Mar.	I fos 18r–v, Cr; RPV p. 172
Westminster	22 Mar.	PRO E28/80/31
Southwark	27, 29 Mar.	I fos 19r, 7*v
Eton	11, 12 Apr.	I fo 19v
Westminster	15 Apr. (at St James Hospt.)	I fo 20v
Windsor	23 Apr.	OG p. 135
Leicester	28 Apr.; 5, 6, 11, 14, 15 May	PRO E28/80/43; I fos 20r, 21v, 8*r
Blackheath	16 May	Flenley p130
Chertsey	11 Jun.	I fo 21v

Winchester	18, 20 Jul.	PRO E28/80.74; I fo 37r
Southwark	30 Jul.	I fo 22r
Westminster	4 Aug.	OG p. 139
Southwark	16 Aug.	I fo 6*v
Eton	17, 22 Aug.	I fo 22r–v
Westminster	28 Aug.	PRO E28/80/86
Southwark	30 Aug.	I fo 22r
Westminster	1 Sep.	PRO C81/1546/54
Southwark	1 Oct.	I fo 2*v(iis)
Guildford	8 Oct.	I fo 22r
Winchester	13, 15, 21, 23, 30, 31 Oct.; 2 Nov.	I fos 23r–v, 8*v,
Southwark	5, 15, 19 Nov.; 4, 14, 19, 20, 27 Dec.	I fos 9*r–v, 23v, 28v–29v, Cv

1451

Southwark	10, 22, 23, 30 Jan.; 4, 5, 11 Feb.; 16 Mar.	I fos 34r–v, 9*v–10*r
Farnham	21 Mar.	I fo Dv
Southwark	7, 8, 14, 19 Apr.	I fos 34r–v, 10*v
Eton	23 Apr.	I fo 35v
Farnham	3 May	I fo 10*v
Southwark	5, 7, 8, 10 May	I fos 10*v, 11*r–v, 12*v
Westminster	18 May	PRO E28/81/12
Southwark	22, 27 May	I fo 10*v
Windsor	29 May	OG p. 137
Westminster	31 May	PRO E28/81/27
Southwark	1, 3 Jun.	I fos 12*r–v
Westminster	5 Jun.	PRO E28/81/30
Southwark	9 Jun.	I fo 13*r
Winchester	2, 3, 5, 10, 12, 13, 15, 20, 24, 26 Jul.	I fos 14*r–v, fo 3r(2s); HMC VI p. 603
Southwark	29 Jul.	I fo 37v
Eton	15 Aug.	I fo 38v
Southwark	13, 16, 20, 31 Aug.	I fos 14*v; 7r(2s)
St Albans	14 Sep.	I fo 14*r–v
Coventry	3 Oct.	I fo 39r
Westminster	14, 22, 24, 29 Oct.; 6, 12, 18, 19,	I fos 39r–40r; C81/1546/57–9
(St James' Hospt.)	24, 27 Nov.	
Eton	10, 13, 16, 22 Dec.	I fos 40r, 41v, 42v
Southwark	28 Dec.	I fo 39v

1452

Westminster	21 Jan.; 11, 14 Feb.	I fo 15*r
(St James' Hospt.)		
Southwark	15, 16 Feb.	I fo 8r(2s)
Westminster	16, 24 Feb.	I fo 42r
Blackheath	27 Feb.	Benet p. 207
Southwark	12, 13, 15 Mar.	I fo 42r
Farnham	20 Mar.; 20, 22, 23, 26 Apr.	I fos 46r, 15*r
Esher	6 May	I fo 46v
Reading	11 May	
Sheen	18 May	PPC p. 127
Southwark	23 Jun.	I fo 46v
Esher	24, 29 Jun.; 4, 18, 28 Jul.	I fos 47r–48v, 15*v
Farnham	5, 6 Aug.	I fo 48v

Bp's Waltham	23, 28, 29 Aug.; 2, 19, 23, 28 Sep.	I fos 16*r, Ev, 49r
Southwark	2 Oct.	I fo 16*v
Esher	12 Oct.	I fo 49v
Southwark	17, 21, 27, 28 Oct.	I fos 49v, 50r, 18*v
Esher	9, 12, 13, 20, 22 Nov.; 16, 23, 24, 26, 28 Dec.	I fos 18*v–19*r, 50r–v, Fr
1453		
Southwark	5, 6, 9 Jan.	I fo 19*r, 56v
Esher	12, 16, 20 Jan.	I fo 57r, 29*r
Southwark	23 Jan.	I fo 57v
Esher	27, 29, 30 Jan.	I fos 57v–58r, 28*v
Southwark	6, 7, 15, 22, 24 Feb.; 1, 2, Mar.	I fos 20*v–22*r, 58r
Esher	4, 5, 6 Mar.	I fos 23*v, 58r
Reading	6, 16 Mar.	RPv p. 227; I fo 59r
Esher	27 Mar.; 8, 9, 22, 23 Apr.	I fos 59r, 25*r–v
Southwark/	26, 28 Apr.; 11, 14, 15, 16, 17, 26 May;	I fos 59v, 25*v, 26*r, PPC 130
Westminster	13, 14, 18, 20, 22 Jun.;	ECR 39/103, I fos 26*v, 61r
	3, 7, 10, 11, 12, 13, 14, 16, 18,	PPC 143; E28/83/12.26.29,
	20, 22 Jul.	30, 33, 29; I fos 27*v, 62r
Esher	10 Aug.	I fo 27*v
Winchester	5, 7, 12, 18, 22 Sep; 3 Oct.	I fos 28*r, 61v, Gv, 9v(2s), 10v(2s)
Westminster	14, 24 Oct.	Stones's chronicle p. 70; PPC p.164
Southwark	5 Nov.	I fo 61v
Esher	10, 11, 13 Nov.	I fos 61v–62r
Southwark	19, 21, 22, 28, 29 Nov.;	I fos 62v, CPR 143; Gx p. 110; PRO C81/1546/71
Southwark/Wmin	1, 5, 6, 9, 10 Dec.	I fos 62v, 28*r; PPC p. 165
Esher	22, 23 Dec.	I fo Gv
1454		
Esher	4, 7 Jan.	I fo 63r
Southwark	22, 26, 28 Jan.; 6, 8, 9, 11, 13, 15, 19, 26 Feb.;	I fos 63r–64v, 29*v; PRO C81/1546/73–5; E28/82/1, 2
	1, 5, 6, 10, 12 Mar.	I fos 64r, 66v, 29*v, 30*r
Esher	13 Mar.	I fo 66v
Southwark	15, 16, 17, 21, 22, 23 Mar.	PRO C81/1546/82; PPC 166; I fos 66v, 30*r
Windsor	25 Mar.	PR V p241
Southwark/Wmin	26, 29, 30 Mar.; 1, 2, 8, 10 Apr.	I fos 67r–v, 30*v PR V, 449–50
Esher	25 Apr.; 2, 3, 7, 8 May	I fos 67v–68v, 30*v
Southwark/Wmin	8, 13, 17, 18, 20, 21, 22, 24, 28, 29, 30, 31 May	I fos 67v, 68r, 31*r, PPC 181, 184, 188, PRO E28/84/7.16. 18, 19, 23, 24, 29, 33, 35
Esher	6, 8 Jun.	I fo 68v
Windsor	9 Jun.	PRO E28/84/49
Westminster	13 Jun.	PRO E28/84/51
Southwark/Wmin	27 Jun.; 5, 7, 8; Jul.	I fos 69r–v, 32*r; PPC 206; PRO E28/84/61
Esher	16 Jul.	I fo 70r
Southwark/Wmin	17, 18, 19, 20, 24 Jul; 7, 8, 9 Aug.	PRO E28/85/47, 51, 53; E28/86/36, 37; C81/1546/84; PPC pp. 208–9

Farnham	11 Aug.	I fo 69v
Bp's Waltham	22, 23 Aug.; 12, 16, 18, 21 Sep.; 3, 9, Oct.	I fos 69v–70r, 33*r–34*v
Esher	23, 29 Oct.	I fos 34*v, 70r
Southwark/Wmin	2, 6, 11, 12, 13, 15, 23, 30 Nov.	I fos 70v, 71r;
		PRO C81/1546/87, 88
Westminster	1, 2, 4, 5 Dec.	PRO C81/1546/90, 92, 94
Esher	21 Dec.	I fo Iv
Westminster	30 Dec.	PRO C81/1546/98

1455

Esher	1 Jan.	I fo 71v
Windsor	9 Jan.	PL 512
Esher	24 Jan.	I fo 34*v
Southwark	4, 6, 9, 12, 19, 20, 28 Feb.; 1, 4 Mar.	I fos 35*r–v, Iv
Esher	21, 27 Mar.; 5, 14, 19, 21 Apr.	I fos 72v, 73r, Kr
Windsor	22 May	OG p155
Eton	23 May	I fo 73r
Esher	26, 29, 30, 31 May; 2, 6 Jun.	I fos 73v, Kr, 36*r–v
Southwark/Wmin	1, 8, 10, 12, 24, 28, 29 Jul.	I fos 37*r, 38*v, 74r,
		PRO C81/1546/109
Merwell	27, 29 Aug.; 3 Sep.	I fo 74r–v
Winchester	20, 27, 29 Sep.; 1 Oct.	I fos 74v, 75r, 38*v, Kv
Farnham	7 Oct.	I fo 75r
Esher	25, 27 Oct.	I fo 75v
Westminster	31 Oct.	PRO C81/1546/109
Southwark	8, 15, 16, 27 Nov.; 2, 3 Dec.	I fos 75v, 38*r
Westminster	5, 6, 9, 12, 13	PRO E28/87/8, 10, 12, 16, 18
Esher	31 Dec.	I fo 77r 1456
Esher	13 Jan.	I fo 77r
Southwark/Wmin	20, 28, 31 Jan.; 5, 6, 7, 13, 25, 26 Feb.	I fos 77r–v, 78r, 38*v; PRO
		C81/1546/99, 115
Southwark	1, 6, 10, 11 Mar.	I fo 78r
Esher	23, 26, 28 Mar.; 5, 10 Apr.	I fo 78v
Southwark	14, 15 Apr.	I fo 79r–v
Esher	18, 19, 20 Apr.	I fo 39*v, Lv
Windsor	22 Apr.	OG p157
Esher	25 Apr.	I fo 79v
Southwark	3 Apr.; 3 May	I fo 78v
Farnham	4 May	I fo 79v
Southwark	6 May	I fo 43*r
Merton	16 May	I fo 79v
Southwark	22 May	I fo 43*r
Farnham	2, 4, 8, 11 Jun.	I fos 39*r, 40*r
Westminster	22 Jun.	PRO C81/1546/116
Farnham	28 Jun.	I fo 80v
Westminster	5, 12 Jul.	PRO C81/1546/117, 118
Farnham	28, 29, 30 Jul.	I fo 80v
Esher	3 Aug.	I fo 43*r
Winchester	5, 7, 11 Aug.	I fo 81r
Bishop's Waltham	16 Aug.	I fo 43*r
Winchester	30 Aug.; 13 Sep.	I fo 81r
Farnham	7 Oct.	I fo 82r
Coventry	11 Oct.	CCR 211

Southwark/Wmin	15, 18, 20–30 Oct.; 3, 4, 6, 7, 8, 10–18, 20, 22–30 Nov.; 1, 2 Dec.	I fo Mr; CCR 150; CPR 324–9, 343, 352; CCR 171, 172; CPR 318, 326–7, 330, 343, 324–9, 352, 331, CCR 153
Esher	3 Dec.	I fo 82r
Southwark	4 Dec.	I fo 76r
Coventry	7, 9, 12, 13 Dec.	CCR 189; CPR 331
Westminster	17, 19, 20 Dec.	CPR 329; 333, 342
Esher	21 Dec.	I fo 40*r
Westminster	22, 23, 28 Dec.	CPR 342, 344
Esher	29 Dec.	I fo 44*v

1457

Westminster	3, 10, 12, 15, 16, 19 Jan.	CPR 332, 669, 671, 678
Esher	20 Jan.	I fo 83r; CCR 201
Southwark/Wmin	22, 24, 25, 27–9, 31 Jan.	I fo 83v; CCR 201; CPR 318, 328, 334, 665
Westminster	1, 3, 5 Feb.	CPR 388, 680, 318
Esher	6 Feb.	I fo 83v
Westminster	7, 8, 9, 11, 12 Feb.	CPR 334, 337, 345; CCR 202
Coventry	13, 14, 15, 16, 18, 21, 23, 24, 25, 26, 28 Feb.	CPR 335–8, 342, 346, 350
	1, 2, 3, 4, 6, 8, 9, 10, 11, 12 Mar.	CPR 335–6, 338–9
but Esher	2, 8 Mar.	I fo Mr, 84r
Warwick	12, 13 Mar.	CCR 210; CPR 335
Banbury	14 Mar.	CPR 339
Esher	15 Mar.	I fo 84r
Westminster	18, 19, 20, 21, 23, 25, 26, 27 Mar.	CPR 328, 334, 336, 339, 341, 669. T.p. 310
Esher	31 Mar.; 2 Apr.	I fo 84r, 41*r
Westminster	3, 4, 8, 12 Apr.	CPR 331, 345, 337, 353
Esher	13 Apr.	I fo 84r
Westminster	15 Apr.	CPR 345
Esher	16, 20, 22, 24 Apr.	I fo 84v, Nv; Gx p. 110
Westminster	24, 26, 30 Apr.	CCR 214; CPR 340, 347, 349
Esher	31 Apr.	I fo Nv
Southwark/Wmin	1–4, 9–14, 17–22, 24–31 May; 2 Jun.	CCR 222, 272, CPR 319, 320, 328, 343, 353, 673, I fo 41r
Coventry	7, 8, 9, 10 Jun.	CPR 351–2
Oxford	13 Jun.	CPR 353
Esher	19 Jun.	I fo 88r
Westminster	20, 23, 25, 27, 28, 20 Jun.	CCR 225; CPR 321
	1, 4, 5, 6, 7, 8, 10, 11, 20 Jul.	CCR 222; P 321–2, 325, 66
Esher	24, 27 Jul.	I fo 88v
Westminster	1, 2, 3 Aug.	CPR 361, 367
Esher	3 Aug.	I fo 88v
Westminster	5, 7, 8, 9, 12, 13, 15, 17, 22 Aug.; 4, 9 Sep.	CCR 221, 231; CPR 341, 361, 370, 666, 671
Bp's Waltham	12, 23, 24, 25, 29 Sep.	II fos 88v, 89r, CPR 362
Westminster	4, 5, 10–18, 20, 21, 26–31 Oct.	I fo 89r; CCR 232, 248, 253, 266; PPR 373–5, 663, 667
	3, 4, 8–11, 15, 17, 23, 24, 26, 28 Nov.; 1 Dec.	I fo 90r; CCR 262; CPR 373–5, 663, 667, 671

Esher	2, 12 Dec.	I fos 90r, 45*v
Westminster	17, 21, 26 Dec.	CPR 342, 666, 678

1458

Southwark/Wmin	3–6, 8, 13, 18, 20, 24, 26–30 Jan.	CPR 378, 398, 411, 413–5, 433, 331, 681; I fo 90r
	1–10, 12–15, 18–25 Feb.	CPR 379, 414–5, 416–7, 419, 422, 435, 437; I fos 44*v, 47*r, 90v
	1, 4, 6, 8, 11, 13–18, 20, 23–4, 27, 29 Mar.	CPR 387, 416, 418–9, 423, 427, 436, 438–9, 662, 666 PRO E28/88/81 I fos 45*r, 90v
	4, 5, 6, 8, 10–12, 14, 17–21, 24, 25, 27–30 Apr.	CR 319; CPR 380–1, 419–20, 388, 432, 671; I fos 53*v, 90v
	2–7, 9–12, 14–17 May	CCR 312; CPR 388, 421, 423–4, 426, 429; PRO E28/88/52; I fo 90v
Esher	18, 21 May	I fo 91r–v
Southwark/Wmin	21, 24, 27, 29–31 May	I fo 45*v; CCR 311; CPR 430, 438, 440
	1, 4, 6, 8–12, 14–16, 19–20, 22, 26, 28, 30 Jun.	CCR 311; CPR 388, 425, 427–8, 430, 434; I fos 92v, 47*v, 48*v, 53*v
Westminster	1–8, 10–13, 16, 19, 20 Jul.	CPR 432, 425–6, 441, 443, 661, 678
Woodstock	21 Jul.	CPR 433
Witney	23 Jul.	CPR 443
Westminster	24, 15, 27, 28, 29 Jul.	CCR 329; CPR 433, 443
Esher	30, 31 Jul.	I fo 92r
Westminster	31 Jul.; 5 Aug.	CPR 434
Berkhampsted	8, 9 Aug.	CPR 434, 444
Esher	14 Aug.	I fo 53*v
Westminster	17 Aug.	CPR 432
Esher	19 Aug.	I fo 53*v
Southwark/Wmin	20, 22–27 Aug.	CPR 432, 434, 442–4; CCR 351; I fo 92r
Esher	31 Aug.; 2, 9, 12 Sep.	I fos 53*v, 92r–v, 93r
Westminster	12, 16–18, 26 Sep.	CPR 458, 678; CCR 342
Esher	29 Sep.	I fo 93r
Southwark/Wmin	9, 10, 12, 13, 20, 30 Oct.	CPR 445–8, 458–60; CCR 315; I fos 53*r, 93r–v
	2, 4, 5, 7–11, 13–25, 27–31 Nov.; 1, 3 Dec.	CPR 447–51, 459, 661, 663, 66, 673; CCR 316, 326, 349, 368; I fos 55*r, 93v
Esher	4, 5 Dec.	I fo 56*r
Westminster	6, 7, 12, 13, 18 Dec.	CPR 662, 677; CCR 319, 344, 363
Esher	28 Dec.	I fo 94r

1459

Esher	11 Jan.	I fo 94r
Westminster	12, 15 Jan.	CPR 475, 678
Esher	15, 16 Jan.	I fo 56*v, 94r
Westminster	19, 20 Jan.	CPR 472, 478

Esher	20 Jan.	I fo 94r
Southwark/Wmin	25, 27, 28, 30 Jan.	CPR 472–3, 480; I fos 96v, 57*r
	4–6, 8–16, 18–28 Feb.; 1–4 Mar.	CCR 322, 354; CPR 462, 473–4, 476–9, 482–3, 492–5; I fo 96v
London	6 Mar.	I fo Vr
Westminster	8, 10, 12 Mar.	CCR 323; CPR 494
Esher	13 Mar.	I fo 97v
Wstminster	15–18, 20, 23, 26–8, 30 Mar.	CCR 324; CPR 481–2, 496
Esher	31 Mar.	I fo 98r
Berkhampsted	3 Apr.	CCR 350
Southwark/Wmin	5, 6, 8, 10–12 Apr.	CCR 376; CPR 479, 485, 506, 672
Esher	12 Apr.	I fo 98r
Southwark/Wmin	14, 17, 18, 20–21, 23–30 Apr.	CPR 462, 476, 480, 484–6, 497–8; I fo 98v
	1–10, 12, 16–19 May	CCR 322; CPR 483, 385–7, 496; 498, 516
Esher	19–20 May	I fos 58*v, 91r
Westminster	22 May	CPR 499
Esher	24, 26 May	I fos 58*v, 98v
Southwark/Wmin	31 May; 1–3, 5, 7–8, 11, 14–15 Jun.	CCR 319, 325, 379; CPR 485, 487, 500, 681; I fo 58*v
Coventry	18 Jun.	CPR 678
Southwark/Wmin	21, 24, 26–30 Jun.; 3 Jul.	CPR 49, 502, 508–9, 514, 674; CCR 402; I fos 58*r, 99r
Coventry	6–8, 10–12, 14–20, 22–26 Jul.	CPR 504–9, 511–12; 517 CCR 399
Westminster	28, 29 Jul.	CCR 393; CPR 505
Wycombe	29 Jul.	CPR 661
Westminster	30 Jul.; 1 Aug.	CPR 509; CCR 331
Esher	4 Aug.	I fo 99v
Westminster	5–8, 13 Aug.	CPR 506, 509–10
Eton	14, 16 Aug.	CPR 510, 514
Farnham	17, 19, 20 Aug.	CPR 510, 678; I fo 99v
Southwark/Wmin	22, 26 Aug.	CPR 511; I fo 92r
Winchester	27, 28, 29 Aug.; 7, 8, 24 Sep.	CPR 511, 680, 665; I fos 99v, 59*v
Leominster	9 Oct.	CCR 420
Westminster	20 Oct.	CPR 519
Winchester	21 Oct.	I fo 100v
Farnham	23 Oct.	I fo 100v
Winchester	26 Oct.	I fo 100v
Farnham	30 Oct.	I fo 100v
Westminster	30 Oct.	CCR 422
Farnham	2 Nov.	I fo 99v
Westminster	3 Nov.	CPR 527
Farnham	5 Nov.	I fo 100v
Westminster	6, 8, 11, 15, 16 Nov.	CPR 519–20
Coventry	20 Nov.	CCR 422
Westminster	21, 22 Nov.	CPR 519
Coventry	24, 26 Nov.	CPR 408, 675
Westminster	27, 28 Nov.	CPR 520
Coventry	28 Nov.; 1, 4 Dec.	CPR 526, 669
Westminster	6 Dec.	CPR 525

Coventry	7–16, 19, 20, 21 Dec.	CPR 525–7, 676; CCR 410–11, 418, 426; *RPv* p. 370
Farnham	26 Dec.	CCR 408

1460

Farnham	7 Jan.	CCR 418
Esher	9 Jan.	I fo 101r
Westminster	13 Jan.	CCR 408
Esher	18, 24, 29 Jan.	I fos 60*r, 101v
Westminster	2 Feb.	CCR 407
Northampton	5 Feb.	CCR 407
Westminster	7 Feb.	CPR 662
Esher	8 Feb.	I fo 101v
Southwark/Wmin	9, 12, 15, 16, 22, 27, 27 Feb.	CCR 405, 407, 422, 444; CPR 663; I fo 60*v
	4, 7, 10, 14–16, 18, 19, 21–26 Mar.	CCR 407–8, 410, 412; CPR 671, 677, 678; I fo 102r
London	1, 5 Apr.	I fo 102v
Esher	7, 23, 25 Apr.	I fos 102v, 63*r
Southwark/Wmin	12–14, 16, 19–20 May	CPR 678; CCR 409, 457; I fos 64*r, 109r
Coventry	24, 25 May	CPR 663; CCR 420
Westminster	26 May	CCR 449
Coventry	1, 8, 11 Jun.	CCR 411, 415, 458,
Southwark/Wmin	14–16 Jun.	CCR 415
Coventry	18, 20, 25 Jun.	CPR 666–7, 682
London	5 Jul.	I fo 104v
Northampton	7 Jul.	CCR 459
Southwark	10 Jul.	I fo 63*r
London	26 Aug.	I fo 104v
Winchester	24, 28–30 Sep.	I fos 104v, 64*r
Farnham	3, 15, 23 Oct.	I fo 64*v
Guildford	2 Nov.	I fo 105r
Southwark	10, 12, 13, 17 Nov.	I fos 105v, 112v
Farnham	26 Nov.; 1, 15, 23, 24 Dec.	I fos 64*v, 106r–v, 107r

1461

Farnham	11 Jan.	I fo 107v
Taunton	18, 24 Mar.	I fo 108v; Gx p. 115
Westminster	28 Jun.	T p. 289
Southwark	2, 7, 8, 14, 19, 27, 31 Jul.	I fos 66*v, 110v–111r; Gx p. 116
Farnham	4, 9 Aug.	I fos 67*r, 111r
Winchester	11, 16, 21 Sep.; 6, 9, 12, 14, 15, 16, 26 Oct.	I fos 67*v, 68*r–v, 111v, 12v (2s); Gx p. 117
Aulton	29 Oct.	I fos 68*v
Southwark	2, 4, 11, 14, 17, 19, 28, 30 Nov.	I fos 112r–113v, 68*v, 69*r; Fane fragment fo 101
	1, 2, 4, 8, 9, 10, 11, 18 Dec.	I fo 112r, fo Zv

1462

Winchester	7, 12, 13 Jan.; 1, 3, 11, 12 Feb.	I fos 69*v, 70*r, 113v, 115r, A*r
Guildford	1 Mar.	I fos 115v
Southwark	13, 15, 26, 31 Mar.; 6 Apr.	I fos 70*r–71*v, 116r

Winchester	20 Apr.	I fo 118v
Kingston	24 Apr.	I fo 118v
Southwark	7, 11, 15 May	I fos 72*v, 119r
Windsor	17 May	OG p. 173
Southwark	21, 26, 20 May; 26, 30 Jun.;	I fos 71*v, 119r, 121r,
	3, 10, 17, 20, 26, 31 Jul.; 6 Aug.	72*r–73*v, 121v–122r
Farnham	9, 15 Aug.	I fos 73*v, 122r
Winchester	23 Aug.	I fo 123r
Bp's Waltham	24, 25 Aug.	I fos 73*v, 122r
Winchester	27, 31 Aug.; 2, 4, 6, 9, 25 Sep.; 9, 22 Oct.	I fo 122v–123v, 74*r
Southwark	29, 31 Sep.; 4, 5, 8 Nov.	I fos 74*v, 123r–124v
Winchester	18 Nov.; 15, 21, 23 Dec.	I fos 124v, 74*v

1463

Winchester	3, 4, 13, 26, 27, 28, 29 Jan.	I fos 124v–125r, 74*v, 16v(2s)
	5, 8, 12, 16, 18, 20, 23, 28 Feb.	I fos 74*v–75*v, 125r–v, B*v
	4, 5, 6 Mar.; 1, 6 Apr.	I fos 75*v, 125v–126r
Windsor	22 Apr.	OG 177
Southwark	27, 28 Apr.; 13, 14, 16, 20, 23, 26 May;	
	6 Jun.	I fos 76*r–v, 78*r, 126r–v
Winchester	25 Jun.	I fo 126v
Southwark	16, 20 Jul.	I fos 126v, 78v
Winchester	12, 16, 20, 23, 31 Aug.; 9, 12 Sep.	I fos 128r–v, 78*r, 79*r
	10, 14, 20, 28 Oct.; 2, 7, 9, 10, 16 Nov.;	
	5, 7 Dec.	I fos 131r–v, 135r, 80*r–v
Bp's Waltham	20, 22 Dec.	I fo 135v
Winchester	30 Dec.	I fo 80*v

1464

Winchester	20, 25 Jan.; 9, 18, 22, 24, 29 Feb.,	I fo 132r–133r
	12, 15, 31 Mar.; 13, 18, 24 Apr.; 1, 12 May	I fos 81*r, 82*–83*v, 133r
Cheriton	17 May	I fo 133v
Winchester	24 May	I fo 133v
East Meon	1 Jun.	I fo 82*r
Farnham	8 Jun.	I fo 133v
Esher	13, 17 Jun.	I fo 133v–134r
Chertsey	22 Jun.	I fo 82*r
Farnham	3 Jul.	I fo 83*r
Esher	11 Jul.	I fo 134r
Highclere	31 Jul.	I fo 134v
Stamford	11 Aug.	I fo 83*r
Southwark	22 Aug.	I fo 134r
Esher	27 Aug.	I fo 84r
Highclere	10 Sep.	I fo 134r
Waltham	14 Sep.	I fo 134v
Reading	20, 25 Sep.	I fo 134v
Bp's Waltham	12, 30 Oct.	I fos 84*r, F*v
Winchester	1, 10 Nov.	I fo 134v
Bp's Waltham	16, 28 Nov.	I fo I*v
Winchester	24, 25 Nov.	I fo 135r
Bp's Waltham	5 Dec.	I fo 84*r
Winchester	17, 18 Dec.	I fo 135r–v
Bp's Waltham	18 Dec.	I fo 135v

1465

Bp's Waltham	6, 16 Jan.	I fos 84*v, 135v
Southwark	21, 26 Jan.; 7, 8, 20 Feb.	I fos 85*r–86*r, 136v,
	2, 4, 6, 15, 19, 21, 24 Mar.	I fos 85*–86*v, 137r–v, 140v, 142r; Gx p. 122
Esher	27 Mar.	I fo 141r
Bp's Waltham	3, 4, 21, 23, 24 Apr.	I fo 86*r, 141r
Winchester	30 Apr.	I fo 141r
Bp's Waltham	6 May	I fo 86*r
Winchester	7 May	I fo 141v
Bp's Waltham	13 May	I fo 86*r
Southwark	22, 28 May	I fo 142r
Esher	29, 30 May	I fo 86*r–v
Bp's Waltham	1, 5, 6, 10, 14, 16, 23 Jun.; 16, 18, 20 Jul.	I fos 142r–v, 86*v–87*r; Gx p. 122
	9, 26, 30 Aug.	I fo 87*r
Winchester	9 Sep.	I fo 142v
Bp's Waltham	21, 24, 28 Sep.; 2 Oct.	I fo 87*r, H*v
Romsey	9 Oct.	I fo 143r
Bp's Waltham	15 Oct.	I fo 143r
East Meon	17 Oct.	I fo 143r
Bp's Waltham	20, 24 Oct.	I fo 87*v
Southwark	4, 18, 21 Nov.	I fo 143r–v
Esher	24 Nov.	I fo 143v
Bp's Waltham	14, 18, 22 Dec.	I fo 143v

1466

Bp's Waltham	8, 26 Jan.	I fo 87*v
Esher	31 Jan.	I fo 144r
Southwark	6 Feb.	I fo 144r
Esher	26 Feb.	I fo 144r
Bp's Waltham	11, 21, 22 Mar.; 2, 9 Apr.	I fo 144r–v
Alton	6 Jun.	I fo 145v
Esher	12, 16, 19 Jun.	I fo 146v
Southwark	25, 26 Jun.; 3, 4 Jul.	I fo 146r
Esher	10 Jul.	I fo 148r
Guildford	16 Jul.	I fo 147v
Esher	19, 20, 21 Jul.	I fo 148r
Farnham	23 Jul.	I fo 148r
Bp's Waltham	29 Jul.	I fo 148r
Winchester	12, 14 Aug.	I fo 148r–v
Bp's Waltham	25 Sep.; 6 Oct.	I fo 148v

1467

Bp's Waltham	17 Jan.; 11 Feb.	I fo 150r
Eton	19 Feb.	I fo 150r
Esher	2, 3 Mar.	I fo 151r
Farnham	6 Apr.	I fo 151r
Windsor	24 Apr.	I fo 151r
Bp's Waltham	23, 32 Apr.; 7 May	I fos 151r–v, L*r
Brommer	16 May	I fo 151v
Bp's Waltham	20, 26 May	I fo 151v
Southwark	3, 5 Jun.; 3 Jul.	I fos 154r, 156v
Esher	4, 5 Jul.	I fo 156v

Winchester	14 Jul.	Wilkins, *Concilia* III, p. 610
Esher	25 Jul.; 13 Aug.	I fos 156v, 89*v
Bp's Waltham	3 Sep.	I fo 157r
Esher	9, 13 Oct.	I fo 90*r, 157r
Farnham	19 Oct.	I fo 91*r
Bp's Waltham	27, 28 Oct.; 19, 20, 25 Nov.; 9, 10, 12, 15 Dec.	I fos 90*r–92*r, 157r

1468

Bp's Waltham	27 Feb.; 16, 28, 29 Mar.; 1, 6, 7 Apr.	I fos 92*v, 94*r, 159r; Gx p. 123
Southwark	10, 13, 19, 22, 24 May	I fos 94*v, 159r–v
Esher	8, 13, 23 Jun.; 3, 11 Jul.	I fos 95*r–v, 159v
Farnham	8, 19 Aug.; 12 Sep.	I fos 95*r, 161v
Southwark	6 Oct.	I fo 161v
Esher	13, 15 Oct.	I fo 162r
Southwark	23 Nov.	I fo 96*r
Esher	24 Nov.	I fo 162r
Ripley	1 Dec.	I fo 162r
Alresford	2 Dec.	I fo 162v
Winchester	7 Dec.	I fo 162v
Southwark	11, 19 Dec.	I fo 162v

1469

Bp's Waltham	23, 28 Mar.	I fos 157v, 163r
Winchester	1 Apr.	I fo 163v
Bp's Waltham	7, 8, 13, 14 Apr.	I fo 96*v
Esher	2 May	I fo 161r
Southwark	15 May	I fo 164r
Farnham	7, 8 Jun.	I fo 96*v
Southwark	27 Jun.; 4, 8 Jul.	I fo 164r–v
Esher	29 Jul.	I fo 164v
Farnham	31 Jul.	I fo 164v
Bp's Waltham	6 Aug.	I fo 164v
Southwark	7 Oct.; 14, 24 Nov.; 2, 9, 12 Dec.	I fos 97*r–98*r, O*r

1470

Bp's Waltham	14 Jan.	I fo 98*r
Southwark	27 Jan.	I fo O*v
Esher	18, 28 Feb.; 5, 8, 17, 31 Mar.; 1, 5 Apr.; 6 May	I fos O*v, P*r, 98*v; II fo 1r
Southwark	27 Jun.; 1, 5, 9, 14 Jul.; 2, 6, 8, 9 Aug.	II fos 2v, 3r, 143r–v; *PL* 252
Esher	13, 21 Aug.	Fos Q*r; II fos 3v, 144r
Southwark	26 Aug.; 23, 29 Sep.; 10, 17, 20, 24, 26 Nov.	II fos 144r–v, 4r–v, Q*r

1471

Esher	7, 26 Jan.; 11 Feb.	II fo 4v, 5r
Southwark	11, 14 Mar.	II fo 11r
Esher	16, 20, 28 Mar.	II fos 5r, 146t
London	31 Mar.	II fo 5r
Southwark	6 Apr.	II fo 146v
Esher	9 Apr.	II fo 1r
Southwark	19, 20 Apr.	II fos 5v, 6r

Esher	6 May; 6, 8 Jun.	II fo 2v
Bp's Waltham	9 Jun.	II fo 5v
Esher	15, 17, 23, 24 Jun.	II fos 5v, 147r
Southwark	4, 12 Jul.	II fo 6r
Esher	15 Jul.	II fo 147r
Southwark	1 Aug.	II fo 6v
Farnham	2, 11 Aug.	II fo 6v
Bp's Waltham	22, 23, 25 Aug.; 6, 17, 20, 28 Sep.; 1, 4, 5 Oct.	II fos 6v, 7r, 8v, 146v, 147r, 148r, 149v
Southwark	4, 6, 9, 21, 29 Nov.; 1 Dec.	II fos 9v, 10r, 148v
Bp's Waltham	4, 12, 22, 23 Dec.	II fos 10r, 53r, 150r

1472

Bp's Waltham	13, 15, 18 Jan.	II fos 149r, 10r; Gx p. 124
Southwark	18, 22 Feb.; 3, 11, 14 Mar.	II fos 10v, 11r, 149v, 168v
Bp's Waltham	12, 16 Apr.	II fos 11v, 150v
Eton	24 Apr.	II fo 11v
Southwark	29, 31 Apr.; 1, 4 May; 19, 25 Jun.; 6, 8 Jul.	II fos 11v, 12r, 14r, 151v, 152r
Farnham	9 Jul.	II fo 152r
Southwark	10, 19 Jul.	II fos 14r, 151v
Esher	27, 30 Jul.; 9, 13 Aug.	II fos 14r–v, 15r
Farnham	17, 20, 23, 29 Aug.	II fos 152r, 153r
Esher	11 Sep.; 2 Oct.	II fos 17v, 18v
Southwark	9, 21, 22 Oct.	II fo 18v
Framlingham	16, 17 Nov.	*PL* 358
Bp's Waltham	23 Dec.	II fo 156r

1473

Bp's Waltham	4 Jan.	Gx p. 125
Winchester	13 Jan.	II fo 21r
Southwark	5, 16, 19, 20 Feb.; 4, 10, 12, 13, 18, 23 Mar.	II fos 21v, 22r–v, 23r
	5, 6 Apr.	II fos 23r, 157v
Winchester	14 Apr.	II fo 159r
Bp's Waltham	3, 7, 8, 11 May	II fos 23v, 24r
Esher	11, 14 May	II fo 160r
Southwark	20, 21, 24, 30 May	II fos 24r, 160r
Esher	11, 23 Jun.	II fo 161r
Southwark	3 Jul.	II fo 163v
Eton	11 Jul.	II fo 24r
Southwark	13 Jul.	II fo 163v
Esher	16 Jul.	II fo 163v
Bp's Waltham	17, 20 Aug.; 1 Sep.	II fo 24v
Southwark	28 Oct.; 4, 5, 26 Nov.	II fos 24v, 25r
Bp's Waltham	25 Dec.	II fo 25r

1474

Bp's Waltham	3, 24 Jan.; 3, 18, 23 Feb.; 5, 7, 22, 31 Mar.	II fos 25v, 26r; Gx p. 132
	1, 6, 7 Apr.	II fos 26v, 27r
Windsor	10 Apr.	*OG* p. 201
Bp's Waltham	12 Apr.	II fo 27r
Southwark	12 May	II fo 27r
Esher	14 May	II fo 27r

Southwark	24 May; 11, 19 Jun.; 2, 4 Jul; 1 Aug.	II fos 27v, 28r, 172v
Winchester	6 Aug.	II fo 29r
Bp's Waltham	8 Aug.	II fo 28v
Winchester	26 Aug.	II fo 29r
Bp's Waltham	1, 5, 6 Sep.	II fo 29r
Southwark	7, 8, 11 Nov.	II fo 29r
Bp's Waltham	3, 5, 6 Dec.	II fo 29r
Esher	12 Dec.	II fo 71v

1475

Sutton	23 Jan.	II fo 30r
Esher	28 Jan.; 1 Feb.	II fo 30r
Southwark	2, 5, 8, 10 Mar.	II fo 30v
Esher	22 Mar.; 4, 7, 12 Apr.; 2, 5, 6, 22 May	II fos 31v, 32r, 33r–v
Southwark	5, 8, 21 Jun.; 6, 7, 11 Jul.	II fos 33r, 34r–v
Esher	25 Jul.	II fo 35r
Bp's Waltham	25, 30 Aug.; 1 Sep.	II fo 130r, 35r
Winchester	5 Sep.	II fo 35r
Bp's Waltham	23, 24 Sep.	II fo 35r
Esher	30 Sep.	II fo 35v
Bp's Waltham	10, 25 Oct.	II fo 36v
Southwark	29 Oct.	II fo 144v
Bp's Waltham	6 Nov.; 6, 20 Dec.	II fos 36r, 144v; Gx p. 142

1476

Bp's Waltham	1 Jan.	Gx p. 126
Southwark	7, 9 Feb.	II fos 36v, 37r
Bp's Waltham	6, 11, 12, 18 Mar.	II fo 39r–v
Southwark	4, 6 May	II fo 39v
Esher	18 Jun.	II fo 40r
Bp's Waltham	28 Jun.	II fo 40r
Winchester	13 Jul.	II fo 40r
Bp's Waltham	10, 13, 30 Aug.	II fo 40v
Winchester	4 Oct.	II fo 40v
Oxford	26 Oct.	II fo 41r
Southwark	31 Oct.; 20, 27, 29, 30 Nov.	II fo 41r–v
Bp's Waltham	7, 15, 29, 31 Dec.	II fos 41v, 42r

1477

Bp's Waltham	2, 16	II fo 42r
Southwark	31 Jan.; 12, 13, 21 Feb.	II fo 42v
Bp's Waltham	7, 15, 21, 29 Apr.; 1, 2, 10, 13, 18, 24 May	II fos 43v, 44r, Gx P143
Esher	6, 23, 27 Jun.	II fo 44v
Southwark	8, 14 Jul.	II fo 45v
Bp's Waltham	4, 5, 20 Aug.; 1, 10, 16 Sep.; 8 Oct.	II fos 45v, 46r–v
Esher	24 Oct.	II fo 47r
Southwark	3, 6 Nov., 16 Dec.	II fos 47r, 49v, 53r
Chichester	27 Dec.	II fo 53r
Bp's Waltham	31 Dec.	II fo 42r

1478

| Southwark | 16 Jan. | II fo 53r |
| Winchester | 7 Mar. | II fo 54r |

Bp's Waltham	16, 19, 20 Mar.; 4, 16, 20, 21 Apr.	II fos 54r–v, 55r; Gx p. 133
	17, 31 May.; 11, 28 Jun.	II fo 55r
Horsedown	3 Jul.	II fo 57r
Southwark	6 Jul.	II fo 57r
Horsedown	8, 13 Jul.	II fo 63r
Romsey	7, 8 Aug.	II fo 64r
Bp's Waltham	12, 15 Aug.; 11, 16, 18, 20, 25 Sep.	II fos 63r–v, 64r, 81r, Gx p. 133
	9, 24 Oct.; 15, 16 Dec.	II fo 81r–v

1479

Southwark	31 Jan.	II fo 81v
Bp's Waltham	1, 16, 18 Mar.; 5, 15, 23, 26 Apr.;	
	4, 22, 27 May	II fos 81v, 82r–v
Witney	4, 10 Nov.	II fo 83v; Gx p. 137

1480

Southwark	3, 4, 9, 20 Feb.; 16 Mar.	II fo 83r–v; Gx p. 134
Winchester	27 Apr.	II fo 83v
Southwark	3 Jul.	II fo 83v
Oxford	23, 24 Aug.	MC Reg A fo 1r–v
Bp's Waltham	23 Sep.; 16, 20 Oct.	II fo 83r
Southwark	10 Nov.	II fo 84r
Eltham	11 Nov.	BL Add MS 6113
Southwark	23 Nov.	II fo 83r

1481

Bp's Waltham	9, 11 Jan.; 1, 10, 16, 23 Mar.;	
	15, 21, 26 May	II fos 84r–v, 85r–v; Gx p. 135
Sutton	28 May	II fo 85v
Bp's Waltham	21, 28, 30 Jul.; 3, 4, 20 Aug.; 7, 9 Sep.	II fos 85v, 86r
Oxford	20, 21, 22, 23 Sep.; 16 Oct.	II fo 86v; MC Reg A fo 7v
Southwark	15, 25 Nov.	II fos 86v, 87r
Bp's Waltham	7, 16, 17, 26 Dec.	II fos 86v, 87r, Gx p. 139

1482

Bp's Waltham	12 Jan.	II fo 87v
Sutton	17 Jan.	II fo 86v
Southwark	6 Feb.	II fo 86v
Bp's Waltham	24 Feb.; 13, 20 Mar.	II fos 86v, 88r
	1, 4, 17, 22, 24, 26, 27, 30 Apr.;	
	15, 16 May	II fos 88r–v, 89r
	7, 8 Jun.; 6 Jul.; 2 Aug.; 5, 6, 29 Sep.	II fos 89r–v, 90r, 91r
	17 Oct.	II fo 91r
Ashthrop	1 Nov.	II fo 91r
Bp's Waltham	20 Dec.	II fo 91r

1483

Southwark	4, 15 Feb.	II fo 92r
Bp's Waltham	11, 17 Mar.; 5 May	II fo 92r
Windsor	17 Apr.	*Archaeologia* I p. 350
Ashthorp	28, 30 Apr.	II fos 92v, 93r
Southwark	2, 5, 27 May	II fo 92v
Ashthorp	10 May	II fo 92v
Oxford	22, 24, 25 Jul.; 19 Aug.; 3, 29 Sep.	II fo 93r–v; MC Reg A fo 27v
Bp's Waltham	6, 7, 14 Oct.; 11 Nov.; 10 Dec.	II fo 93v

1484

Bp's Waltham	7, 8 Jan.	II fo 94r
Southwark	1 Mar.	Gx p. 141
Esher	11, 17 Mar.; 7, 16 May; 27, 28 Jun.; 12 Jul.	II fos 94r, 95v
Southwark	12 Aug.; 7 Sep.	II fo 95v
Esher	15 Oct.	II fo 96r

1485

Esher	29 Jan.; 1, 13, 18 Feb.; 7, 15, 18, 31 Mar.	II fos 101v, 103r, 104r, Gx p. 143; MC Reg A fo 9r
Bp's Waltham	1 Apr.	Gx p. 149
Esher	14, 19, 31 May; 10 Jun.; 8, 30 Jul.	II fo 104r–v
Bp's Waltham	4 Sep.	II fo 105r
Esher	4, 5, 13, 14, 19 Oct.	II fos 104v, 105r; Gx p. 145
Southwark	28 Oct.; 4, 11, 29 Nov.; 3, 5, 7, 19 Dec.	II fos 106r; 110v, 111v; Gx p. 143
Bp's Waltham	27 Dec.	II fo 111r

1486

Bp's Waltham	3, 4, 8, 11, 12, 31 Jan.; 1, 4, 14, 23, 24, 25, 26 Feb.;	II fos 112r–v, 113r, 116r, 121v, Gx p. 144, 147–8
	3, 4 Mar.; 4, 8, 11, 12, 13 Apr.;	II fos 116r–v, 117r–v;
	6, 9, 23 May;	Gx pp. 146, 148
	7 Jun.; 19, 20, 26, 29 Jul.; 7, 9, 11 Aug.	II fos 118r, 140r–v; Gx pp. 149–50

Waynflete died at Bishop's Waltham on 11 August.

List of Sources

A UNPRINTED SOURCES

London, Public Record Office
C1   Early Chancery Proceedings
C47   Chancery Miscellanea
C81   Chancery Warrants
C85   Significations of Excommunication
E28   Exchequer TR, Council and Privy Seal
E101 Exchequer KR, Various Accounts
E135 Exchequer, Ecclesiastical
E404 Exchequer of Receipt, Warrants for Issues
SC1   Special Collections, Ancient Correspondence
SC8   Special Collections, Ancient Petitions

London, British Library
Additional Manuscripts 4839–44, 15381–5
Egerton MSS 2031, 2576, 2892
Harleian MS 2077
Cotton Vesp. B.XVI

London, Lambeth Palace Library
MS 450
Register of John Stafford

Winchester, Hampshire Record Office
Register of William Waynflete
EC/2/159438–44 (Pipe Rolls)
EC/2/155827–46 (Ministers' Accounts)
EC/2/159516, box 157

Winchester, Winchester College
WCM 22992   *Liber Albus*
WCM 22117–25 Bursars' accounts
WCM 22824–30 Hall books
WCM 829–31

Lincoln Archives Office
Register of Philip Repington
Register of Richard Fleming

Cambridge, Trinity College
King's Hall account books vols 7, 8

Cambridge, Corpus Christi College
MS 170, Letter Book.

Oxford, Bodleian Library
MS Rawl Q.C.14   Statutes of Magdalen College
MS e.Mus.229   Customs of Southwark Stews
Lincoln Coll MS 117   Theological Dictionary of Thomas Gascoigne

Oxford, Magdalen College
Register A
Liber computi i
CP/8/49   Bursary book 1477–86
CP/2/67/1,2   Building accounts
CP/2/55   Funeral expenses, John Waynflete
MS Latin 277   College statutes
MS 367   Letter book
Chartae Regiae 50   Foundation Charter, Magdalen Hall
Chartae Regiae 81   Foundation Charter, Magdalen College
Chartae Regiae 43   Waynflete's will
MC Receivers Accounts, Box D, nos 11,17
MC deeds   Appropriations 1a, 2, 3, 5, 7, 8, 19, 22, 26; Aynho 4; Beenham Valence
3; Brackley B.207; Bursary Book 1477–80; Candlesby 43, 43a, 54b, 65a; Chalgrove
34A; Chartae Regiae 50.8.ii; Chartae Concessae 63, 58; Clifton & Deddington 24;
Corton 19; Cowfold 20; Cromwell Papers 317, 354, 357, 425–7; East New Hall 7, 3;
East Bridgeford 10, 14, 17, 21, 25, 33; Enham A89, B191; Fastolf Paper 97; Ford
and Taunton 2, 7; Henton 3d, 9b, 14c, 44c, 41a, 30a, 31a, 32a, 51c, 56, 56d;
Multon Hall 10, 48, 60, 62, 70, 77, 98, 136; Norfolk and Suffolk 47; Otterbourne
137, 139; Petersfield 90p, 31, 64; Quinton 67; Romney 9; Saltfleetby 3, 37a; Sele III,
1, 17, 36a, 49, 58, 59, 77, 85, 90, 91, 93, 98, 109; Skyres 89, 81; Slimbridge 26;
Shoreham 2; Sombourne Regia A1; Stainswyke 4, 19, 44; Stanlake 8, 14, 29a; Temple
Bar 52; Tubney 2, 29, 52, 79; Wanborough 29A
MC Estate papers 165/6;
Macray,   Typescript index to college deeds
Woolgar   Typescript index to estate archives.

Eton, Eton College
ECR 38   Building documents
ECR 39   Patent letters
ECR 61   Account rolls
ECR 26/120
ECR 54/10
ECR 60/LB/L College lease book

EARLY PRINTED MATERIAL

Lambeth Palace Library
Maitland Fragment 5   Early printed indulgence

Cambridge, University Library
Anwykyll, John, *Compendium Totius Grammaticae*, Deventer 1489

PRINTED SOURCES

Ancient Fifteenth Century Laws for King's College Cambridge and for the Public School of Eton, ed. J. Heywood and T. Wright, 1850.

Anglia Sacra, ed. H. Wharton, 2 vols, 1691.

'John Benet's Chronicle for the Years 1400–1462', ed. G.L. and M.A. Harriss, *Camden Miscellany* xxiv, Camden Society 1972.

The Building Accounts of Tattershall Castle 1434–1472, ed. W.D. Simpson, Lincolnshire Record Society lv, 1960.

Calendar of Charters and Documents Relating to Selborne and its Priory, ed. W.D. Macray, 2 vols, Hampshire Record Society 1891, 1894.

Calendar of Papal Letters, vols vi–xv, HMSO, 1904–60, Dublin 1978.

Calendar of Close Rolls, HMSO, 1902–54.

Calendar of Patent Rolls, HMSO, 1895–1911.

Cartulary of the Hospital of St John the Baptist, ed. H.E. Salter, 3 vols, OHS 66, 68–9, 1914–20.

'Catalogue of Books Belonging to the College of St Mary Winchester in the Reign of Henry VI', ed. W.H. Gunner, *Archaeological Journal* xv, 1858, 59–74.

'Chantry Certificates Lincolnshire', *Lincolnshire Archaeological Society*, 1947, 281–2.

'The Charter of Incorporation of Wainfleet', ed. R.M. Heanley, *Lincolnshire Notes and Queries* ii, 1890, 11–14.

The Chaundler Manuscripts, ed. M.R. James, Roxburghe Club, 1916.

Early Lincoln Wills, ed. A. Gibbons, Lincoln 1888.

The Early Rolls of Merton College, ed. J.R.L. Highfield, OHS ns xviii, 1963.

Educational Charters and Documents, ed. A.F. Leach, Cambridge 1911.

Epistolae Academicae Oxon, ed. H. Anstey, 2 vols, OHS xxxv–xxxvi, 1898.

Gascoigne, Thomas, *Loci e Libro Veritatum*, ed. J.E. Thorold Rogers, Oxford 1881.

Grace Book A 1454–88, ed. S.M. Leathes, Cambridge 1897.

Historical Manuscript Commission, Reports, 4th, De Lisle and Dudley, Hastings, Various.

Historical Register of the University of Oxford to 1900, Oxford 1900.

Issues of the Exchequer, ed. F. Devon, 1837.

Itineraries of William Worcester, ed. J.H. Harvey, Oxford 1969.

Langland, Piers the Ploughman, ed. J.F. Goodridge, 1959.

Les Liggenen et Autures Archives de la Guilde de Saint Luc, ed. P. Rombout, Antwerp 1872.

Lyndwood, W. *Provinciale*, Oxford 1689.

Merton Muniments, ed. P.S. Allen and H.W. Garrod, OHS 86, 1928.

The Ministers' Accounts of the Warwickshire Estates of the Duke of Clarence, ed. R. Hilton, Dugdale Society 1952.

Notes from the Muniments of Mary Magdalen College Oxford, ed. W.D. Macray, Oxford 1882.

Official Correspondence of Thomas Beckington, ed. G. Williams, 2 vols RS 1872.

The Paston Letters 1422–1509, ed. J. Gairdner, 6 vols, 1904.

Paston Letters and Papers of the Fifteenth Century, ed. N. Davis, 2 vols, Oxford 1971–6.

Proceedings and Ordinances of the Privy Council of England 1386–1542, ed. N.H. Nicolas, Record Commissioners, 7 vols, 1834–7.

The Register of the Common Seal of the Priory of St Swithun, Winchester, ed. J. Greatrex, Hampshire Record Series 2, Hampshire County Council 1979.

Register of Henry Chichele 1413–43, ed. E.F. Jacob, 4 vols, Canterbury & York Society xlii, xlv–xlvii, 1943–7.

Registrum Johannis Stanbury episcopi Herefordensis, ed. A.T. Bannister, Canterbury & York Society xxv, 1919, p. ix.

Registrum Cancellarii Oxoniensis 1434–69, ed. H.E. Salter, 2 vols, OHS 93–4, 1930–31.

Rous, John, 'A Mid-Fifteenth Century List of Oxford Halls', Appendix F in '*Survey of the Antiquities of the City of Oxford' Composed in 1661–6 by Anthony Wood*, i, ed. A. Clark, OHS 93, 1889, 638–41.

Statutes of the Colleges of Oxford, 3 vols, 1853–6, ii, 5–91.

Syllabus of Rymer's Foedera, ed. T.D. Hardy, 3 vols, 1869–85.

Taxatio Ecclesiastica Angliae et Walliae Auctoritate Pope Nicholai IV 1291, 1802.

Valor Ecclesiasticus, ed. J. Caley and J. Hunter, 6 vols, 1810–34.

The Winchester Anthology [BL MS Add 60577], ed. I. Fenlon and E. Wilson, 1981.

William Worcestre, *Itineraries*, ed. J.H. Harvey, Oxford 1969.

SECONDARY WORKS

Agnew, G., 'Pictures', in *Treasures of Eton*, ed. J. McConnell, 1967, 115–31.

Anstis, J., *Register of the Order of the Garter*, 2 vols, 1724.

Aston, T.H., 'Oxford's Medieval Alumni', *Past & Present* lxxiv, 1977, 36–40.

Baker, N. and R. Birley, 'The Story of Jane Shore', *Etoniana*, 1972, 342–4.

Bedford, W.K.R., *The Blazon of Episcopacy*, 2nd edn, Oxford 1897.

Betcherman, L.R., 'The Making of Bishops in the Lancastrian Period', *Speculum* xli, 1966, 397–419.

Beveridge, W., 'Wages in the Winchester Manors, *Economic History Review* viii, 1936, 22–43.

Birch, W.G., *Catalogue of Seals in the Department of Manuscripts in the British Museum*, 6 vols, 1887–1900.

Birley, R., 'The History of Eton College Library', *The Library* v series, xi, 1956, 231–61.

Bloxam, J.R., *A Register of the Presidents and Other Members of Magdalen College Oxford*, 7 vols, Oxford 1853–85.

Bonaventure, Br, 'The Teaching of Latin in Later Medieval England', *Mediaeval Studies* xxiii, 1961, 1–20.

Bond, M., 'Chapter Adminstration and Archives at Windsor', *Journal of Ecclesiastical History* viii, 1957, 166–81.

Bowers, R., 'Obligation, Agency and Laisser-Faire: the Promoton of Polyphonic Composition for the Church in Fifteenth Century England', in I. Fenlon, ed., *Music in Medieval and Early Modern Europe*, Cambridge 1981, 1–20.

Bowker, M., *The Secular Clergy in the Diocese of Lincoln 1495–1520*, Cambridge 1968.

Boyle, L.E., 'The Constitution *Cum ex eo* of Boniface VIII', *Mediaeval Studies* xxiv, 1962, 263–302.

Brady, W.M., *The Episcopal Succession in England, Scotland and Wales*, 3 vols, Rome 1876–7.

Budden, J., *Gulielmi Patteni, Wintoniensis Ecclesie Presulis Vita Obitusque*, Oxford 1602.

Buxton, J. and Williams, P., *New College Oxford 1379–1979*, Oxford 1979.

Carter, H., *Oxford University Press: a History*, Oxford 1975.

Chandler, R., *The Life of William Waynflete, Bishop of Winchester*, 1811.

Chitty, H., 'William Waynflete', *Notes and Queries* ix series, i, 1905, 461–2.

Clay, R.M., *The Medieval Hospitals of England*, 1909.

Clifton-Taylor, A., *English Brickwork*, 1979.

Clough, C.H. (ed.), *Profession, Vocation and Culture in Later Medieval England: Essays Dedicated to the Memory of A.R. Myers*, Liverpool 1982.

Cobban, A., *The King's Hall Within the University of Cambridge in the Later Middle Ages*, Cambridge 1969.

————, *The Medieval English Universities: Oxford and Cambridge to c.1500*, Aldershot, 1988.

————, 'Colleges and Halls 1380–1500', in *Late Medieval Oxford: The History of the University of Oxford II*, ed. J.I. Catto and R. Evans, Oxford 1992.

Colvin, H., *The History of the King's Works*, 3 vols, HMSO, 1963.

Cokayne, G.E. and Doubleday, H.A., *The Complete Peerage*, 13 vols, 1910–59.

Cook, G.H., *Medieval Chantries and Chantry Chapels*, 1947.

Courtenay, W., *Schools and Learning in the Fourteenth Century*, Princeton 1987.

Coxe, H.O., *Catologus Codicum Mss. qui in Collegiis Aulisque Oxoniensibus Hodie Adservantur*, 2 vols, Oxford 1852.

Davies, R.G., 'The Episcopate', in C.H. Clough, ed. *Profession, Vocation and Culture in Later Medieval England: Essays Dedicated to the Memory of A.R. Myers*, Liverpool 1982.

Davies, R.R., 'Baronial Accounts, Incomes and Arrears in the Late Middle Ages', *Economic History Review* ii series, xxi, 1968, 211–29.

Davis, N., 'The Epistolary Uses of William Worcester', in D. Pearsall and R.A. Waldron, eds, *Medieval Literature and Civilisation*, 1969, 249–74.

Davis, V., 'William Waynflete and the Educational Revolution of the Fifteenth Century', in *People, Politics and Community in the Later Middle Ages*, ed. J. Rosenthal and C. Richmond, Gloucester 1987, 40–59.

————, 'Rivals for Ministry? Ordinations of Secular and Regular Clergy in Southern England, c.1300–1500', *Ministry, Clerical and Lay*, ed. D. Wood, Studies in Church History xxvi, Oxford 1989, 99–109.

————, 'William Waynflete and the Wars of the Roses', *Southern History* xi, 1989, 1–22.

————, 'Medieval English Clergy Database', *History and Computing* ii, 1990, 75–87.

————, 'The Making of English Collegiate Statutes in the Later Middle Ages', *History of Universities* xiii, 1993, 1–23.

Denholm-Young, D., *Seigniorial Administration in England*, Oxford 1937.

Du Boulay, F.R.H., *The Lordship of Canterbury*, 1966.

Duff, E.G., *Fifteenth Century English Books*, Oxford 1917.

Dunham, W.H., 'Lord Hastings' Indentured Retainers 1461–1483', *Transactions of the Connecticut Academy of Arts and Sciences* xxxix, 1955.

Dyer, C., *Lords and Peasants in a Changing Society*, Cambridge 1978.

Emden, A.B., *A Biographical Register of the University of Oxford to A.D.1500*, 3 vols, Oxford 1957–9.

————, *A Medieval Oxford Hall*, Oxford 1927.

————, *A Biographical Register of the University of Cambridge to 1500*, Cambridge 1963.

Fenlon, I., 'Instrumental Music, Songs and Verse from Sixteenth Century Winchester,

British Library Additional MS 60577', in Fenlon, ed., *Music in Medieval and Early Modern Europe*, Cambridge 1981, 93–116.

Fletcher, J., 'A Fifteenth Century Benefaction to Magdalen College Library', *Bodleian Library Record* ix, 1974, 169–72.

Floyer, J.K., 'The Ancient Manor House of the Bishops of Winchester at Esher Place', *Proceedings of the Society of Antiquaries* xxxii, 1920, 121–32.

Foot, M., 'English Decorated Bookbindings', in J. Griffith and D. Pearsall, eds, *Book Production and Publishing in Britain*, Cambridge 1989, 65–86

Friedrichs, R.L., 'The Two Last Wills of Ralph, Lord Cromwell', *Nottingham Medieval Studies* xxxiv, 1990, 93–112.

Fuller, T., *The Worthies of England* (1662), ed. John Freeman, London, 1952.

Garth, H.M., *Saint Mary Magdalene in Medieval Literature*, Baltimore 1950.

Gray, H.L., 'Greek Visitors to England 1455–1456', *Anniversary Essays in Medieval History by Students of C.H.Haskins*, ed. C.H. Taylor and J.L. LaMonte, Boston 1929.

Green, V.H., *The Commonwealth of Lincoln College 1427–1977*, Oxford 1979.

Griffiths, R.A., *The Reign of Henry VI*, 1981.

———, 'The King's Council and the First Protectorate of the Duke of York', *EHR* lcix, 1984.

Haines, R.M., 'The Education of the English Clergy in the Later Middle Ages', *Canadian Journal of History* iv, 1969, 1–22.

Hall, H., 'A List of the Rent Rolls of the Bishopric of Winchester', *Economica* x, 1924, 52–61.

Harrison, F., *Music in Medieval Britain*, 1958.

Harriss, G.L., *Cardinal Beaufort*, Oxford 1988.

Harvey, J., 'Winchester College', *Journal of the British Archaeological Association* xxviii, 1965, 107–28.

———, 'Winchester College Muniments', *Archives* v, 1962, 201–16.

———, 'Architecture in Oxford 1350–1500', in J.I. Catto and R. Evans, eds, *Late Medieval Oxford: The History of the University of Oxford II*, Oxford 1992, 764–7.

Harvey J. and A. Oswald, *English Medieval Architects: a Biographical Dictionary Down to 1550*, 2nd edn, Gloucester 1984.

Heal, F., *Of Prelates and Princes*, Cambridge 1980.

Heylin, P., *Memorial of Bishop Waynflete*, ed. J.R. Bloxam, Caxton Society 1851.

Highfield, J., 'The Promotion of William of Wickham to the See of Winchester', *JEH* iv, 1953, 37–54.

Hoberg, H., *Taxae pro Communibus Servitiis 1295–1455*, Rome 1938.

Holingshead, R., *Chronicles* (1577), ed. H. Ellis, 6 vols, London 1807–8, ii.

Hope, W.H. St J., 'The Episcopal Ornaments of William of Wykeham and William of Waynfleet, Sometime Bishops of Winchester and of Certain Bishops of St Davids', *Archaeologia* lx, 1907, 465–92.

Humphridus, L., *Epistola de Graecis Literis et Homeri Lectione*, Basle 1558.

Jackson-Stops, G., 'The Building of the Medieval College', in *New College Oxford 1379–1979*.

Jacob, E.F., *Archbishop Henry Chichele*, 1967.

———, 'Founders and Foundations in the Middle Ages', in *Essays in the later Middle Ages*, Manchester 1968.

James, M.R. and Tristram, E.W., 'The Wall Paintings in Eton College Chapel and in the Lady Chapel of Winchester Cathedral', *The Walpole Society* xvii, 1928–9, 1–43.

———, *The Frescoes of Eton College*, 1907.

Jewell, H., 'English Bishops as Educational Benefactors in the Later Fifteenth Century', in R.B. Dobson, ed., *Church, Politics and Patronage in England and France in the Fifteenth Century*, Gloucester, 1984, 146–67.

Ker, N., 'The Virgin and Child Binder and William Horman', *The Library* v series, xvii, 1962, 77–85.

Kirby, T.F., *Annals of Winchester*, 1892.

Knecht, R.J., 'The Episcopate and the Wars of the Roses', *University of Birmingham Historical Journal* vi, 1957–8, 108–31.

Knoop, D. and G.P. Jones, 'The Building of Eton College 1442–60', *Transactions Quatuor Coronati Lodge* xlvi, 1933, 3–43.

Knowles, D. and R.N. Hadcock, *Medieval Religious Houses: England and Wales*, 2nd ed. 1971.

Lambert, G., *Esher Place*, 1884.

Le Faye, D., 'Selborne Priory 1233–1486', *Proceedings of the Hampshire Field Club and Archaeological Society* xxx, 1973, 1–68.

Leach, A.L., *The Schools of Medieval England*, 2nd edn, London, 1916.

———, 'Eton College', in *VCH Buckinghamshire* ii, 147–70.

Leader, D., 'Philosophy at Oxford and Cambridge in the Fifteenth Century', *History of Universities* iv, 1984, 25–46.

———, 'Grammar in Late Medieval Oxford and Cambridge', *History of Education*, xii, 1983, 9–14.

Leedy, W., 'King's College, Cambridge: Observations on its Context and Foundations', in E. Fernie and P. Crossley, eds, *Medieval Architecture and its Intellectual Context: Studies in Honour of Peter Kidson*, 1990, 209–17.

Levett, A.E., *The Black Death on the Estates of the See of Winchester*, Oxford 1916.

———, 'The Financial Organisation of the Manor', *Economic History Review* i, 1927, 65–86.

Lindley, P., 'Figure-Sculpture at Winchester in the Fifteenth Century; a New Chronology', in D. Williams, ed., *England in the Fifteenth Century: Proceedings of the 1986 Harlaxton Symposium*, Woodbridge 1987, 153–66.

———, 'The Great Screen of Winchester Cathedral II: Style and Date', in *Burlington Magazine*, forthcoming.

Little, A.G., *The Grey Friars in Oxford*, OHS xx, 1892.

Lunt, W.E., *Financial Relations of the Papacy with England 1327–1534*, Cambridge Mass., 1962.

Lyndwood's Provinciale, ed. J.V. Bullard and H.C. Bell, 1929.

MacNamara, F.N., *Memorials of the Danvers Family*, 1895.

McFarlane, K.B., *England in the Fifteenth Century: Collected Essays*, 1981.

Macray, W.D., *Register of the Presidents and Other Members of Magdalen College Oxford: New Series – Fellows 1458–1915*, 8 vols, Oxford 1894–1915.

Maddan, F., *The Early Oxford Press 1468–1640*, Oxford 1895.

[A.C. de La Mare] *Duke Humphrey and English Humanism in the Fifteenth Century*, Catalogue of an exhibition held in the Bodleian Library Oxford 1970.

Mare, A.C. de La, 'Humanistic Hands in England', in *Catalogue of the R.W. Hunt Memorial Exhibition*, Bodleian Library Oxford 1980.

Marks, R., 'The Glazing of the Collegiate Church of the Holy Trinity Tattershall: a Study of Late Fifteenth Century Glass Painting Workshops', *Archaeologia* cvi, 1979, 133–56.

Maxwell-Lyte, H.C., *A History of Eton College*, 4th edn, 1911.

Moran, J.H., 'Clerical Recruitment in the Diocese of York, 1340–1530', *JEH* xxxiv, 1983, 19–54.

Myatt-Price, E., 'Ralph, Lord Cromwell', *The Lincolnshire Historian* ii, 1957, 4–13.

Nelson, W., *John Skelton, Laureate*, Columbia 1939.

Oldfield, E., *A Topographical and Historical Account of Wainfleet in the County of Lincoln*, 1829.

Orme, N., *English Schools in the Middle Ages*, 1973.

Orme, N., 'An Early-Tudor Oxford Schoolbook', in N. Orme, *Education and Society in Medieval and Renaissance England*, 1989, 121–51.

Parry-Jones, B., *Five Hundred Years of Magdalen College School, Wainfleet 1484–1984*, Wainfleet 1984.

Peckham, W.D., 'John Waynflete, Dean of Chichester', *Sussex Notes and Queries* xii, 1949, 7–9.

Pevsner, N., *The Buildings of England: Buckinghamshire*, 1960.

Pevsner, N., and Nairn, I., *Surrey*, 1963.

Pollard, G., 'The Names of Some Fifteenth Century English Binders', *The Library* v series, xxv, 1970, 193–218.

Raban, S., *Mortmain Legislation and the English Church*, Cambridge 1982.

Rawcliffe, C., *The Staffords, Earls of Stafford and Dukes of Buckingham*, Cambridge 1978.

Richmond, C., *John Hopton* Cambridge 1981.

———, 'A letter of 19 April 1483 from John Gigur to William Wainfleet', *Historical Research* lxv, 1992, 112–116.

Rhodes, D.E., *A Catalogue of Oxford Incunabula Outside the Bodleian*, Oxford 1982.

Rosenthal, J.T., 'The Training of an Elite Group: English Bishops in the Fifteenth Century', *Transactions of the American Philosophical Society* ns lx, pt v, 1970.

Rosenthal, J.T., 'The Fifteenth Century Episcopate: Careers and Bequests', in D. Baker, ed., *Studies in Church History* x, 1973, 117–28.

Russell, E., 'The Influx of Commoners into the University of Oxford before 1581: an Optical Illusion?', *EHR* lcii, 1977, 721–45.

St John Hope, *Report on Bishops Waynflete's Chapel in Winchester College*, privately printed, Burlington House, 1898.

Saltmarsh, J., 'The Founder's Statutes of King's College Cambridge', *Studies presented to Sir Hilary Jenkinson*, ed. J. Conway Davies, 1957, 337–60.

———, *King Henry VI and the Royal Foundations*, Cambridge 1972.

Salzman, L., *Building in England down to 1540*, 1952.

Simon, J., *Education and Society in Tudor England*, Cambridge 1966.

Smith, T.P., *The Medieval Brickmaking Industry in England 1400–1450*, British Archaeological Reports cxxxviii, 1988.

Stanier, R., *Magdalen School*, OHS iii, 1940.

Storey, R.L., *Thomas Langley and the Bishopric of Durham 1406–37*, 1961.

———, 'Recruitment of English Clergy in the Period of the Conciliar Movement', *Annuarium Historiae Conciliorum* vii, 1975, 290–313.

———, 'The Foundation of the Medieval College', in J. Buxton, J. and P. Williams, *New College Oxford 1379–1979*, Oxford 1979.

———, 'Cardinal Beaufort's Greek Doctor', *Nottingham Medieval Studies* xxix, 1985, 109–14.

Stubbs, W., *Registrum Sacrum Anglicanum*, 2nd edn, Oxford 1897.

Swanson, R.N., 'Episcopal Income from Spiritualities in the Diocese of Exeter in the Early Sixteenth Century', *JEH* 39, 1988, 520–30.

———, 'Episcopal Income from Spiritualities in Later Medieval England: the Evidence for the Diocese of Coventry and Lichfield', *Midland History* xiv, 1988, 1–20.

Thomas, D., 'Grammar in England in the Late Middle Ages', in *Catalogue of the R.W. Hunt Memorial Exhibition*, Oxford 1980.

Thompson, J.A.F., 'Bishop Lionel Woodville and Richard III', *BIHR* lix, 1986, 130–35.

Thompson, M.W., 'The Date of "Fox's Tower", Farnham Castle, Surrey', *Surrey Archaeological Collections* lvii, 1960, 85–92.

Thomson, D., *A Descriptive Catalogue of Middle English Grammatical Texts*, 1979.

Titow, J.Z., *Winchester Yields*, Cambridge 1972.

Vernhagen, H., *De Duobus Foliis Libri Cuiusdam Anglici*, Erlangen 1906.

Virgoe, R., 'Some Ancient Indictments in the King's Bench Referring to Kent 1450–52', in F.R.H. DuBoulay, ed., *Kent Records; Documents Illustrative of Medieval Kentish Society*, Ashford 1964, 214–65.

———, 'The Composition of the King's Council 1437–61', *BIHR* xliii, 1970, 134–60.

Walcott, M., *William of Wykeham and his Colleges*, 1854.

[Wavell] J., *The History and Antiquities of Winchester*, 2 vols, Winchester 1773, ii, 1909.

Weiss, R., *Humanism in England in the Fifteenth Century*, 3rd edn, Oxford 1967.

Wight, J., *Brick Building in England from the Middle Ages Down to 1550*, 1972.

Williams, G., 'Ecclesiastical Vestments, Books and Furniture in the Collegiate Church of King's College Cambridge in the Fifteenth Century', *The Ecclesiologist* xx, 1859, 305–6.

Willis, R. and Clark, J.W., *The Architectural History of the Colleges of Cambridge and Eton*, 4 vols, Cambridge 1886.

Wilson, E., 'A Poem Presented to William Waynflete as Bishop of Winchester', in *Middle English Studies Presented to Norman Davis*, ed. E.G. Stanley and D. Gray, Oxford 1983, 127–51.

Wolffe, B., *Henry VI*, 1981.

Wood, M., *The English Medieval House*, 1965.

Woodman, F., *The Architectural History of King's College Cambridge*, 1986.

Unpublished Theses

Bridges, S.F., 'Thomas Chaundler', Oxford B.Litt., 1949.

Davis, V.G., 'The Life and Career of William Waynflete', Dublin Ph.D., 1985.

Keir, G.I., 'The Ecclesiastical Career of George Neville 1432–76', Oxford B.Litt., 1970.

Mills, J., 'The Foundation, Endowment and Early Administration of Magdalen College Oxford', Oxford B.Litt., 1973.

Swift, E., 'The Machinery of Manorial Administration with Special Reference to the Lands of the Bishopric of Winchester 1208–1454', London MA, 1930.

Index